ANCIENT LEGENDS, MYSTIC CHARMS AND SUPERSTITIONS OF IRELAND

ANCIENT LEGENDS, MYSTIC CHARMS AND SUPERSTITIONS OF IRELAND

LADY WILDE

This edition published in 2024 by Arcturus Publishing Limited
26/27 Bickels Yard, 151–153 Bermondsey Street,
London SE1 3HA

Copyright © Arcturus Holdings Limited

All rights reserved. No part of this publication may be reproduced, stored in a retrieval system, or transmitted, in any form or by any means, electronic, mechanical, photocopying, recording or otherwise, without prior written permission in accordance with the provisions of the Copyright Act 1956 (as amended). Any person or persons who do any unauthorised act in relation to this publication may be liable to criminal prosecution and civil claims for damages.

AD012430UK

Printed in China

CONTENTS

Foreword	9
Preface	13
Introduction	17
The Legend of Ballytowtas Castle	31
A Wolf Story	37
The Evil Eye	40
The Stolen Bride	50
Fairy Music	52
The Fairy Dance	53
Fairy Justice	55
The Priest's Soul	57
The Fairy Race	62
The Trial by Fire	65
The Lady Witch	66
Ethna the Bride	68
The Fairies' Revenge	72
Fairy Help – the Phouka	75
The Farmer Punished	77
The Farmer's Wife	80
The Midnight Ride	82
The Leprehaun	85
The Bride's Death-Song	89
The Fairy Child	91
The Doom	95
The Clearing From Guilt	97
The Holy Well and the Murderer	98
Legends of Innis-Sark – a Woman's Curse	99

LEGENDS OF THE DEAD IN THE WESTERN ISLANDS
The Death Sign 106
Kathleen 107
November Eve 109
The Dance of the Dead 111
Superstitions Concerning the Dead 113
The Fatal Love-Charm 115
The Fenian Knights 117
Rathlin Island 119
The Strange Guests 119
The Dead Soldier 120
The Three Gifts 121
The Fairies as Fallen Angels 122
The Fairy Changeling 123
Fairy Wiles 125
Shaun-Mor 126

THE CAVE FAIRIES
The Tuatha-de-Danann 129
Edain the Queen 130
The Royal Steed 132

EVIL SPELLS
Cathal the King 135
The Poet's Malediction 137
Drimial Agus Thorial 138
An Irish Adept of the Islands 139
The May Festival 140
May-Day Superstitions 146

FESTIVALS
Candlemas 149
Whitsuntide 149
Whitsuntide Legend of the Fairy Horses 150
November Spells 151
November Eve 152
A Terrible Revenge 155

MIDSUMMER
The Baal Fires and Dances 156

The Fairy Doctress	157
Marriage Rites	159
The Dead	161
The Wake Orgies	164
The Power of the Word	169
The Poet and the King	170
The *Sidhe* Race	172
Music	174
Poet Inspiration – Eodain the Poetess	175
The Banshee	176
Queen Maeve	179
Death Signs	180
The Hartpole Doom	181
Superstitions	182
The Fairy Rath	184
Fairy Nature	184
Irish Nature	186

LEGENDS OF ANIMALS

Concerning Dogs	190
Concerning Cats	195
The King of the Cats	198
The Demon Cat	200
Cat Nature	202
Seanchan the Bard and the King of the Cats	205
The Bards	210
King Arthur and the Cat	214
Concerning Cows	217
Fairy Wiles	220
The Dead Hand	222
The Wicked Widow	223
The Butter Mystery	226

CONCERNING BIRDS

The Magpie	228
The Wren	229
The Raven and Water Wagtail	229
The Cuckoo and Robin Redbreast	229

CONCERNING LIVING CREATURES
The Cricket...231
The Beetle 231
The Hare..232
The Weasel 233

OMENS AND SUPERSTITIONS
Omens that Forbode Evil 236
To Attract Bees..238

SUPERSTITIONS OF THE ISLANDS
Concerning the Dead...239
The Coastguard's Fate...240
Relics...241

MYSTERIES OF FAIRY POWER
The Evil Stroke 242
The Changeling 244
The Fairy Doctor...246
The Poet's Spell 248
Charm for the Fairy Stroke 248
The Farmer's Fate 249
The Fairy Rath 250

FOREWORD

Lady Wilde, born Jane Francesca Agnes Elgee in Wexford, was as passionate about Irish folklore as her famous son, the playwright Oscar Wilde. The 1887 publication of *Ancient Legends, Mystic Charms and Superstitions of Ireland* built on her reputation in the area, having previously written on the subject for periodicals. Three years subsequent to publication, poet and Nobel Laureate W.B. Yeats would be thanking Lady Wilde for permission to use some of the tales given here in his own anthology of legends entitled *Fairy and Folk Tales of Ireland*.

In early editions of the work, there was addended a chapter called Sketches of the Irish Past and another by her husband, Sir William Wilde, entitled The Ancient Race of Ireland. These we have not reproduced in this edition for the reason that the content within those chapters falls significantly outside the remit of the title *Ancient Legends, Mystic Charms and Superstitions of Ireland*. Those chapters, while still occasionally referring back to the beliefs given in earlier chapters, seem to break from the flow of folk legends and beliefs that precede them in the original work and instead concentrate on historical and archaeological finds about the peoples of Ireland. Her husband's chapter seems even more jarring in content, given that he wrote *Irish Popular Superstitions* in 1852 and extracts from that work would have been far better suited to this than the politically charged nature of the add-on chapter. The chapter may have been added due to Lady Wilde wishing to honour her late husband's memory or to acknowledge that much of the material in the book was collected by him from the peasantry when commissioner for three censuses between 1851 and 1871.

Charles Gavan Duffy, editor of The Nation newspaper in which Lady Wilde's poems appeared, had become notorious as the nationalist poet 'Speranza'. His pro-revolutionary verses led to his arrest by the British authorities. In this collection, Lady Wilde, with purpose, but greater discretion, attempted to show the unique character and culture of the Irish peasantry.

A number of nationalists at that time were attracted to folklore as a way of embracing and elevating the idea of a cohesive Irish identity, irrespective of religious background. The enormity of the horror of the Great Famine also quickened the demands for Irish nationhood, in light of the failure of the British government to come to Ireland's aid. Sir William Wilde's collecting of folklore, especially in 1851, would have been a good contemporary account of how the Famine had affected beliefs in the land, especially given the argument put forward by some English commentators at the time that the potato blight was a divinely ordained punishment on the Irish.

However, we rarely turn to such material when examining that troubling time in Irish history. Historian Cathal Portéir, in his essay *Folk Memory and the Famine*, writes 'the reluctance of many historians to engage with the evidence of folklore seems to be based on the false premise that the folklore of the Famine, by dint of its nature as folklore, carries a nationalist interpretation of the causes, events and effects of the calamity.' Lady Wilde, from her days as the nation's poet Speranza, would have been conscious of the power of sentiment that tales of ancient Ireland would invoke for the generation whose parents experienced – and may well have been displaced by – the Great Famine. Although she does, in her preface, claim not to be appealing to any sense of nostalgia for times past, there is no doubt that there would have been an appetite for books about 'the old country' in particular among the American Irish diaspora.

The heady mix of legends, charms and superstitions are such that she sometimes digresses from the section she is on and so you find the tale of 'The Dead Hand' (page 222) in the midst of a chapter on animals. This is testament to the tangled mix of stories told, the blend

FOREWORD

of Pagan hangovers and the Christianization of ancient beliefs. There are too many interesting tales to tell in too logical a manner; much like a storyteller of old would entrance his audience around the fire with asides and additions to the main narrative, Lady Wilde knows what will hold her reader's attention. As such, we have retained the original ordering of the stories within this edition, even where it may seem eccentric, in order to remain true to the intentions of the author.

PREFACE

The three great sources of knowledge respecting the shrouded part of humanity are the language, the mythology, and the ancient monuments of a country.

From the language one learns the mental and social height to which a nation had reached at any given period in arts, habits, and civilization, with the relation of man to man, and to the material and visible world.

The mythology of a people reveals their relation to a spiritual and invisible world; while the early monuments are solemn and eternal symbols of religious faith – rituals of stone in cromlech, pillar, shrine and tower, temples and tombs.

The written word, or literature, comes last, the fullest and highest expression of the intellect and culture, and scientific progress of a nation.

The Irish race were never much indebted to the written word. The learned class, the ollamhs, dwelt apart and kept their knowledge sacred. The people therefore lived entirely upon the traditions of their forefathers, blended with the new doctrines taught by Christianity; so that the popular belief became, in time, an amalgam of the pagan myths and the Christian legend, and these two elements remain indissolubly united to this day. The world, in fact, is a volume, a serial rather, going on for six thousand years, but of which the Irish peasant has scarcely yet turned the first page.

The present work deals only with the mythology, or the fantastic creed of the Irish respecting the invisible world – strange and mystical superstitions, brought thousands of years ago from their Aryan home, but which still, even in the present time, affect all the modes of thinking and acting in the daily life of the people.

ANCIENT LEGENDS, MYSTIC CHARMS AND SUPERSTITIONS OF IRELAND

Amongst the educated classes in all nations, the belief in the supernatural, acting directly on life and constantly interfering with the natural course of human action, is soon dissipated and gradually disappears, for the knowledge of natural laws solves many mysteries that were once inexplicable; yet much remains unsolved, even to the philosopher, of the mystic relation between the material and the spiritual world. Whilst to the masses – the uneducated – who know nothing of the fixed eternal laws of nature, every phenomenon seems to result from the direct action of some non-human power, invisible though ever present; able to confer all benefits, yet implacable if offended, and therefore to be propitiated.

The superstition, then, of the Irish peasant is the instinctive belief in the existence of certain unseen agencies that influence all human life; and with the highly sensitive organization of their race, it is not wonderful that the people live habitually under the shadow and dread of invisible powers which, whether working for good or evil, are awful and mysterious to the uncultured mind that sees only the strange results produced by certain forces, but knows nothing of approximate causes.

Many of the Irish legends, superstitions, and ancient charms now collected were obtained chiefly from oral communications made by the peasantry themselves, either in Irish or in the Irish-English which preserves so much of the expressive idiom of the antique tongue.

These narrations were taken down by competent persons skilled in both languages, and as far as possible in the very words of the narrator; so that much of the primitive simplicity of the style has been retained, while the legends have a peculiar and special value as coming direct from the national heart.

In a few years such a collection would be impossible, for the old race is rapidly passing away to other lands, and in the vast working-world of America, with all the new influences of light and progress, the young generation, though still loving the land of their fathers, will scarcely find leisure to dream over the fairy-haunted hills and lakes and raths of ancient Ireland.

PREFACE

I must disclaim, however, all desire to be considered a melancholy *Laudatrix temporis acti*. These studies of the Irish past are simply the expression of my love for the beautiful island that gave me my first inspiration, my quickest intellectual impulses, and the strongest and best sympathies with genius and country possible to a woman's nature.

FRANCESCA SPERANZA WILDE

INTRODUCTION

The ancient legends of all nations of the world, on which from age to age the generations of man have been nurtured, bear so-striking a resemblance to each other that we are led to believe there was once a period when the whole human family was of one creed and one language. But with increasing numbers came the necessity of dispersion; and that ceaseless migration was commenced of the tribes of the earth from the Eastern cradle of their race which has now continued for thousands of years with undiminished activity.

From the beautiful Eden-land at the head of the Persian Gulf, where creeds and culture rose to life, the first migrations emanated, and were naturally directed along the line of the great rivers, by the Euphrates and the Tigris and southward by the Nile; and there the first mighty cities of the world were built, and the first mighty kingdoms of the East began to send out colonies to take possession of the unknown silent world around them. From Persia, Assyria, and Egypt, to Greece and the Isles of the Sea, went forth the wandering tribes, carrying with them, as signs of their origin, broken fragments of the primal creed, and broken idioms of the primal tongue – those early pages in the history of the human race, eternal and indestructible, which hundreds of centuries have not been able to obliterate from the mind of man.

But as the early tribes diverged from the central parent stock, the creed and the language began to assume new forms, according as new habits of life and modes of thought were developed amongst the wandering people, by the influence of climate and the contemplation of new and striking natural phenomena in the lands where they found a resting-place or a home. Still, amongst all nations a basis remained of the primal creed and language, easily to be traced through all the mutations caused by circumstances in human thought, either by higher culture or by the debasement to which both language and symbols are subjected amongst rude and illiterate tribes.

To reconstruct the primal creed and language of humanity from these scattered and broken fragments, is the task which is now exciting so keenly the energies of the ardent and learned ethnographers of Europe; as yet, indeed, with but small success as regards language, for not more, perhaps, than twenty words which the philologists consider may have belonged to the original tongue have been discovered; that is, certain objects or ideas are found represented in all languages by the same words, and therefore the philologist concludes that these words must have been associated with the ideas from the earliest dawn of language; and as the words express chiefly the relations of the human family to each other, they remained fixed in the minds of the wandering tribes, untouched and unchanged by all the diversities of their subsequent experience of life.

Meanwhile, in Europe there is diligent study of the ancient myths, legends, and traditions of the world, in order to extract from them that information respecting the early modes of thought prevalent amongst the primitive race, and also the lines of the first migrations, which no other monuments of antiquity are so well able to give. Traditions, like rays of light, take their colour from the medium through which they pass; but the scientific mythographic student knows how to eliminate the accidental addition from the true primal basis, which remains fixed and unchangeable; and from the numerous myths and legends of the nations of the earth, which bear so striking a conformity to each other that they point to a common origin, he will be able to reconstruct the first articles of belief in the creed of humanity, and to pronounce almost with certainty upon the primal source of the lines of human life that now traverse the globe in all directions. This source of all life, creed, and culture now on earth, there is no reason to doubt, will be found in Iran or Persia as we call it, and in the ancient legends and language of the great Iranian people, the head and noblest type of the Aryan races.

INTRODUCTION

Endowed with splendid physical beauty, noble intellect, and a rich musical language, the Iranians had also a lofty sense of the relation between man and the spiritual world. They admitted no idols into their temples; their God was the One Supreme Creator and Upholder of all things, whose symbol was the sun and the pure, elemental fire. But as the world grew older and more wicked the pure primal doctrines were obscured by human fancies, the symbol came to be worshipped in place of the God, and the debased idolatries of Babylon, Assyria, and the Canaanite nations were the result. Egypt – grave, wise, learned, mournful Egypt – retained most of the primal truth; but truth was held by the priests as too precious for the crowd, and so they preserved it carefully for themselves and their own caste. They alone knew the ancient and cryptic meaning of the symbols; the people were allowed only to see the outward and visible sign.

From Egypt, philosophy, culture, art, and religion came to Greece, but the Greeks moulded these splendid elements after their own fashion, and poured the radiance of beauty over the grave and gloomy mysticism of Egypt. Everything hideous, terrible, and revolting was banished from the Greek Mythology. The Greeks constructed no theory of a devil, and believed in no hell, as a distinct and eternal abode for the lost souls of men. The Greek gods were divinely beautiful, and each divinity in turn was ready to help the mortal that invoked him. The dead in Hades mourned their fate because they could no longer enjoy the glorious beauty of life, but no hard and chilling dogmas doomed them there to the tortures of eternal punishment. Earth, air, the heavens and the sea, the storms and sunshine, the forests and flowers and the purple grapes with which they crowned a god, were all to the Greek poet-mind the manifestations of an all-pervading spiritual power and life. A sublime Pantheism was their creed, that sees gods in everything, yet with one Supreme God over all. Freedom, beauty, art, light, and joy, were the elements of the Greek religion, while the Eternal Wisdom, the Great Athene of the Parthenon, was the peculiar and selected divinity of their own half divine race.

Meanwhile other branches of the primal Iranian stock were spreading over the savage central forests of Europe, where they laid the foundation of the great Teuton and Gothic races, the destined world-rulers; but Nature to them was a gloomy and awful mother, and life seemed an endless warfare against the fierce and powerful elemental demons of frost and snow and darkness, by whom the beautiful Sun-god was slain, and who reigned triumphant in that fearful season when the earth was iron and the air was ice, and no beneficent God seemed near to help. Hideous idols imaged these unseen powers, who were propitiated by sanguinary rites; and the men and the god they fashioned were alike as fierce and cruel as the wild beasts of the forest, and the aspects of the savage nature around them.

Still the waves of human life kept rolling westward until they surged over all the lands and islands of the Great Sea, and the wandering mariners, seeking new homes, passed through the Pillars of Hercules out into the Western Ocean, and coasting along by the shores of Spain and France, founded nations that still bear the impress of their Eastern origin, and are known in history as the Celtic race; while the customs, usages, and traditions which their forefathers had learnt in Egypt or Greece were carefully preserved by them, and transmitted as heirlooms to the colonies they founded. From Spain the early mariners easily reached the verdant island of the West in which we Irish are more particularly interested. And here in our beautiful Ireland the last wave of the great Iranian migration finally settled. Further progress was impossible – the unknown ocean seemed to them the limits of the world. And thus the wanderers of the primal race, with their fragments of the ancient creed and mythic poet-lore, and their peculiar dialect of the ancient tongue, formed, as it were, a sediment here which still retains its peculiar affinity with the parent land – though the changes and chances of three thousand years have swept over the people, the legends, and the language. It is, therefore, in Ireland, above all, that the nature and origin of the primitive races of Europe should be studied. Even the form of the Celtic head shows a decided conformity to that of the Greek races, while it differs essentially from the Saxon and Gothic

INTRODUCTION

types. This is one of the many proofs in support of the theory that the Celtic people in their westward course to the Atlantic travelled by the coasts of the Mediterranean, as all along that line the same cranial formation is found. Philologists also affirm that the Irish language is nearer to Sanskrit than any other of the living and spoken languages of Europe; while the legends and myths of Ireland can be readily traced to the far East, but have nothing in common with the fierce and weird superstitions of Northern mythology.

This study of legendary lore, as a foundation for the history of humanity, is now recognized as such an important branch of ethnology that a journal entirely devoted to comparative mythology has been recently started in Paris, to which all nations are invited to contribute – Sclaves, Teutons, and Celts, Irish legends being considered specially important, as containing more of the primitive elements than those of other Western nations. All other countries have been repeatedly overwhelmed by alien tribes and peoples and races, but the Irish have remained unchanged, and in place of adopting readily the usages of invaders they have shown such remarkable powers of fascination that the invaders themselves became *Hibernicis ipsis Hiberniores*. The Danes held the east coast of Ireland for three hundred years, yet there is no trace of Thor or Odin or the Frost Giants, or of the Great Worldserpent in Irish legend; but if we go back in the history of the world to the beginning of things, when the Iranian people were the only teachers of humanity, we come upon the true ancient source of Irish legend, and find that the original materials have been but very slightly altered, while amongst other nations the ground-work has been overlaid with a dense palimpsest of their own devising, suggested by their peculiar local surroundings.

Amongst the earliest religious symbols of the world are the Tree, the Woman, and the Serpent – memories, no doubt, of the legend of Paradise; and the reverence for certain sacred trees has prevailed in Persia from the most ancient times, and become diffused among all the Iranian nations. It was the custom in Iran to hang costly garments on the branches as votive offerings; and it is recorded that Xerxes before going to battle invoked victory by the Sacred Tree and hung jewels and rich robes on the boughs. And the poet Saadi narrates an anecdote concerning trees which has the true Oriental touch of mournful suggestion: He was once, he says, the guest of a very rich old man who had a son remarkable for his beauty. One night the old man said to him, 'During my whole life I never had but this son. Near this place is a Sacred Tree to which men resort to offer up their petitions. Many nights at the foot of this tree I besought God until He bestowed on me this son.' Not long after Saadi overheard this young man say in a low voice to his friend, 'How happy should I be to know where that Sacred Tree grows, in order that I might implore God for the death of my father.'

The poorer class in Persia, not being able to make offerings of costly garments, are in the habit of tying bits of coloured stuffs on the boughs, and these rags are considered to have a special virtue in curing diseases. The trees are often near a well or by a saint's grave, and are then looked upon as peculiarly sacred.

This account might have been written for Ireland, for the belief and the ceremonial are precisely similar, and are still found existing to this day both in Iran and in Erin. But all trees were not held sacred – only those that bore no eatable fruit that could nourish men; a lingering memory of the tree of evil fruit may have caused this prejudice, while the Tree of Life was eagerly sought for, with its promised gift of immortality. In Persia the plane-tree was specially reverenced; in Egypt, the palm; in Greece, the wild olive; and the oak amongst the Celtic nations.

Sometimes small tapers were lit amongst the branches, to simulate by fire the presence of divinity. It is worthy of note, while on the subject of Irish and Iranian affinities, that the old Persian word for tree is *dar*, and the Irish call their sacred tree, the oak, *darragh*.[1]

---

[1] The terms Dryad and Druid may be compared as containing the same root and reference..

INTRODUCTION

The belief in a race of supernatural beings, midway between man and the Supreme God, beautiful and beneficent, a race that had never known the weight of human life, was also part of the creed of the Iranian people. They called them Peris, or Feroüers (fairies); and they have some pretty legends concerning the beautiful Dukhtari Shah Periân, the 'Daughter of the King of the Fairies,' for a sight of whose beauty men pine away in vain desire, but if it is granted to them once to behold her, they die. Every nation believes in the existence of these mysterious spirits, with mystic and powerful influence over human life and actions, but each nation represents them differently, according to national habits and national surroundings. Thus, the Russians believe in the phantom of the Ukraine, a beautiful young girl robed in white, who meets the wanderer on the lonely snow steppes, and lulls him by her kisses into that fatal sleep from which he never more awakens. The legends of the Scandinavians, also, are all set in the framework of their own experiences; the rending and crash of the ice is the stroke of the god Thor's hammer; the rime is the beard of the Frost Giant; and when Balder, their Sun-god, is beginning to die at Midsummer, they kindle pine-branches to light him on his downward path to hell; and when he is returning to the upper world, after the winter solstice, they burn the Yule-log, and hang lights on the fir-trees to illuminate his upward path. These traditions are a remnant of the ancient sun worship, but the peasants who kindle the Baal fires at Midsummer, and the upper classes who light up the brilliant Christmas-tree, have forgotten the origin of the custom, though the world-old symbol and usage is preserved.

The *Sidhe*, or Fairies, of Ireland, still preserve all the gentle attributes of their ancient Persian race, for in the soft and equable climate of Erin there were no terrible manifestations of nature to be symbolized by new images; and the genial, laughter-loving elves were in themselves the best and truest expression of Irish nature that could have been invented. The fairies loved music and dancing and frolic; and, above all things, to be let alone, and not to be interfered with as regarded their peculiar fairy habits, customs, and pastimes. They had also, like the

Irish, a fine sense of the right and just, and a warm love for the liberal hand and kindly word. All the solitudes of the island were peopled by these bright, happy, beautiful beings, and to the Irish nature, with its need of the spiritual, its love of the vague, mystic, dreamy, and supernatural, there was something irresistibly fascinating in the belief that gentle spirits were around, filled with sympathy for the mortal who suffered wrong or needed help. But the fairies were sometimes wilful and capricious as children, and took dire revenge if any one built over their fairy circles, or looked at them when combing their long yellow hair in the sunshine, or dancing in the woods, or floating on the lakes. Death was the penalty to all who approached too near, or pried too curiously into the mysteries of nature.

To the Irish peasant earth and air were filled with these mysterious beings, half-loved, half-feared by them; and therefore they were propitiated by flattery, and called 'the good people,' as the Greeks call the dread goddesses 'the Eumenides.' Their voices were heard in the mountain echo, and their forms seen in the purple and golden mountain mist; they whispered amidst the perfumed hawthorn branches; the rush of the autumn leaves was the scamper of little elves – red, yellow, and brown – wind-delven, and dancing in their glee; and the bending of the waving barley was caused by the flight of the Elf King and his Court across the fields. They danced with soundless feet, and their step was so light that the drops of dew they danced on only trembled, but did not break. The fairy music was low and sweet, 'blinding sweet,' like that of the great god Pan by the river; they lived only on the nectar in the cups of the flowers, though in their fairy palaces sumptuous banquets were offered to the mortals they carried off – but woe to the mortal who tasted of fairy food; to eat was fatal. All the evil in the world has come by eating; if Eve had only resisted that apple our race might still he in Paradise. The Sidhe look with envy on the beautiful young human children, and steal them when they can; and the children of a Sidhe and a mortal mother are reputed to grow up strong and powerful, but with evil and dangerous natures. There is also a belief that every seven years the fairies are obliged to deliver up a victim to the Evil One, and to save their own people they try to abduct some beautiful young mortal girl, and her they hand over to the Prince of Darkness.

Dogmatic religion and science have long since killed the mythopoetic faculty in cultured Europe. It only exists now, naturally and instinctively, in children, poets, and the childhke races, like the Irish – simple, joyous, reverent, and unlettered, and who have remained unchanged for centuries, walled round by their language from the rest of Europe, through which separating veil science, culture, and the cold mockery of the sceptic have never yet penetrated.

Christianity was readily accepted by the Irish. The pathetic tale of the beautiful young Virgin-Mother and the Child-God, for central objects, touched all the deepest chords of feeling in the tender, loving, and sympathetic Irish heart. The legends of ancient times were not overthrown by it, however, but taken up and incorporated with the new Christian faith. The holy wells and the sacred trees remained, and were even made holier by association with a saint's name. And to this day the old mythology holds its ground with a force and vitality untouched by any symptoms of weakness or decay. The Greeks, who are of the same original race as our people, rose through the influence of the highest culture to the fulness and perfectness of eternal youth; but the Irish, without culture, are eternal children, with all the childlike instincts of superstition still strong in them, and capable of believing all things, because to doubt requires knowledge. They never, like the Greeks, attained to the conception of a race of beings nobler than themselves – men stronger and more gifted, with the immortal fire of a god in their veins; women divinely beautiful, or divinely inspired; but, also, the Irish never defaced the image of God in their hearts by infidelity or irreligion.

One of the most beautiful and sublimely touching records in all human history is that of the unswerving devotion of the Irish people to their ancient faith, through persecutions and penal enactments more insulting and degrading than were ever inflicted in any other land by one Christian sect upon another.

With this peculiarly reverential nature it would be impossible to make the Irish a nation of sceptics, even if a whole legion of German Rationalists came amongst them to preach a crusade against all belief in the spiritual and the unseen. And the old traditions of their race have likewise taken firm hold in their hearts, because they are an artistic people, and require objects for their adoration and love, not mere abstractions to be accepted by their reason. And they are also a nation of poets; the presence of God is ever near them, and the saints and angels, and the shadowy beings of earth and air are perpetually drawing their minds, through mingled love and fear, to the infinite and invisible world. Probably not one tradition or custom that had its origin in a religious belief has been lost in Ireland during the long course of ages since the first people from Eastern lands arrived and settled on our shores. The Baal fires are still lit at Midsummer, though no longer in honour of the sun, but of St John; and the peasants still make their cattle pass between two fires – not, indeed, as of old, in the name of Moloch, but of some patron saint. That all Irish legends point to the East for their origin, not to the North, is certain; to a warm land, not one of icebergs, and thunder crashes of the rending of ice-bound rivers, but to a region where the shadow of trees, and a cool draught from the sparkling well were life-giving blessings. Well-worship could not have originated in a humid country like Ireland, where wells can be found at every step, and sky and land are ever heavy and saturated with moisture. It must have come from an Eastern people, wanderers in a dry and thirsty land, where the discovery of a well seemed like the interposition of an angel in man's behalf.

We are told also by the ancient chroniclers that serpent-worship once prevailed in Ireland, and that St Patrick hewed down the serpent idol Crom-Cruadh (the great worm) and cast it into the Boyne (from whence arose the legend that St Patrick banished all venomous things from the island). Now as the Irish never could have seen a serpent, none existing in Ireland, this worship must have come from the far East, where this beautiful and deadly creature is looked upon as the symbol of the Evil One, and worshipped and propitiated by votive offerings, as all evil things were in the early world, in the hope of turning away their evil hatred from man, and to induce them to show mercy and pity; just as the Egyptians propitiated the sacred crocodile by subtle flatteries and hung costly jewels in its ears. The Irish, indeed, do not seem to have originated any peculiar or national cultus.

Their funeral ceremonies recall those of Egypt and Greece and other ancient Eastern climes, from whence they brought their customs of the Wake, the death chant, the mourning women, and the funeral games. In Sparta, on the death of a king or great chief, they had a wake and 'keen' not common to the rest of Greece, but which they said they learned from the Phoenicians; and this peculiar usage bears a striking resemblance to the Irish practice. All the virtues of the dead were recited, and the Greek 'Eleleu,' the same cry as the 'Ul-lu-lu' of the Irish, was keened over the corpse by the chorus of hired mourning women. The custom of selecting women in place of men for the chorus of lamentation prevailed throughout all the ancient world, as if an open display of grief was thought beneath the dignity of man. It was Cassandra gave the keynote for the wail over Hector, and Helen took the lead in reciting praises to his honour. The death chants in Egypt, Arabia, and Abyssinia all bear a marked resemblance to the Irish; indeed the mourning cry is the same in all, and the Egyptian lamentation 'Hi-loo-loo! Hi-loo-loo!' cried over the dead, was probably the original form of the Irish wail.

The Greeks always endeavoured to lessen the terrors of death, and for this reason they established funeral games, and the funeral ceremonies took the form of a festival, where they ate and drank and poured libations of wine in honour of the dead. The Irish had also their funeral games and peculiar dances, when they threw off their upper garments, and holding hands in a circle, moved in a slow measure round a woman crouched in the centre, with her hands covering her face. Another singular part of the ceremony was the entrance of a woman wearing a cow's head and horns, as Io appears upon the scene in the Prometheus of Aeschylus. This woman was probably meant to represent the horned or crescented moon, the antique Diana, the Goddess of Death. The custom of throwing off the garments no doubt originally signified the casting off the garment of the flesh. We brought nothing into this world, and it is certain we carry nothing out. The soul must stand unveiled before God.

In the islands off the West Coast of Ireland, where the most ancient superstitions still exist, they have a strange custom. No funeral wail is allowed to be raised until three hours have elapsed from the moment of death, because, they say, the sound of the cries would hinder the soul from speaking to God when it stands before Him, and waken up the two great dogs that are watching for the souls of the dead in order that they may devour them – and the Lord of Heaven Himself cannot hinder them if once they waken. This tradition of watching by the dead in silence, while the soul stands before God, is a fine and solemn superstition, which must have had its origin amongst a people of intense faith in the invisible world, and is probably of great antiquity.

The sound of the Irish keen is wonderfully pathetic. No one could listen to the long-sustained minor wail of the 'Ul-lu-lu' without strong emotion and even tears; and once heard it can never be forgotten. Nor is there anything derogatory to grief in the idea of hired mourners; on the contrary, it is a splendid tribute to the dead to order their praises to be recited publicly before the assembled friends; while there is something indescribably impressive in the aspect of the mourning women crouched around the bier with shrouded heads, as they rock themselves to and fro and intone the solemn, ancient death-song with a measured cadence, sometimes rising to a piercing wail. They seem like weird and shadowy outlines of an old-world vision, and at once the imagination is carried back to the far-distant East, and the time when all these funeral symbols had a mysterious and awful meaning. Sometimes a wail of genuine and bitter grief interrupts the chant of the hired mourners. An Irish keen which was taken down from the lips of a bereaved mother some years ago, runs thus in the literal English version –

'O women, look on me! Look on me, women! Have you ever seen any sorrow like mine? Have you ever seen the like of me in my sorrow? Arrah, then, my darling, my darling, 'tis your mother that calls you.

INTRODUCTION

How long you are sleeping. Do you see all the people round you, my darling, and I sorely weeping? Arrah, what is this paleness on your face? Sure there was no equal to it in Erin for beauty and fairness, and your hair was heavy as the wing of a raven, and your skin was whiter than the hand of a lady. Is it the stranger must carry me to my grave, and my son lying here?'

This touching lament is so thoroughly Greek in form and sentiment that it might be taken for part of a chorus from the Hecuba of Euripides. Even the 'Arrah' reminds one of a Greek word used frequently by the Greeks when commencing a sentence or asking a question, although the resemblance may be only superficial.

The tales and legends told by the peasants in the Irish vernacular are much more weird and strange, and have much more of the old-world colouring than the ordinary fairy tales narrated in English by the people, as may be seen in many stories, translated from the Irish, and said to be centuries old.

THE LEGEND OF BALLYTOWTAS CASTLE

The next tale I shall select is composed in a lighter and more modern spirit. All the usual elements of a fairy tale are to be found in it, but the story is new to the nursery folk, and, if well illustrated, would make a pleasant and novel addition to the rather worn-out legends on which the children of many generations have been hitherto subsisting.

In old times there lived where Ballytowtas Castle now stands a poor man named Towtas. It was in the time when manna fell to the earth with the dew of evening, and Towtas lived by gathering the manna, and thus supported himself, for he was a poor man, and had nothing else.

One day a pedlar came by that way with a fair young daughter.

'Give us a night's lodging,' he said to Towtas, 'for we are weary.'

And Towtas did so.

Next morning, when they were going away, his heart longed for the young girl, and he said to the pedlar, 'Give me your daughter for my wife.'

'How will you support her?' asked the pedlar.

'Better than you can,' answered Towtas, 'for she can never want.'

Then he told him all about the manna; how he went out every morning when it was lying on the ground with the dew, and gathered it, as his father and forefathers had done before him, and lived on it all their lives, so that he had never known want nor any of his people.

Then the girl showed she would like to stay with the young man, and the pedlar consented, and they were married, Towtas and the fair young maiden; and the pedlar left them and went his way. So years went on, and they were very happy and never wanted; and they had one son, a bright, handsome youth, and as clever as he was comely.

But in due time old Towtas died, and after her husband was buried, the woman went out to gather the manna as she had seen him do, when the dew lay on the ground; but she soon grew tired and said to herself, 'Why should I do this thing every day? I'll just gather now enough to do the week and then I can have rest.'

So she gathered up great heaps of it greedily, and went her way into the house. But the sin of greediness lay on her evermore; and not a bit of manna fell with the dew that evening, nor ever again. And she was poor, and faint with hunger, and had to go out and work in the fields to earn the morsel that kept her and her son alive; and she begged pence from the people as they went into chapel, and this paid for her son's schooling; so he went on with his learning, and no one in the county was like him for beauty and knowledge.

One day he heard the people talking of a great lord that lived up in Dublin, who had a daughter so handsome that her like was never seen; and all the fine young gentlemen were dying about her, but she would take none of them. And he came home to his mother and said, 'I shall go see this great lord's daughter. Maybe the luck will be mine above all the fine young gentlemen that love her.'

'Go along, poor fool,' said the mother, 'how can the poor stand before the rich?'

But he persisted. 'If I die on the road,' he said, 'I'll try it.'

'Wait, then,' she answered, 'till Sunday, and whatever I get I'll give you half of it.' So she gave him half of the pence she gathered at the chapel door, and bid him go in the name of God.

He hadn't gone far when he met a poor man who asked him for a trifle for God's sake. So he gave him something out of his mother's money and went on. Again, another met him, and begged for a trifle to buy food, for the sake of God, and he gave him something also, and then went on.

'Give me a trifle for God's sake,' cried a voice, and he saw a third poor man before him.

'I have nothing left,' said Towtas, 'but a few pence; if I give them,

THE LEGEND OF BALLYTOWTAS CASTLE

I shall have nothing for food and must die of hunger. But come with me, and whatever I can buy for this I shall share with you.' And as they were going on to the inn he told all his story to the beggar man, and how he wanted to go to Dublin, but had now no money. So they came to the inn, and he called for a loaf and a drink of milk. 'Cut the loaf,' he said to the beggar.

'You are the oldest.'

'I won't,' said the other, for he was ashamed, but Towtas made him.

And so the beggar cut the loaf, but though they ate, it never grew smaller, and though they drank as they liked of the milk, it never grew less. Then Towtas rose up to pay, but when the landlady came and looked, 'How is this?' she said. 'You have eaten nothing. I'll not take your money, poor boy,' but he made her take some; and they left the place, and went on their way together.

'Now,' said the beggar man, 'you have been three times good to me to-day, for thrice I have met you, and you gave me help for the sake of God each time. See, now, I can help also,' and he reached a gold ring to the handsome youth. 'Wherever you place that ring, and wish for it, gold will come – bright gold, so that you can never want while you have it.'

Then Towtas put the ring first in one pocket and then in another, until all his pockets were so heavy with gold that he could scarcely walk; but when he turned to thank the friendly beggar man, he had disappeared.

So, wondering to himself at all his adventures, he went on, until he came at last in sight of the lord's palace, which was beautiful to see; but he would not enter in until he went and bought fine clothes, and made himself as grand as any prince; and then he went boldly up, and they invited him in, for they said, 'Surely he is a king's son.' And when dinner-hour came the lord's daughter linked her arm with Towtas, and smiled on him.

And he drank of the rich wine, and was mad with love; but at last the wine overcame him, and the servants had to carry him to his bed; and in going into his room he dropped the ring from his finger, but knew it not.

Now, in the morning, the lord's daughter came by, and cast her eyes upon the door of his chamber, and there close by it was the ring she had seen him wear.

'Ah,' she said, 'I'll tease him now about his ring.' And she put it in her box, and wished that she were as rich as a king's daughter, that so the king's son might marry her; and, behold, the box filled up with gold, so that she could not shut it; and she put it from her into another box, and that filled also; and then she was frightened at the ring, and put it at last in her pocket as the safest place.

But when Towtas awoke and missed the ring, his heart was grieved.

'Now, indeed,' he said, 'my luck is gone.'

And he inquired of all the servants, and then of the lord's daughter, and she laughed, by which he knew she had it; but no coaxing would get it from her, so when all was useless he went away, and set out again to reach his old home.

And he was very mournful and threw himself down on the ferns near an old fort, waiting till night came on, for he feared to go home in the daylight lest the people should laugh at him for his folly. And about dusk three cats came out of the fort talking to each other.

'How long our cook is away,' said one.

'What can have happened to him?' said another.

And as they were grumbling a fourth cat came up.

'What delayed you?' they all asked angrily.

Then he told his story – how he had met Towtas and given him the ring. 'And I just went,' he said, 'to the lord's palace to see how the young man behaved; and I was leaping over the dinner table when the lord's knife struck my tail and three drops of blood fell upon his plate, but he never saw it and swallowed them with his meat. So now he has three kittens inside him and is dying of agony, and can never be cured until he drinks three draughts of the water of the well of Ballytowtas.'

So when young Towtas heard the cats talk he sprang up and went and told his mother to give him three bottles full of the water of the Towtas well, and he would go to the lord disguised as a doctor and cure him.

THE LEGEND OF BALLYTOWTAS CASTLE

So off he went to Dublin. And all the doctors in Ireland were round the lord, but none of them could tell what ailed him, or how to cure him. Then Towtas came in and said, 'I will cure him.' So they gave him entertainment and lodging, and when he was refreshed he gave of the well water three draughts to his lordsnip, when out jumped the three kittens. And there was great rejoicing, and they treated Towtas like a prince. But all the same he could not get the ring from the lord's daughter, so he set off home again quite disheartened, and thought to himself, 'If I could only meet the man again that gave me the ring who knows what luck I might have?' And he sat down to rest in a wood, and saw there not far off three boys fighting under an oak-tree.

'Shame on ye to fight so,' he said to them. 'What is the fight about?'

Then they told him. 'Our father,' they said, 'before he died, buried under this oak-tree a ring by which you can be in any place in two minutes if you only wish it; a goblet that is always full when standing, and empty only when on its side; and a harp that plays any tune of itself that you name or wish for.'

'I want to divide the things,' said the youngest boy, 'and let us all go and seek our fortunes as we can.'

'But I have a right to the whole,' said the eldest.

And they went on fighting, till at length Towtas said –

'I'll tell you how to settle the matter. All of you be here tomorrow, and I'll think over the matter tonight, and I engage you will have nothing more to quarrel about when you come in the morning.'

So the boys promised to keep good friends till they met in the morning, and went away.

When Towtas saw them clear off, he dug up the ring, the goblet, and the harp, and now said he, 'I'm all right, and they won't have anything to fight about in the morning.'

Off he set back again to the lord's castle with the ring, the goblet, and the harp; but he soon bethought himself of the powers of the ring, and in two minutes he was in the great hall where all the lords and ladies were just sitting down to dinner; and the harp played the sweetest music, and they all listened in delight; and he drank out of the goblet which was never empty, and then, when his head began to grow a little light, 'It is enough,' he said; and putting his arm round the waist of the lord's daughter, he took his harp and goblet in the other hand, and murmuring – 'I wish we were at the old fort by the side of the wood' – in two minutes they were both at the desired spot. But his head was heavy with the wine, and he laid down the harp beside him and fell asleep. And when she saw him asleep she took the ring off his finger, and the harp and the goblet from the ground and was back home in her father's castle before two minutes had passed by.

When Towtas awoke and found his prize gone, and all his treasures beside, he was like one mad; and roamed about the country till he came by an orchard, where he saw a tree covered with bright, rosy apples. Being hungry and thirsty, he plucked one and ate it, but no sooner had he done so than horns began to sprout from his forehead, and grew larger and longer till he knew he looked like a goat, and all he could do, they would not come off. Now, indeed, he was driven out of his mind, and thought how all the neighbours would laugh at him; and as he raged and roared with shame, he spied another tree with apples, still brighter, of ruddy gold.

'If I were to have fifty pairs of horns I must have one of those,' he said; and seizing one, he had no sooner tasted it than the horns fell off, and he felt that he was looking stronger and handsomer than ever.

'Now, I have her at last,' he exclaimed. 'I'll put horns on them all, and will never take them off until they give her to me as my bride before the whole Court.'

Without further delay he set off to the lord's palace, carrying with him as many of the apples as he could bring off the two trees. And when they saw the beauty of the fruit they longed for it; and he gave to them all, so that at last there was not a head to be seen without horns in the whole dining-hall. Then they cried out and prayed to have the horns taken off, but Towtas said –

'No; there they shall be till I have the lord's daughter given to me for my bride, and my two rings, my goblet, and my harp all restored to me.'

And this was done before the face of all the lords and ladies; and his treasures were restored to him; and the lord placed his daughter's hand in the hand of Towtas, saying –

'Take her; she is your wife; only free me from the horns.' Then Towtas brought forth the golden apples; and they all ate, and the horns fell off; and he took his bride and his treasures, and carried them off home, where he built the Castle of Ballytowtas, in the place where stood his father's hut, and enclosed the well within the walls. And when he had filled his treasure-room with gold, so that no man could count his riches, he buried his fairy treasures deep in the ground, where no man knew, and no man has ever yet been able to find them until this day.

A WOLF STORY

Transformation into wolves is a favourite subject of Irish legend, and many a wild tale is told by the peasants round the turf fire in the winter nights of strange adventures with wolves.

Stories that had come down to them from their forefathers in the old times long ago; for there are no wolves existing now in Ireland.

A young farmer, named Connor, once missed two fine cows from his herd, and no tale or tidings could be heard of them anywhere. So he thought he would set out on a search throughout the country; and he took a stout blackthorn stick in his hand, and went his way. All day he travelled miles and miles, but never a sign of the cattle. And the evening began to grow very dark, and he was wearied and hungry, and no place near to rest in; for he was in the midst of a bleak, desolate heath, with never a habitation at all in sight, except a long, low, rude shieling, like the den of a robber or a wild beast. But a gleam of light came from a chink between the boards, and Connor took heart and went up and knocked at the door. It was opened at once by a tall, thin, grey-haired old man, with keen, dark eyes.

'Come in,' he said, 'you are welcome. We have been waiting for you. This is my wife,' and he brought him over to the hearth, where was seated an old, thin, grey woman, with long, sharp teeth and terrible glittering eyes.

'You are welcome,' she said. 'We have been waiting for you – it is time for supper. Sit down and eat with us.'

Now Connor was a brave fellow, but he was a little dazed at first at the sight of this strange creature. However, as he had his stout stick with him, he thought he could make a fight for his life any way, and, meantime, he would rest and eat, for he was both hungry and weary, and it was now black night, and he would never find his way home even if he tried. So he sat down by the hearth, while the old grey woman stirred the pot on the fire. But Connor felt that she was watching him all the time with her keen, sharp eyes.

Then a knock came to the door. And the old man rose up and opened it. When in walked a slender, young black wolf, who immediately went straight across the floor to an inner room, from which in a few moments came forth a dark, slender, handsome youth, who took his place at the table and looked hard at Connor with his glittering eyes.

'You are welcome,' he said, 'we have waited for you.'

Before Connor could answer another knock was heard, and in came a second wolf, who passed on to the inner room like the first, and soon after, another dark, handsome youth came out and sat down to supper with them, glaring at Connor with his keen eyes, but said no word.

'These are our sons,' said the old man, 'tell them what you want, and what brought you here amongst us, for we live alone and don't care to have spies and strangers coming to our place.'

Then Connor told his story, how he had lost his two fine cows, and had searched all day and found no trace of them; and he knew nothing of the place he was in, nor of the kindly gentleman who asked him to supper; but if they just told him where to find his cows he would thank them, and make the best of his way home at once.

Then they all laughed and looked at each other, and the old hag looked more frightful than ever when she showed her long, sharp teeth.

On this, Connor grew angry, for he was hot tempered; and he grasped his blackthorn stick firmly in his hand and stood up, and bade them open the door for him; for he would go his way, since they would give no heed and only mocked him.

Then the eldest of the young men stood up. 'Wait,' he said, 'we are fierce and evil, but we never forget a kindness. Do you remember, one day down in the glen you found a poor little wolf in great agony and like to die, because a sharp thorn had pierced his side? And you gently extracted the thorn and gave him a drink, and went your way leaving him in peace and rest?'

'Aye, well do I remember it,' said Connor, 'and how the poor little beast licked my hand in gratitude.'

'Well,' said the young man, 'I am that wolf, and I shall help you if I can, but stay with us tonight and have no fear.'

So they sat down again to supper and feasted merrily, and then all fell fast asleep, and Connor knew nothing more till he awoke in the morning and found himself by a large hay-rick in his own field.

'Now surely,' thought he, 'the adventure of last night was not all a dream, and I shall certainly find my cows when I go home; for that excellent, good young wolf promised his help, and I feel certain he would not deceive me.'

But when he arrived home and looked over the yard and the stable and the field, there was no sign nor sight of the cows. So he grew very sad and dispirited. But just then he espied in the field close by three of the most beautiful strange cows he had ever set eyes on. 'These must have strayed in,' he said, 'from some neighbour's ground;' and he took his big stick to drive them out of the gate off the field. But when he reached the gate, there stood a young black wolf watching; and when the cows tried to pass out at the gate he bit at them, and drove them back. Then Connor knew that his friend the wolf had kept his word. So he let the cows go quietly back to the field; and there they remained, and grew to be the finest in the whole country, and their descendants are flourishing to this day, and Connor grew rich and prospered; for a kind deed is never lost, but brings good luck to the doer for evermore, as the old proverb says;

'Blessings are won,
By a good deed done.'

But never again did Connor find that desolate heath or that lone shieling, though he sought far and wide, to return his thanks, as was due to the friendly wolves; nor did he ever again meet any of the family, though he mourned much whenever a slaughtered wolf was brought into the town for the sake of the reward, fearing his excellent friend might be the victim. At that time the wolves in Ireland had increased to such an extent, owing to the desolation of the country by constant wars, that a reward was offered and a high price paid for every wolf's skin brought into the court of the justiciary; and this was in the time of Queen Elizabeth, when the English troops made ceaseless war against the Irish people, and there were more wolves in Ireland than men; and the dead lay unburied in hundreds on the highways, for there were no hands left to dig them graves.

THE EVIL EYE

There is nothing more dreaded by the people, nor considered more deadly in its effects, than the Evil Eye.

It may strike at any moment unless the greatest precautions are taken, and even then there is no true help possible unless the fairy doctor is at once summoned to pronounce the mystic charm that can alone destroy the evil and fatal influence.

There are several modes in which the Evil Eye can act, some much more deadly than others. If certain persons are met the first thing in the morning, you will be unlucky for the whole of that day in all you do. If the evil-eyed comes in to rest, and looks fixedly on anything, on cattle or on a child, there is doom in the glance; a fatality which cannot be evaded except by a powerful counter-charm. But if the evil-eyed mutters a verse over a sleeping child, that child will assuredly die, for the incantation is of the devil, and no charm has power to resist it or turn away the evil. Sometimes the process of bewitching is effected by looking fixedly at the object, through nine fingers; especially is the magic fatal if the victim is seated by the fire in the evening when the moon is full. Therefore, to avoid being suspected of having the Evil Eye, it is necessary at once, when looking at a child, to say 'God bless it.' And when passing a farmyard where the cows are collected for milking, to say, 'The blessing of God be on you and on all your labours.' If this form is omitted, the worst results may be apprehended, and the people would be filled with terror and alarm, unless a counter-charm were not instantly employed.

The singular malific influence of a glance has been felt by most persons in life; an influence that seems to paralyze intellect and speech, simply by the mere presence in the room of some one who is mystically antipathetic to our nature. For the soul is like a fine-toned harp that vibrates to the slightest external force or movement, and the presence and glance of some persons can radiate around us a divine joy, while others may kill the soul with a sneer or a frown. We call these subtle influences mysteries, but the early races believed them to be produced by spirits, good or evil, as they acted on the nerves or the intellect.

Some years ago an old woman was living in Kerry, and it was thought so unlucky to meet her in the morning, that all the girls used to go out after sunset to bring in water for the following day, that so they might avoid her evil glance; for whatever she looked upon came to loss and grief.

There was a man, also, equally dreaded on account of the strange, fatal power of his glance; and so many accidents and misfortunes were traced to his presence that finally the neighbours insisted that he should wear a black patch over the Evil Eye, not to be removed unless by request; for learned gentlemen, curious in such things, sometimes came to him to ask for a proof of his power, and he would try it for a wager while drinking with his friends.

One day, near an old ruin of a castle, he met a boy weeping in great grief for his pet pigeon, which had got up to the very top of the ruin, and could not be coaxed down.

'What will you give me,' asked the man, 'if I bring it down for you?'

'I have nothing to give,' said the boy, 'but I will pray to God for you. Only get me back my pigeon, and I shall be happy.'

Then the man took off the black patch and looked up steadfastly at the bird; when all of a sudden it fell to the ground and lay motionless, as if stunned; but there was no harm done to it, and the boy took it up and went his way, rejoicing.

A woman in the County Galway had a beautiful child, so handsome, that all the neighbours were very careful to say 'God bless it' when they saw him, for they knew the fairies would desire to steal the child, and carry it off to the hills.

But one day it chanced that an old woman, a stranger, came in. 'Let me rest,' she said, 'for I am weary.' And she sat down and looked at the child, but never said 'God bless it.' And when she had rested, she rose up, looked again at the child fixedly, in silence, and then went her way.

All that night the child cried and would not sleep. And all the next day it moaned as if in pain. So the mother told the priest, but he would do nothing for fear of the fairies. And just as the poor mother was in despair, she saw a strange woman going by the door. 'Who knows,' she said to her husband, 'but this woman would help us.' So they asked her to come in and rest. And when she looked at the child she said 'God bless it,' instantly, and spat three times at it, and then sat down.

'Now, what will you give me,' she said, 'if I tell you what ails the child?'

'I will cross your hand with silver,' said the mother, 'as much as you want, only speak,' and she laid the money on the woman's hand. 'Now tell me the truth, for the sake and in the name of Mary, and the good Angels.'

THE EVIL EYE

'Well,' said the stranger, 'the fairies have had your child these two days in the hills, and this is a changeling they have left in its place. But so many blessings were said on your child that the fairies can do it no harm. For there was only one blessing wanting, and only one person gave the Evil Eye. Now, you must watch for this woman, carry her into the house and secretly cut off a piece of her cloak. Then burn the piece close to the child, till the smoke as it rises makes him sneeze; and when this happens the spell is broken, and your own child will come back to you safe and sound, in place of the changeling.'

Then the stranger rose up and went her way.

All that evening the mother watched for the old woman, and at last she spied her on the road.

'Come in,' she cried, 'come in, good woman, and rest, for the cakes are hot on the griddle, and supper is ready.'

So the woman came in, but never said 'God bless you kindly,' to man or mortal, only scowled at the child, who cried worse than ever.

Now the mother had told her eldest girl to cut off a piece of the old woman's cloak, secretly, when she sat down to eat. And the girl did as she was desired, and handed the piece to her mother, unknown to any one. But, to their surprise, this was no sooner done than the woman rose up and went out without uttering a word; and they saw her no more.

Then the father carried the child outside, and burned the piece of cloth before the door, and held the boy over the smoke till he sneezed three times violently: after which he gave the child back to the mother, who laid him in his bed, where he slept peacefully, with a smile on his face, and cried no more with the cry of pain. And when he woke up the mother knew that she had got her own darling child back from the fairies, and no evil thing happened to him any more.

The influence of the mysterious and malign power of the Evil Eye has at all times been as much dreaded in Ireland as it is in Egypt, Greece, or Italy at the present day. Everything young beautiful, or perfect after its kind, and which naturally attracts attention and admiration, is peculiarly liable to the fatal blight that follows the glance of the Evil Eye. It is therefore an invariable habit amongst the peasantry never to praise anything without instantly adding, 'God bless it;' for were this formula omitted, the worst consequences would befall the object praised.

The superstition must be of great antiquity in Ireland, for Balor, the Fomorian giant and hero, is spoken of in an ancient manuscript as able to petrify his enemies by a glance; and how he became possessed of the power is thus narrated:

One day as the Druids were busy at their incantations, while boiling a magical spell or charm, young Balor passed by, and curious to see their work, looked in at an open window. At that moment the Druids happened to raise the lid of the caldron, and the vapour, escaping, passed under one of Balor's eyes, carrying with it all the venom of the incantation. This caused his brow to grow to such a size that it required four men to raise it whenever he wanted to exert the power of his venomed glance over his enemies. He was slain at last in single combat, according to the ancient legend, at the great battle of Magh-Tura[2] (the plain of the towers), fought between the Firbolgs and the Tuatha-de-Dananns for the possession of Ireland several centuries before the Christian era; for before Balor's brow could be lifted so that he could transfix his enemy and strike him dead with the terrible power of his glance, his adversary flung a stone with such violence that it went right through the Evil Eye, and pierced the skull, and the mighty magician fell to rise no more.

An interesting account of this battle, with a remarkable confirmation of the legends respecting it still current in the district, is given by Sir William Wilde, in his work, 'Lough Corrib; its Shores and Islands.' In the ancient manuscript, it is recorded that a young hero having been slain while bravely defending his king, the Firbolg army erected a mound over him, each man carrying a stone, and the monument was henceforth known as the *Carn-in-en-Fhir* (the cairn of the one man). Having examined the locality with a transcript of this manuscript

---

[2] Now called Moytura.

in his hand, Sir William fixed on the particular mound, amongst the many stone tumuli scattered over the plain, which seemed to agree best with the description, and had it opened carefully under his own superintendence.

A large flag-stone was first discovered, laid horizontally; then another beneath it, covering a small square chamber formed of stones, within which was a single urn of baked clay, graceful and delicate in form and ornamentation, containing incinerated human bones, the remains, there can be no reason to doubt, of the Firbolg youth who was honoured for his loyalty by the erection over him of the *Carn-in-en-Fhir* on the historic plains of Mayo.

After Balor, the only other ancient instance of the fatal effects of the malific Eye is narrated of St Silan, who had a poisonous hair in his eyebrow that killed whoever looked first on him in the morning. All persons, therefore, who from long sickness, or sorrow, or the weariness that comes with years, were tired of life, used to try and come in the saint's way, that so their sufferings might be ended by a quick and easy death. But another saint, the holy Molaise, hearing that St Silan was coming to visit his church, resolved that no more deaths should happen by means of the poisoned hair. So he arose early in the morning, before any one was up, and went forth alone to meet St Silan, and when he saw him coming along the path, he went boldly up and plucked out the fatal hair from his eyebrow, but in doing so he himself was struck by the venom, and immediately after fell down dead.

The power of the Evil Eye was recognized by the Brehon laws, and severe measures were ordained against the users of the malign influence. 'If a person is in the habit of injuring things through neglect, or of will, whether he has blessed, or whether he has not blessed, full penalty be upon him, or restitution in kind.' So ran the ancient law.

The gift comes by nature and is born with one, though it may not be called into exercise unless circumstances arise to excite the power. Then it seems to act like a spirit of bitter and malicious envy that radiates a poisonous atmosphere which chills and blights everything within its reach. Without being superstitious every one has felt that there is such a power and succumbed to its influence in a helpless, passive way, as if all self-trust and self-reliant energy were utterly paralyzed by its influence.

Suspected persons are held in great dread by the peasantry, and they recognize them at once by certain signs. Men and women with dark lowering eyebrows are especially feared, and the handsome children are kept out of their path lest they might be overlooked by them.

Red hair is supposed to have a most malign influence, and it has even passed into a proverb: 'Let not the eye of a red-haired woman rest on you.'

Many persons are quite unconscious that their glance or frown has this evil power until some calamity results, and then they strive not to look at any one full in the face, but to avert their eyes when speaking, lest misfortune might fall upon the person addressed.[3]

The saving invocation, 'God bless it!' is universally used when praise is bestowed, to prevent danger, and should a child fall sick some one is immediately suspected of having omitted the usual phrase out of malice and ill-will. Nothing is more dreaded by the peasantry than the full, fixed, direct glance of one suspected of the Evil Eye, and should it fall upon them, or on any of their household, a terrible fear and trembling of heart takes possession of them, which often ends in sickness or sometimes even in death.

Some years ago a woman living in Kerry declared that she was overlooked by the Evil Eye. She had no pleasure in her life and no comfort, and she wasted away because of the fear that was on her, caused by the following singular circumstance:

Every time that she happened to leave home alone, and that no one was within call, she was met by a woman totally unknown to her, who, fixing her eyes on her in silence, with a terrible expression, cast her to the ground and proceeded to beat and pinch her till she was nearly senseless; after which her tormentor disappeared.

---

[3] There is a strange idea current in Europe at the present time that one of the most remarkable potentates now living has this fatal gift and power of the Evil Eye.

THE EVIL EYE

Having experienced this treatment several times, the poor woman finally abstained altogether from leaving the house, unless protected by a servant or companion; and this precaution she observed for several years, during which time she never was molested. So at last she began to believe that the spell was broken, and that her strange enemy had departed for ever.

In consequence she grew less careful about the usual precaution, and one day stepped down alone to a little stream that ran by the house to wash some clothes.

Stooping down over her work, she never thought of any danger, and began to sing as she used to do in the light-hearted days before the spell was on her, when suddenly a dark shadow fell across the water, and looking up, she beheld to her horror the strange woman on the opposite side of the little stream, with her terrible eyes intently fixed on her, as hard and still as if she were of stone.

Springing up with a scream of terror, she flung down her work, and ran towards the house; but soon she heard footsteps behind her, and in an instant she was seized, thrown down to the ground, and her tormentor began to beat her even worse than before, till she lost all consciousness; and in this state she was found by her husband, lying on her face and speechless. She was at once carried to the house, and all the care that affection and rural skill could bestow were lavished on her, but in vain. She, however, regained sufficient consciousness to tell them of the terrible encounter she had gone through, but died before the night had passed away.

It was believed that the power of fascination by the glance, which is not necessarily an evil power like the Evil Eye, was possessed in a remarkable degree by learned and wise people, especially poets, so that they could make themselves loved and followed by any girl they liked, simply by the influence of the glance. About the year 1790, a young man resided in the County Limerick, who had this power in a singular and unusual degree. He was a clever, witty rhymer in the Irish language; and, probably, had the deep poet eyes that characterize warm and passionate poet-natures – eyes that even without necromancy have been known to exercise a powerful magnetic influence over female minds.

One day, while travelling far from home, he came upon a bright, pleasant-looking farmhouse, and feeling weary, he stopped and requested a drink of milk and leave to rest. The farmer's daughter, a young, handsome girl, not liking to admit a stranger, as all the maids were churning, and she was alone in the house, refused him admittance.

The young poet fix'd his eyes earnestly on her face for some time in silence, then slowly turning round left the house, and walked towards a small grove of trees just opposite. There he stood for a few moments resting against a tree, and facing the house as if to take one last vengeful or admiring glance, then went his way without once turning round.

The young girl had been watching him from the windows, and the moment he moved she passed out of the door like one in a dream, and followed him slowly, step by step, down the avenue. The maids grew alarmed, and called to her father, who ran out and shouted loudly for her to stop, but she never turned or seemed to heed. The young man, however, looked round, and seeing the whole family in pursuit, quickened his pace, first glancing fixedly at the girl for a moment. Immediately she sprang towards him, and they were both almost out of sight, when one of the maids espied a piece of paper tied to a branch of the tree where the poet had rested. From curiosity she took it down, and the moment the knot was untied, the farmer's daughter suddenly stopped, became quite still, and when her father came up she allowed him to lead her back to the house without resistance.

When questioned, she said that she felt herself drawn by an invisible force to follow the young stranger wherever he might lead, and that she would have followed him through the world, for her life seemed to be bound up in his; she had no will to resist, and was conscious of nothing else but his presence. Suddenly, however, the spell was broken, and then she heard her father's voice, and knew how strangely she had acted. At the same time the power of the young man over her vanished, and the impulse to follow him was no longer in her heart.

The paper, on being opened, was found to contain five mysterious words written in blood, and in this order –

THE EVIL EYE

Sator.
Arepo.
Tenet.
Opera.
Rotas.

These letters are so arranged that read in any way, right to left, left to right, up or down, the same words are produced; and when written in blood with a pen made of an eagle's feather, they form a charm which no woman (it is said) can resist; but the incredulous reader can easily test the truth of this assertion for himself.

These popular stories are provokingly incomplete, and one cannot help regretting that the romance of 'The Poet and the Farmer's Daughter' was not brought to a happy termination; but the Irish tales are in general rather incoherent, more like remembered fragments of ancient stories than a complete, well-organized dramatic composition, with lights well placed, and a striking catastrophe. The opening is usually attractive, with the exciting formula, 'Once upon a time,' from which one always expects so much; and there is sure to be an old woman, weird and witchlike, capable of the most demoniacal actions, and a mysterious man who promises to be the unredeemed evil spirit of the tale; but in the end they both turn out childishly harmless, and their evil actions seldom go beyond stealing their neighbours' butter, or abducting a pretty girl, which sins mere mortals would be quite equal to, even without the aid of 'the gods of the earth' and their renowned leader, Finvarra, the King of the Fairies. The following tale, however, of a case of abduction by fairy power, is well constructed. The hero of the narrative has our sympathy and interest, and it ends happily, which is considered a great merit by the Irish, as they dislike a tale to which they cannot append, as an epilogue, the hearty and outspoken 'Thank God.'

THE STOLEN BRIDE

About the year 1670 there was a fine young fellow living at a place called Querin, in the County Clare. He was brave and strong and rich, for he had his own land and his own house, and not one to lord it over him. He was called the Kern of Querin. And many a time he would go out alone to shoot the wild fowl at night along the lonely strand and sometimes cross over northward to the broad east strand, about two miles away, to find the wild geese.

One cold frosty November Eve he was watching for them, crouched down behind the ruins of an old hut, when a loud splashing noise attracted his attention. 'It is the wild geese,' he thought, and raising his gun, waited in death-like silence the approach of his victim.

But presently he saw a dark mass moving along the edge of the strand. And he knew there were no wild geese near him. So he watched and waited till the black mass came closer, and then he distinctly perceived four stout men carrying a bier on their shoulders, on which lay a corpse covered with a white cloth. For a few moments they laid it down, apparently to rest themselves, and the Kern instantly fired; on which the four men ran away shrieking, and the corpse was left alone on the bier. Kern of Querin immediately sprang to the place, and lifting the cloth from the face of the corpse, beheld by the freezing starlight, the form of a beautiful young girl, apparently not dead but in a deep sleep.

Gently he passed his hand over her face and raised her up, when she opened her eyes and looked around with wild wonder, but spake never a word, though he tried to soothe and encourage her. Then, thinking it was dangerous for them to remain in that place, he raised her from the bier, and taking her hand led her away to his own house. They arrived safely, but in silence. And for twelve months did she remain with the Kern, never tasting food or speaking word for all that time.

When the next November Eve came round, he resolved to visit the east strand again, and watch from the same place, in the hope of meeting with some adventure that might throw light on the history of the beautiful girl. His way lay beside the old ruined fort called *Lios-na-*

fallainge (the Fort of the Mantle), and as he passed, the sound of music and mirth fell on his ear. He stopped to catch the words of the voices, and had not waited long when he heard a man say in a low whisper –

'Where shall we go to-night to carry off a bride?'

And a second voice answered –

'Wherever we go I hope better luck will be ours than we had this day twelvemonths.'

'Yes,' said a third; 'on that night we carried off a rich prize, the fair daughter of O'Connor; but that clown, the Kern of Querin, broke our spell and took her from us. Yet little pleasure has he had of his bride, for she has neither eaten nor drank nor uttered a word since she entered his house.'

'And so she will remain,' said a fourth, 'until he makes her eat off her father's table-cloth, which covered her as she lay on the bier, and which is now thrown up over the top of her bed.'

On hearing all this, the Kern rushed home, and without waiting even for the morning, entered the young girl's room, took down the table-cloth, spread it on the table, laid meat and drink thereon, and led her to it. 'Drink,' he said, 'that speech may come to you.' And she drank, and ate of the food, and then speech came. And she told the Kern her story – how she was to have been married to a young lord of her own country, and the wedding guests had all assembled, when she felt herself suddenly ill and swooned away, and never knew more of what had happened to her until the Kern had passed his hand over her face, by which she recovered consciousness, but could neither eat nor speak, for a spell was on her, and she was helpless.

Then the Kern prepared a chariot, and carried home the young girl to her father, who was like to die for joy when he beheld her. And the Kern grew mightily in O'Connor's favour, so that at last he gave him his fair young daughter to wife; and the wedded pair lived together happily for many long years after, and no evil befell them, but good followed all the work of their hands.

This story of Kern of Querin still lingers in the faithful, vivid Irish memory, and is often told by the peasants of Clare when they gather round the fire on the awful festival of *Samhain*, or November Eve, when the dead walk, and the spirits of earth and air have power over mortals, whether for good or evil.

FAIRY MUSIC

The evil influence of the fairy glance does not kill, but it throws the object into a death-like trance, in which the real body is carried off to some fairy mansion, while a log of wood, or some ugly, deformed creature is left in its place, clothed with the shadow of the stolen form. Young women, remarkable for beauty, young men, and handsome children, are the chief victims of the fairy stroke. The girls are wedded to fairy chiefs, and the young men to fairy queens; and if the mortal children do not turn out well, they are sent back, and others carried off in their place. It is sometimes possible, by the spells of a powerful fairy-man, to bring back a living being from Fairy-land. But they are never quite the same after. They have always a spirit-look, especially if they have listened to the fairy music. For the fairy music is soft and low and plaintive, with a fatal charm for mortal ears

One day a gentleman entered a cabin in the County Clare, and saw a young girl about twenty seated by the fire, chanting a melancholy song, without settled words or music. On inquiry he was told she had once heard the fairy harp, and those who hear it lose all memory of love or hate, and forget all things, and never more have any other sound in their ears save the soft music of the fairy harp, and when the spell is broken, they die.

It is remarkable that the Irish national airs – plaintive, beautiful, and unutterably pathetic – should so perfectly express the spirit of the Céol-Sidhe (the fairy music), as it haunts the fancy of the people and mingles with all their traditions of the spirit world. Wild and capricious as the fairy nature, these delicate harmonies, with their mystic, mournful rhythm, seem to touch the deepest chords of feeling, or to fill the sunshine with laughter, according to the mood of the players; but, above all things, Irish music is the utterance of a Divine sorrow; not stormy or passionate, but like that of an exiled spirit, yearning and wistful, vague and unresting; ever seeking the unattainable, ever shadowed, as it were, with memories of some lost good, or some dim foreboding of a coming fate – emotions that seem to find their truest expression in the sweet, sad, lingering wail of the pathetic minor in a genuine Irish air. There is a beautiful phrase in one of the ancient manuscripts descriptive of the wonderful power of Irish music over the sensitive human organization: 'Wounded men were soothed when they heard it, and slept; and women in travail forgot their pains.' There are legends concerning the subtle charm of the fairy music and dance, when the mortal under their influence seems to move through the air with 'the naked, fleshless feet of the spirit,' and is lulled by the ecstasy of the cadence into forgetfulness of all things, and sometimes into the sleep of death.

THE FAIRY DANCE

The following story is from the Irish, as told by a native of one of the Western Isles, where the primitive superstitions have still all the freshness of young life.

One evening late in November, which is the month when spirits have most power over all things, as the prettiest girl in all the island was going to the well for water, her foot slipped and she fell. It was an unlucky omen, and when she got up and looked round it seemed to her as if she were in a strange place, and all around her was changed as if by enchantment. But at some distance she saw a great crowd gathered round a blazing fire, and she was drawn slowly on towards them, till at last she stood in the very midst of the people; but they kept silence, looking fixedly at her; and she was afraid, and tried to turn and leave them, but she could not. Then a beautiful youth, like a prince, with a red sash, and a golden band on his long yellow hair, came up and asked her to dance.

'It is a foolish thing of you, sir, to ask me to dance,' she said, 'when there is no music.'

Then he lifted his hand and made a sign to the people, and instantly the sweetest music sounded near her and around her, and the young man took her hand, and they danced and danced till the moon and the stars went down, but she seemed like one floating on the air, and she forgot everything in the world except the dancing, and the sweet low music, and her beautiful partner.

At last the dancing ceased, and her partner thanked her, and invited her to supper with the company. Then she saw an opening in the ground, and a flight of steps, and the young man, who seemed to be the king amongst them all, led her down, followed by the whole company. At the end of the stairs they came upon a large hall, all bright and beautiful with gold and silver and lights; and the table was covered with everything good to eat, and wine was poured out in golden cups for them to drink. When she sat down they all pressed her to eat the food and to drink the wine; and as she was weary after the dancing, she took the golden cup the prince handed to her, and raised it to her lips to drink. Just then, a man passed close to her, and whispered –

'Eat no food, and drink no wine, or you will never reach your home again.'

So she laid down the cup, and refused to drink. On this they were angry, and a great noise arose, and a fierce, dark man stood up, and said –

'Whoever comes to us must drink with us.'

And he seized her arm, and held the wine to her lips, so that she almost died of fright. But at that moment a red-haired man came up, and he took her by the hand and led her out.

'You are safe for this time,' he said. 'Take this herb, and hold it in

---

[4] In Ancient Egypt the ivy was sacred to Osiris and a safeguard against evil.

your hand till you reach home, and no one can harm you.' And he gave her a branch of a plant called the *Athair-Luss* (the ground ivy).[4]

This she took, and fled away along the sward in the dark night; but all the time she heard footsteps behind her in pursuit. At last she reached home and barred the door, and went to bed, when a great clamour arose outside, and voices were heard crying to her –

'The power we had over you is gone through the magic of the herb; but wait – when you dance again to the music on the hill, you will stay with us for evermore, and none shall hinder.'

However, she kept the magic branch safely, and the fairies never troubled her more; but it was long and long before the sound of the fairy music left her ears which she had danced to that November night on the hillside with her fairy lover.

FAIRY JUSTICE

A LEGEND OF SHARK ISLAND

The 'Red-haired Man,' although he is considered very unlucky in actual life, yet generally acts in the fairy world as the benevolent *Deus ex machina*, that saves and helps and rescues the unhappy mortal, who himself is quite helpless under the fairy spells.

There was a man in Shark Island who used to cross over to Boffin[5] to buy tobacco, but when the weather was too rough for the boat his ill-temper was as bad as the weather, and he used to beat his wife, and fling all the things about, so that no one could stand before him. One day a man came to him.

'What will you give me if I go over to Boffin,' said he, 'and bring you the tobacco?'

---

[5] The correct names for these islands are Innis-Erk (the Island of St Erk), and Innis-bo-finn (the Island of the White Cow).

'I will give you nothing,' said the other. 'Whatever way you go I can go also.'

'Then come with me to the shore,' said the first man, 'and I'll show you how to get across; but as only one can go, you must go alone.'

And as they went down to the sea, they saw a great company of horsemen and ladies galloping along, with music and laughter.

'Spring up now on a horse and you will get across,' said the first man.

So the other sprang up as he was told, and in an instant they all jumped right across the sea and landed at Boffin. Then he ran to buy the tobacco and was back again in a minute, and found all the same company by the sea-shore. He sprang again upon a horse and they all jumped right into the sea, but suddenly stopped midway between the two islands, where there was a great rock, and beyond this they could not force the horses to move. Then there was great disquietude amongst them, and they called a council.

'There is a mortal amongst us,' they said. 'Let us drown him.'

And they carried the man up to the top of the rock and cast him down; and when he rose to the surface again they caught him by the hair, and cried –

'Drown him! Drown him! We have the power over life and death; he must be drowned.'

And they were going to cast him down a second time, when a red-haired man pleaded for him, and carried him off with a strong hand safe to shore.

'Now,' said he, 'you are safe, but mind, the spirits are watching you, and if ever again you beat your poor good wife, and knock about the things at home just to torment her out of her life, you will die upon that rock as sure as fate.' And he vanished, So from that time forth the man was as meek as a mouse, for he was afraid; and whenever he went by the rock in his boat he always stopped a minute, and said a little prayer for his wife with a 'God bless her.' And this kept away the evil, and they both lived together happily ever after to a great old age.

This is but a rude tale. Yet the moral is good, and the threat of retributive justice shows a laudable spirit of indignation on the part of the fairy race against the tyranny of man over the weaker vessel.

THE PRIEST'S SOUL

An ethical purpose is not often to be detected in the Irish legends; but the following tale combines an inner meaning with the incidents in a profound and remarkable manner. The idea that underlies the story is very subtle and tragic; Calderon or Goethe might have founded a drama on it; and Browning's genius would find a fitting subject in this contrast between the pride of the audacious, self-relying sceptic in the hour of his triumph and the moral agony that precedes his punishment and death.

In former days there were great schools in Ireland where every sort of learning was taught to the people, and even the poorest had more knowledge at that time than many a gentleman has now. But as to the priests, their learning was above all, so that the fame of Ireland went over the whole world, and many kings from foreign lands used to send their sons all the way to Ireland to be brought up in the Irish schools.

Now at this time there was a little boy learning at one of them who was a wonder to every one for his cleverness. His parents were only labouring people, and of course very poor; but young as he was, and poor as he was, no king's or lord's son could come up to him in learning. Even the masters were put to shame, for when they were trying to teach him he would tell them something they never heard of before, and show them their ignorance. One of his great triumphs was in argument; and he would go on till he proved to you that black was white, and then when you gave in, for no one could beat him in talk, he would turn round and show you that white was black, or may be that there was no colour at all in the world. When he grew up his poor father and mother were so proud of him that they resolved to make him a priest, which they did at last, though they nearly starved themselves to get the money. Well, such another learned man was not in Ireland, and he was as great in argument as ever, so that no one could stand before him. Even the Bishops tried to talk to him, but he showed them at once they knew nothing at all.

Now there were no schoolmasters in those times but it was the priests taught the people; and as this man was the cleverest in Ireland all the foreign kings sent their sons to him as long as he had house-room to give them. So he grew very proud, and began to forget how low he had been, and worst of all, even to forget God, who had made him what he was. And the pride of arguing got hold of him, so that from one thing to another he went on to prove that there was no Purgatory, and then no Hell, and then no Heaven, and then no God; and at last that men had no souls, but were no more than a dog or a cow, and when they died there was an end of them. 'Who ever saw a soul?' he would say. 'If you can show me one, I will believe.' No one could make any answer to this; and at last they all came to believe that as there was no other world, every one might do what they liked in this; the priest setting the example, for he took a beautiful young girl to wife. But as no priest or bishop in the whole land could be got to marry them, he was obliged to read the service over for himself. It was a great scandal, yet no one dared to say a word, for all the kings' sons were on his side, and would have slaughtered any one who tried to prevent his wicked goings-on. Poor boys! They all believed in him, and thought every word he said was the truth. In this way his notions began to spread about, and the whole world was going to the bad, when one night an angel came down from Heaven, and told the priest he had but twenty-four hours to live. He began to tremble, and asked for a little more time.

But the angel was stiff, and told him that could not be.

'What do you want time for, you sinner?' he asked.

'Oh, sir, have pity on my poor soul!' urged the priest.

'Oh, ho! You have a soul, then,' said the angel. 'Pray, how did you find that out?'

THE PRIEST'S SOUL

'It has been fluttering in me ever since you appeared,' answered the priest. 'What a fool I was not to think of it before.'

'A fool indeed,' said the angel. 'What good was all your learning, when it could not tell you that you had a soul?'

'Ah, my lord,' said the priest, 'if I am to die, tell me how soon I may be in Heaven?'

'Never,' replied the angel. 'You denied there was a Heaven.'

'Then, my lord, may I go to Purgatory?'

'You denied Purgatory also; you must go straight to Hell,' said the angel.

'But, my lord, I denied Hell also,' answered the priest, 'so you can't send me there either.'

The angel was a little puzzled.

'Well,' said he, 'I'll tell you what I can do for you. You may either live now on earth for a hundred years enjoying every pleasure, and then be cast into Hell for ever; or you may die in twenty-four hours in the most horrible torments, and pass through Purgatory, there to remain till the Day of Judgment, if only you can find some one person that believes, and through his belief mercy will be vouchsafed to you and your soul will be saved.' The priest did not take five minutes to make up his mind.

'I will have death in the twenty-four hours,' he said, 'so that my soul may be saved at last.'

On this the angel gave him directions as to what he was to do, and left him.

Then, immediately, the priest entered the large room where all his scholars and the kings' sons were seated, and called out to them –

'Now, tell me the truth, and let none fear to contradict me. Tell me what is your belief. Have men souls?'

'Master,' they answered, 'once we believed that men had souls; but, thanks to your teaching, we believe so no longer. There is no Hell, and no Heaven, and no God. This is our belief, for it is thus you taught us.'

Then the priest grew pale with fear and cried out – 'Listen! I taught you a lie. There is a God, and man has an immortal soul. I believe now all I denied before.'

But the shouts of laughter that rose up drowned the priest's voice, for they thought he was only trying them for argument.

'Prove it, master,' they cried, 'prove it. Who has ever seen God? Who has ever seen the soul?'

And the room was stirred with their laughter.

The priest stood up to answer them, but no word could he utter; all his eloquence, all his powers of argument had gone from him, and he could do nothing but wring his hands and cry out –

'There is a God, there is a God! Lord have mercy on my soul!'

And they all began to mock him, and repeat his own words that he had taught them –

'Show him to us; show us your God.'

And he fled from them groaning with agony, for he saw that none believed, and how then could his soul be saved?

But he thought next of his wife.

'She will believe,' he said to himself. 'Women never give up God.'

And he went to her; but she told him that she believed only what he taught her, and that a good wife should believe in her husband first, and before and above all things in heaven or earth.

Then despair came on him, and he rushed from the house and began to ask every one he met if they believed. But the same answer came from one and all – 'We believe only what you have taught us,' for his doctrines had spread far and wide through the county.

Then he grew half mad with fear, for the hours were passing. And he flung himself down on the ground in a lonesome spot, and wept and groaned in terror, for the time was coming fast when he must die.

Just then a little child came by.

'God save you kindly,' said the child to him.

The priest started up.

'Child, do you believe in God?' he asked.

'I have come from a far country to learn about Him,' said the child. 'Will your honour direct me to the best school that they have in these parts?'

THE PRIEST'S SOUL

'The best school and the best teacher is close by,' said the priest, and he named himself.

'Oh, not to that man,' answered the child, 'for I am told he denies God, and Heaven, and Hell, and even that man has a soul, because we can't see it; but I would soon put him down.'

The priest looked at him earnestly. 'How?' he inquired.

'Why,' said the child, 'I would ask him if he believed he had life to show me his life.'

'But he could not do that, my child,' said the priest, 'Life cannot be seen; we have it, but it is invisible.'

'Then if we have life, though we cannot see it, we may also have a soul, though it is invisible,' answered the child.

When the priest heard him speak these words he fell down on his knees before him, weeping for joy, for now he knew his soul was safe; he had met at last one that believed. And he told the child his whole story: all his wickedness, and pride, and blasphemy against the great God; and how the angel had come to him and told him of the only way in which he could be saved, through the faith and prayers of some one that believed.

'Now then,' he said to the child, 'take this penknife and strike it into my breast, and go on stabbing the flesh until you see the paleness of death on my face. Then watch – for a living thing will soar up from my body as I die, and you will then know that my soul has ascended to the presence of God. And when you see this thing, make haste and run to my school and call on all my scholars to come and see that the soul of their master has left the body, and that all he taught them was a lie, for that there is a God who punishes sin, and a Heaven and a Hell, and that man has an immortal soul, destined for eternal happiness or misery.'

'I will pray,' said the child, 'to have courage to do this work.'

And he kneeled down and prayed. Then when he rose up he took the penknife and struck it into the priest's heart, and struck and struck again till all the flesh was lacerated; but still the priest lived though the agony was horrible, for he could not die until the twenty-four hours had expired. At last the agony seemed to cease, and the stillness of death settled on his face. Then the child, who was watching, saw a beautiful living creature, with four snow white wings, mount from the dead man's body into the air and go fluttering round his head.

So he ran to bring the scholars; and when they saw it they all knew it was the soul of their master, and they watched with wonder and awe until it passed from sight into the clouds.

And this was the first butterfly that was ever seen in Ireland; and now all men know that the butterflies are the souls of the dead waiting for the moment when they may enter Purgatory, and so pass through torture to purification and peace.

But the schools of Ireland were quite deserted after that time, for people said, What is the use of going so far to learn when the wisest man in all Ireland did not know if he had a soul till he was near losing it; and was only saved at last through the simple belief of a little child?

The allusion in this clever tale to the ancient Irish schools is based on historical fact. From the seventh to the tenth century Ireland was the centre of learning. The great Alfred of England was a student at one of the famous Irish seminaries, along with other royal and noble youths, and there formed a life-long friendship with the learned Adamnanl who often afterwards was a welcome guest at the Court of King Alfred. Other eminent Irishmen are known to history as the teachers and evangelizers of Europe. Alcuin, the Irish monk, became the friend and secretary of Charlemagne, and founded, at Aix-la-Chapelle, the first Grammar School in the imperial dominions. And the celebrated Clemens and Albinus, two Irishmen of distinguished ability and learning, aided the emperor not only in educating the people, but also to found a school for the nobles within his own palace.

THE FAIRY RACE

The *Sidhe* or spirit race, called also the *Feadh-Ree*, or fairies, are supposed to have been once angels in heaven, who were cast out by

THE FAIRY RACE

Divine command as a punishment for their inordinate pride.

Some fell to earth, and dwelt there, long before man was created, as the first gods of the earth. Others fell into the sea, and they built themselves beautiful fairy palaces of crystal and pearl underneath the waves; but on moonlight nights they often come up on the land, riding their white horses, and they hold revels with their fairy kindred of the earth, who live in the clefts of the hills, and they dance together on the greensward under the ancient trees, and drink nectar from the cups of the flowers, which is the fairy wine.

Other fairies, however, are demoniacal, and given to evil and malicious deeds; for when cast out of heaven they fell into hell, and there the devil holds them under his rule, and sends them forth as he wills upon missions of evil to tempt the souls of men downward by the false glitter of sin and pleasure. These spirits dwell under the earth and impart their knowledge only to certain evil persons chosen of the devil, who gives them power to make incantations, and brew love potions, and to work wicked spells, and they can assume different forms by their knowledge and use of certain magical herbs.

The witch women who have been taught by them, and have thus become tools of the Evil One, are the terror of the neighbourhood; for they have all the power of the fairies and all the malice of the devil, who reveals to them secrets of times and days, and secrets of herbs, and secrets of evil spells; and by the power of magic they can effect all their purposes, whether for good or ill.

The fairies of the earth are small and beautiful. They passionately love music and dancing, and live luxuriously in their palaces under the hills and in the deep mountain caves; and they can obtain all things lovely for their fairy homes, merely by the strength of their magic power. They can also assume all forms, and will never know death until the last day comes, when their doom is to vanish away – to be annihilated for ever. But they are very jealous of the human race who are so tall and strong, and to whom has been promised immortality. And they are often tempted by the beauty of a mortal woman and greatly desire to have her as a wife.

The children of such marriages have a strange mystic nature, and generally become famous in music and song. But they are passionate, revengeful and not easy to live with. Every one knows them to be of the Sidhe or spirit race, by their beautiful eyes and their bold, reckless temperament.

The fairy king and princes dress in green, with red caps bound on the head with a golden fillet. The fairy queen and the great court ladies are robed in glittering silver gauze, spangled with diamonds, and their long golden hair sweeps the ground as they dance on the greensward.

Their favourite camp and resting-place is under a hawthorn tree, and a peasant would die sooner than cut down one of the ancient hawthorns sacred to the fairies, and which generally stands in the centre of a fairy ring. But the people never offer worship to these fairy beings, for they look on the Sidhe as a race quite inferior to man. At the same time they have an immense dread and fear of the mystic fairy power, and never interfere with them nor offend them knowingly.

The Sidhe often strive to carry off the handsome children, who are then reared in the beautiful fairy palaces under the earth, and wedded to fairy mates when they grow up.

The people dread the idea of a fairy changeling being left in the cradle in place of their own lovely child; and if a wizened little thing is found there, it is sometimes taken out at night and laid in an open grave till morning, when they hope to find their own child restored, although more often nothing is found save the cold corpse of the poor outcast.

Sometimes it is said the fairies carry off the mortal child for a sacrifice, as they have to offer one every seven years to the devil in return for the power he gives them. And beautiful young girls are carried off, also, either for sacrifice or to be wedded to the fairy king.

The fairies are pure and cleanly in their habits, and they like above all things a pail of water to be set for them at night in case they may wish to bathe.

They also delight in good wines, and are careful to repay the donor in blessings, for they are truly upright and honest. The great lords of Ireland, in ancient times, used to leave a keg of the finest Spanish wine frequently at night out on the window-sill for the fairies, and in the morning it was all gone.

Fire is a great preventative against fairy magic, for fire is the most sacred of all created things, and man alone has power over it. No animal has ever yet attained the knowledge of how to draw out the spirit of fire from the stone or the wood, where it has found a dwelling-place. If a ring of fire is made round cattle or a child's cradle, or if fire is placed under the churn, the fairies have no power to harm. And the spirit of the fire is certain to destroy all fairy magic, if it exists.

THE TRIAL BY FIRE

The ordeal by fire is the great test adopted by the peasants to try if a child or any one is fairy-struck. There was a man in Mayo who was bedridden for months and months, and though he ate up all the food they brought him, he never grew a bit stronger, and on Sundays when they went to mass, they locked him up and left him alone in the place with plenty of food. Now there was a fine field close by, and one Sunday, coming home from mass earlier than usual, they saw a great company of people bowling in the field, and the sick man amongst them, but at that moment he vanished away; and when the family reached home, there was the sick man lying fast asleep in his bed.

'Get up,' they said, 'for we have seen you bowling with the fairies, and you shan't eat or drink any more at our expense.'

But he refused, and said he was too ill to move. Then they made down a large fire of turf and said, 'Get up, or we'll lay you on the fire and break the fairy spell.' And they took hold of him to burn him. Then he was frightened, and rose up and went out at the door, and they watched him till he stopped in the field where the hurlers played, and lay down there in the grass; but when they went up to him he was dead.

A man going to his work one morning early saw two women going up to a house, and one said, 'There is a beautiful boy in this house, go in and hand it out to me, and we'll leave the dead child in its place.' And the other went in at the window as she was told, and handed out a sleeping child, and took the dead child and laid it in the bed within. Now the man saw it was fairy work, and he went over and made the sign of the cross on the sleeping child, whereupon the two women shrieked as if they had been struck, and fled away, dropping the child on the grass. Then the man took it up gently, and put it under his coat, and went away to his wife.

'Here,' he said, 'take care of this child till I come back, and burn a turf beside the cradle to keep off the fairies.'

When he passed by the house again, where he had seen the two women, he heard a great crying and lamentation; and he entered in and asked what ailed them.

'See here,' said the mother, 'my child is dead in its cradle. It died in the night, and no one near.' And she wept bitterly.

'Be comforted' said the man; 'this is a fairy changeling, your child is safe!' and he told her the story. 'Now,' he said, 'if you don't believe me, just lay this dead child on the fire, and we'll see what will happen.'

So she made down a good fire, and took the dead child in her arms, and laid it on the hot turf, saying, 'Burn, burn, burn – if of the devil, burn; but if of God and the Saints, be safe from harm.' And the child no sooner felt the fire than it sprang up the chimney with a cry and disappeared.

THE LADY WITCH

About a hundred years ago there lived a woman in Joyce County, of whom all the neighbours were afraid, for she had always plenty of money, though no one knew how she came by it; and the best of eating and drinking went on at her house, chiefly at night – meat and fowls and Spanish wines in plenty for all comers. And when people asked how it all came, she laughed and said, 'I have paid for it,' but would tell them no more.

THE LADY WITCH

So the word went through the county that she had sold herself to the Evil One, and could have everything she wanted by merely wishing and willing, and because of her riches they called her 'The Lady Witch.'

She never went out but at night, and then always with a bridle and whip in her hand; and the sound of a horse galloping was heard often far on in the night along the roads near her house.

Then a strange story was whispered about, that if a young man drank of her Spanish wines at supper and afterwards fell asleep, she would throw the bridle over him and change him to a horse, and ride him all over the country, and whatever she touched with her whip became hers. Fowls, or butter, or wine, or the new-made cakes – she had but to wish and will and they were carried by spirit hands to her house, and laid in her larder. Then when the ride was done, and she had gathered enough through the country of all she wanted, she took the bridle off the young man, and he came back to his own shape and fell asleep; and when he awoke he had no knowledge of all that had happened, and the Lady Witch bade him come again and drink of her Spanish wines as often as it pleased him.

Now there was a fine brave young fellow in the neighbourhood, and he determined to make out the truth of the story. So he often went back and forwards, and made friends with the Lady Witch, and sat down to talk to her, but always on the watch. And she took a great fancy to him and told him he must come to supper some night, and she would give him the best of everything, and he must taste her Spanish wine.

So she named the night, and he went gladly, for he was filled with curiosity. And when he arrived there was a beautiful supper laid, and plenty of wine to drink; and he ate and drank, but was cautious about the wine, and spilled it on the ground from his glass when her head was turned away. Then he pretended to be very sleepy, and she said –

'My son, you are weary. Lie down there on the bench and sleep, for the night is far spent, and you are far from your home.'

So he lay down as if he were quite dead with sleep, and closed his eyes, but watched her all the time.

And she came over in a little while and looked at him steadily, but he never stirred, only breathed the more heavily.

Then she went softly and took the bridle from the wall, and stole over to fling it over his head; but he started up, and, seizing the bridle, threw it over the woman, who was immediately changed into a spanking grey mare. And he led her out and jumped on her back and rode away as fast as the wind till he came to the forge.

'Ho, smith,' he cried, 'rise up and shoe my mare, for she is weary after the journey.'

And the smith got up and did his work as he was bid, well and strong. Then the young man mounted again, and rode back like the wind to the house of the Witch; and there he took off the bridle, and she immediately regained her own form, and sank down in a deep sleep.

But as the shoes had been put on at the forge without saying the proper form of words, they remained on her hands and feet, and no power on earth could remove them.

So she never rose from her bed again, and died not long after of grief and shame. And not one in the whole country would follow the coffin of the Lady Witch to the grave; and the bridle was burned with fire, and of all her riches nothing was left but a handful of ashes, and this was flung to the four points of earth and the four winds of heaven; so the enchantment was broken and the power of the Evil One ended.

ETHNA THE BRIDE

The fairies, as we know, are greatly attracted by the beauty of mortal women, and Finvarra the king employs his numerous sprites to find out and carry off when possible the prettiest girls and brides in the country. These are spirited away by enchantment to his fairy palace at Knockma in Tuam, where they remain under a fairy spell, forgetting all about the

ETHNA THE BRIDE

earthly life and soothed to passive enjoyment, as in a sweet dream, by the soft low melody of the fairy music, which has the power to lull the hearer into a trance of ecstasy.

There was once a great lord in that part of the country who had a beautiful wife called Ethna, the loveliest bride in all the land. And her husband was so proud of her that day after day he had festivals in her honour; and from morning till night his castle was filled with lords and ladies, and nothing but music and dancing and feasting and hunting and pleasure was thought of.

One evening while the feast was merriest, and Ethna floated through the dance in her robe of silver gossamer clasped with jewels, more bright and beautiful than the stars in heaven, she suddenly let go the hand of her partner and sank to the floor in a faint.

They carried her to her room, where she lay long quite insensible; but towards the morning she woke up and declared that she had passed the night in a beautiful palace, and was so happy that she longed to sleep again and go there in her dreams. And they watched by her all day, but when the shades of evening fell dark on the castle, low music was heard at her window, and Ethna again fell into a deep trance from which nothing could rouse her.

Then her old nurse was set to watch her; but the woman grew weary in the silence and fell asleep, and never awoke till the sun had risen. And when she looked towards the bed, she saw to her horror that the young bride had disappeared. The whole household was roused up at once, and search made everywhere, but no trace of her could be found in all the castle, nor in the gardens, nor in the park. Her husband sent messengers in every direction, but to no purpose – no one had seen her; no sign of her could be found, living or dead.

Then the young lord mounted his swiftest steed and galloped right off to Knockma, to question Finvarra, the fairy king, if he could give any tidings of the bride, or direct him where to search for her; for he and Finvarra were friends, and many a good keg of Spanish wine had been left outside the window of the castle at night for the fairies to carry away, by order of the young lord. But he little dreamed now that Finvarra himself was the traitor; so he galloped on like mad till he reached Knockma, the hill of the fairies.

And as he stopped to rest his horse by the fairy rath, he heard voices in the air above him, and one said –

'Right glad is Finvarra now, for he has the beautiful bride in his palace at last; and never more will she see her husband's face.'

'Yet,' answered another, 'if he dig down through the hill to the centre of the earth, he would find his bride; but the work is hard and the way is difficult, and Finvarra has more power than any mortal man.'

'That is yet to be seen,' exclaimed the young lord. 'Neither fairy, nor devil, nor Finvarra himself shall stand between me and my fair young wife;' and on the instant he sent word by his servants to gather together all the workmen and labourers of the country round with their spades and pickaxes, to dig through the hill till they came to the fairy palace.

And the workmen came, a great crowd of them, and they dug through the hill all that day till a great deep trench was made down to the very centre. Then at sunset they left off for the night; but next morning when they assembled again to continue their work, behold, all the clay was put back again into the trench, and the hill looked as if never a spade had touched it – for so Finvarra had ordered; and he was powerful over earth and air and sea.

But the young lord had a brave heart, and he made the men go on with the work; and the trench was dug again, wide and deep into the centre of the hill. And this went on for three days, but always with the same result, for the clay was put back again each night and the hill looked the same as before, and they were no nearer to the fairy palace.

Then the young lord was ready to die for rage and grief, but suddenly he heard a voice near him like a whisper in the air, and the words it said were these –

'Sprinkle the earth you have dug up with salt, and your work will be safe.'

On this, new life came into his heart and he sent word through all the country to gather salt from the people; and the clay was sprinkled

ETHNA THE BRIDE

with it that night, when the men had left off their work at the hill.

Next morning they all rose up early in great anxiety to see what had happened, and there to their great joy was the trench all safe, just as they had left it, and all the earth round it was untouched.

Then the young lord knew he had power over Finvarra, and he bade the men work on with a good heart, for they would soon reach the fairy palace now in the centre of the hill. So by the next day a great glen was cut right through deep down to the middle of the earth, and they could hear the fairy music if they put their ear close to the ground, and voices were heard round them in the air.

'See now,' said one, 'Finvarra is sad, for if one of those mortal men strike a blow on the fairy palace with their spades, it will crumble to dust, and fade away like the mist.'

'Then let Finvarra give up the bride,' said another, 'and we shall be safe.'

On which the voice of Finvarra himself was heard, clear like the note of a silver bugle through the hill.

'Stop your work,' he said. 'Oh, men of earth, lay down your spades, and at sunset the bride shall be given back to her husband. I, Finvarra, have spoken.'

Then the young lord bade them stop the work, and lay down their spades till the sun went down. And at sunset he mounted his great chestnut steed and rode to the head of the glen, and watched and waited; and just as the red light flushed all the sky, he saw his wife coming along the path in her robe of silver gossamer, more beautiful than ever; and he sprang from the saddle and lifted her up before him, and rode away like the storm wind back to the castle. And there they laid Ethna on her bed; but she closed her eyes and spake no word. So day after day passed, and still she never spake or smiled, but seemed like one in a trance.

And great sorrow fell upon every one, for they feared she had eaten of the fairy food, and that the enchantment would never be broken. So her husband was very miserable. But one evening as he was riding home late, he heard voices in the air, and one of them said –

'It is now a year and a day since the young lord brought home his beautiful wife from Finvarra; but what good is she to him? She is speechless and like one dead; for her spirit is with the fairies though her form is there beside him.'

Then another voice answered –

'And so she will remain unless the spell is broken. He must unloose the girdle from her waist that is fastened with an enchanted pin, and burn the girdle with fire, and throw the ashes before the door, and bury the enchanted pin in the earth; then will her spirit come back from Fairy-land, and she will once more speak and have true life.'

Hearing this the young lord at once set spurs to his horse, and on reaching the castle hastened to the room where Ethna lay on her couch silent and beautiful like a waxen figure. Then, being determined to test the truth of the spirit voices, he untied the girdle, and after much difficulty extracted the enchanted pin from the folds. But still Ethna spoke no word; then he took the girdle and burned it with fire, and strewed the ashes before the door, and he buried the enchanted pin in a deep hole in the earth, under a fairy thorn, that no hand might disturb the spot. After which he returned to his young wife, who smiled as she looked at him and held forth her hand. Great was his joy to see the soul coming back to the beautiful form, and he raised her up and kissed her; and speech and memory came back to her at that moment, and all her former life, just as if it had never been broken or interrupted; but the year that her spirit had passed in Fairy-land seemed to her but as a dream of the night, from which she had just awoke.

After this Finvarra made no further efforts to carry her off; but the deep cut in the hill remains to this day, and is called 'The Fairy's Glen.' So no one can doubt the truth of the story as here narrated.

THE FAIRIES' REVENGE

The fairies have a great objection to the fairy raths, where they meet at night, being built upon by mortal man. A farmer called Johnstone,

THE FAIRIES' REVENGE

having plenty of money, bought some land, and chose a beautiful green spot to build a house on, the very spot the fairies loved best.

The neighbours warned him that it was a fairy rath; but he laughed and never minded (for he was from the north), and looked at such things as mere old-wives' tales. So he built the house and made it beautiful to live in; and no people in the country were so well off as the Johnstones, so that the people said the farmer must have found a pot of gold in the fairy rath.

But the fairies were all the time plotting how they could punish the farmer for taking away their dancing ground, and for cutting down the hawthorn bush where they held their revels when the moon was full. And one day when the cows were milking, a little old woman in a blue cloak came to Mrs Johnstone and asked her for a porringer of milk.

'Go away,' said the mistress of the house, 'you shall have no milk from me. I'll have no tramps coming about my place.' And she told the farm servants to chase her away.

Some time after, the best and finest of the cows sickened and gave no milk, and lost her horns and teeth and finally died.

Then one day as Mrs Johnstone was sitting spinning flax in the parlour, the same little woman in the blue cloak suddenly stood before her.

'Your maids are baking cakes in the kitchen,' she said; 'give me some off the griddle to carry away with me.'

'Go out of this,' cried the farmer's wife, angrily; 'you are a wicked old wretch, and have poisoned my best cow.' And she bade the farm servants drive her off with sticks.

Now the Johnstones had one only child; a beautiful bright boy, as strong as a young colt, and as full of life and merriment. But soon after this he began to grow queer and strange, and was disturbed in his sleep; for he said the fairies came round him at night and pinched and beat him, and some sat on his chest and he could neither breathe nor move. And they told him they would never leave him in peace unless he promised to give them a supper every night of a griddle cake and a porringer of milk. So to soothe the child the mother had these things laid every night on a table beside his bed, and in the morning they were gone.

But still the child pined away, and his eyes got a strange, wild look, as if he saw nothing near or around him, only something far, far away that troubled his spirit. And when they asked him what ailed him, he said the fairies carried him away to the hills every night, where he danced and danced with them till the morning, when they brought him back and laid him again in his bed. At last the farmer and his wife were at their wits' end from grief and despair, for the child was pining away before their eyes, and they could do nothing for him to help him. One night he cried out in great agony –

'Mother! mother! send for the priest to take away the fairies, for they are killing me; they are here on my chest, crushing me to death,' and his eyes were wild with terror.

Now the farmer and his wife believed in no fairies, and in no priest, but to soothe the child they did as he asked and sent for the priest, who prayed over him and sprinkled him with holy water.

The poor little fellow seemed calmer as the priest prayed, and he said the fairies were leaving him and going away, and then he sank into a quiet sleep. But when he woke in the morning he told his parents that he had a beautiful dream and was walking in a lovely garden with the angels; and he knew it was heaven, and that he would be there before night, for the angels told him they would come for him.

Then they watched by the sick child all through the night, for they saw the fever was still on him, but hoped a change would come before morning; for he now slept quite calmly with a smile on his lips.

But just as the clock struck midnight he awoke and sat up, and when his mother put her arms round him weeping, he whispered to her – 'The angels are here, mother,' and then he sank back, and so died.

Now after this calamity the farmer never held up his head. He ceased to mind his farm, and the crops went to ruin and the cattle died, and finally before a year and a day were over he was laid in the grave by the side of his little son; and the land passed into other hands, and as no one would live in the house it was pulled down. No one, either, would plant on the rath; so the grass grew again all over it, green and beautiful, and the fairies danced there once more in the moonlight as they used to do in the old time, free and happy; and thus the evil spell was broken for evermore.

But the people would have nothing to do with the childless mother, so she went away back to her own people, a broken-hearted, miserable woman – a warning to all who would arouse the vengeance of the fairies by interfering with their ancient rights and possessions and privileges.

FAIRY HELP

THE PHOUKA

The Phouka is a friendly being, and often helps the farmer at his work if he is treated well and kindly. One day a farmer's son was minding cattle in the field when something rushed past him like the wind; but he was not frightened, for he knew it was the Phouka on his way to the old mill by the moat where the fairies met every night. So he called out, 'Phouka, Phouka! show me what you are like, and I'll give you my big coat to keep you warm.' Then a young bull came to him lashing his tail like mad; but Phadrig threw the coat over him, and in a moment he was quiet as a lamb, and told the boy to come to the mill that night when the moon was up, and he would have good luck.

So Phadrig went, but saw nothing except sacks of corn all lying about on the ground, for the men had fallen asleep, and no work was done. Then he lay down also and slept, for he was very tired: and when he woke up early in the morning there was all the meal ground, though certainly the men had not done it, for they still slept. And this happened for three nights, after which Phadrig determined to keep awake and watch.

Now there was an old chest in the mill, and he crept into this to hide, and just looked through the keyhole to see what would happen. And exactly at midnight six little fellows came in, each carrying a sack of corn upon his back; and after them came an old man in tattered rags of clothes, and he bade them turn the mill, and they turned and turned till all was ground.

Then Phadrig ran to tell his father, and the miller determined to watch the next night with his son, and both together saw the same thing happen.

'Now,' said the farmer, 'I see it is the Phouka's work, and let him work if it pleases him, for the men are idle and lazy and only sleep. So I'll pack the whole set off tomorrow, and leave the grinding of the corn to this excellent old Phouka.'

After this the farmer grew so rich that there was no end to his money, for he had no men to pay, and all his corn was ground without his spending a penny. Of course the people wondered much over his riches, but he never told them about the Phouka, or their curiosity would have spoiled the luck.

Now Phadrig went often to the mill and hid in the chest that he might watch the fairies at work; but he had great pity for the poor old Phouka in his tattered clothes, who yet directed everything and had hard work of it sometimes keeping the little Phoukas in order. So Phadrig, out of love and gratitude, bought a fine suit of cloth and silk and laid it one night on the floor of the mill just where the old Phouka always stood to give his orders to the little men, and then he crept into the chest to watch.

'How is this?' said the Phouka when he saw the clothes.

'Are these for me? I shall be turned into a fine gentleman.'

And he put them on, and then began to walk up and down admiring himself. But suddenly he remembered the corn and went to grind as usual, then stopped and cried out –

'No, no. No more work for me. Fine gentlemen don't grind corn. I'll go out and see a little of the world and show my fine clothes.' And he kicked away the old rags into a corner, and went out.

No corn was ground that night, nor the next, nor the next; all the little Phoukas ran away, and not a sound was heard in the mill. Then Phadrig grew very sorry for the loss of his old friend, and used to go out into the fields and call out, 'Phouka, Phouka! come back to me. Let me see your face.' But the old Phouka never came back, and all his life long Phadrig never looked on the face of his friend again. However, the farmer had made so much money that he wanted no more help; and he sold the mill, and reared up Phadrig to be a great scholar and a gentleman, who had his own house and land and servants. And in time he married a beautiful lady, so beautiful that the people said she must be daughter to the king of the fairies.

A strange thing happened at the wedding, for when they all stood up to drink the bride's health, Phadrig saw beside him a golden cup filled with wine. And no one knew how the golden cup had come to his hand; but Phadrig guessed it was the Phouka's gift, and he drank the wine without fear and made his bride drink also. And ever after their lives were happy and prosperous, and the golden cup was kept as a treasure in the family, and the descendants of Phadrig have it in their possession to this day.

THE FARMER PUNISHED

The fairies, with their free, joyous temperament and love of beauty and luxury, hold in great contempt the minor virtues of thrift and economy, and, above all things, abhor the close, hard, niggardly nature that spends grudgingly and never gives freely.

Indeed, they seem to hold it as their peculiar mission to punish such people, and make them suffer for the sins of the hard heart and niggard hand, as may be seen by the following tale:

A farmer once lived near the Boyne, close to an old churchyard. He was very rich, and had crops and cattle, but was so hard and avaricious that the people hated him for his habit was to get up very early in the morning and go out to the fields to watch that no one took a cabbage or a turnip, or got a cup of milk when the cows were being milked, for the love of God and the saints.

One morning, as he was out as usual by sunrise spying about the place, he heard a child crying bitterly –

'Oh, mother, mother! I am hungry. Give me something, or I'll die.'

'Hush, darling,' said the mother, 'though the hunger is on you, wait; for the farmer's cow will be milked presently, and I'll knock down the pail so the milk will be spilt upon the ground, and you can drink your fill.'[6]

When the farmer heard this he sent a stout man to watch the girl that milked, and to tie the cow's feet that she should not kick. So that time no milk was spilled upon the ground.

Next morning he went out again by sunrise, and he heard the child crying more bitterly even than before –

'Mother, mother! I am hungry. Give me to eat,'

'Wait, my child,' said the mother; 'the farmer's maid bakes cakes today, and I'll make the dish to fall just as she is carrying them from the griddle. So we shall have plenty to eat this time.'

Then the farmer went home and locked up the meal, and said –

'No cakes shall be baked today, not till the night.'

But the cry of the child was in his ears, and he could not rest so early in the morning he was out again, and bitter was the cry of the child as he passed the copse –

'Mother, mother!' it said, 'I have had no milk, I have had no cake; let me lay down my head on your breast and die.'

'Wait,' said the mother, 'some one will die before you, my darling. Let the old man look to his son, for he will be killed in battle before many days are over; and then the curse will be lifted from the poor, and we shall have food in plenty.'

But the farmer laughed. 'There is no war in Ireland now,' he said to himself. 'How then can my son be killed in battle?' And he went home to his own house, and there in the courtyard was his son cleaning his spear and sharpening his arrows. He was a comely youth, tall and slender as a young oak-tree, and his brown hair fell in long curls over his shoulders.

'Father,' he said, 'I am summoned by the king, for he is at war with the other kings. So give me the swiftest horse you have, for I must be off tonight to join the king's men. And see, I have my spears and arrows ready.'

---

[6] The fairies have a right to whatever is spilt or falls upon the ground.

THE FARMER PUNISHED

Now at that time in Ireland there were four great kings, and each of them had two deputies. And the king of Leinster made a great feast for the deputies, and to seven of them he gave a brooch of gold each, but to the eighth only a brooch of silver, for, he said, the man is not a prince like the others. Then the eighth deputy was angry, and he struck the king's page full in the face for handing him the brooch. On this all the knights sprang up and drew their swords, and some took one part and some another, and there was a great fight in the hall. And afterwards the four kings quarrelled, and the king of Leinster sent out messengers to bid all his people come to help him. So the farmer's son got the message as well as the others, and he made ready at once to join the battle with a proud heart for the sake of the king and a young man's love of adventure.

Then the farmer was filled with rage.

'This is the wicked work of the witch woman,' he said; 'but as I would not give her the milk to spill, nor the cakes when baked, so I will not give her the life of my only son.'

And he took large stones and built up great walls the height of a man, round a hut, and set a great stone at the top to close it, only leaving places for a vessel of food to be handed down. And he placed the lad within the hut.

'Now,' he said, 'the king shall not have him, nor the king's men; he is safe from the battle and the spears of the warriors.' So the next morning he rose up quite content, and was out at sunrise as usual; and as he walked by the churchyard, he heard the child laughing. And the mother said –

'Child, you laugh by a grave. For the farmer's son will be laid in that ground before three days are over, and then the curse will be lifted from the poor. He would not let the milk be spilled, nor the cakes to be baked, but he cannot keep his son from death. The spell is on him for evil.'

Then a voice said –

'But his father has walled him round in a hut with strong walls, high as a man. How then can he die in battle?'

And the woman answered –

'I climbed the hut last night and gave him nine stones, and bade him throw them one by one over his left shoulder, and each time a stone of the wall would fall down, till free space was left him to escape, and this he did; and before sunrise this morning he fled away, and has joined the king's army; but his grave is ready, and in three days he will be in this ground, for his doom is spoken.'

When the farmer heard these words, he rushed like mad to the hut, and called his son by name; but no answer came. Then he climbed up and looked in through the hole at the top, but no sign of his son was there. And he wrung his hands in despair, and went home and spake no word, but sat moaning with his head buried in his hands.

And on the third day he heard the steps of men outside, and he rose up, for he knew they were bearing the body of his dead son to the door. And he went out to meet them, and there lay the corpse of the young man on the bier, pale and beautiful, struck through and through by a spear, even as he had died in battle.

And they laid him in the churchyard, just as the witch-woman had foretold, while all the people wept, for the young man was noble to look upon, and of a good and upright spirit.

But the father neither spoke nor wept. His mind was gone, and his heart was broken. And soon he lay down and died, unpitied by all; for he was hard and cruel in his life, and no man wept for him; and all the riches he had gathered by grinding down the poor melted away, and his race perished from the land, and his name was heard of no more, and no blessing rested on his memory.

THE FARMER'S WIFE

Down in the South there lived another rich farmer and his wife, who were both of them hated by the people for their stingy, hard-hearted ways. Never a word of kindness was on their lips, and never a blessing

THE FARMER'S WIFE

from the poor was invoked on their heads.

One day an old woman came to the door to beg a little food – a cake from the griddle, or a few potatoes, or a handful of meal; but she was harshly refused by the farmer's wife and turned away.

Then she came back in a little while, and begged for a drink of milk, for she was faint and weary, she said, and had travelled far. This was also refused, and she was ordered to leave the place at once. But the woman still begged hard for leave to rest herself a little, and for even a drink of butter milk, for it was churning day and she knew there must be plenty in the house. Then the farmer's wife grew very angry, and said she would turn the dogs on her if she didn't go away, and that no tramp should get anything from her. On this the woman muttered some words, with her hand on the lintel of the door, and then went her way. Soon after, being much heated by the violence of her anger, the farmer's wife went to the dairy for a drink; but as she poured out the draught she saw something black in the cup, and she tried to take it out with her finger, but it always escaped her. Then, being very thirsty, she drank off the milk, and still another and another cup, and in the drinking the black object disappeared.

That night, however, she felt nigh to death, for her body began to swell, and turned black all over. Medical aid was sent for, but the doctor could make out nothing of the cause or nature of the strange disease. Then the priest was summoned, and he at once, having heard the story, said there was witchcraft in it; and he proceeded to pray, and to exorcise the evil spirit in the woman. Besides this he made her be placed in a hot bath, into which he poured some holy water.

At first the woman uttered fierce cries, and said her body seemed rent and torn; but gradually she became calmer, and the blackness slowly went down from head to feet, and finally disappeared, leaving the body fair and whole, all except one hand, and this remained still as black as ink. The holy water was poured on it, and the priest prayed, but nothing would remove the devil's mark.

So the priest told her at last that the blackness would remain as a sign and token of her sins against the poor; and from that day forth to her death the mark of the evil spell remained on her, but she grew kinder to the poor, for her heart was shaken by terror. And when she came to die there was no blackness on her hand, for the tears of the poor she had succoured and befriended had washed all the devil's mark away, before the moment came when her soul was to appear before God.

THE MIDNIGHT RIDE

A PEASANT'S TALE

One evening a man called Shawn Ruadh was out looking for a red cow that had strayed away, when he heard voices round him, and one said 'Get me a horse,' and another cried 'Get me a horse.' 'And get me a horse, too,' said Shawn, 'since they seem so plenty, for I'd like a ride along with you,' and with that he found himself on the instant mounted on a fine grey horse beside another man who rode a black horse. And they rode away and away till they came to a great city.

'Now, do you know where you are?' said the black horseman. 'You are in London, and whatever you want you can have.'

'Thank you kindly, my friend,' said the other, 'so, with your leave, I'll just have a good suit of clothes, for I'm much in want of that same. Can I have them?'

'By all means,' said the black horseman; 'there, go into that merchant's shop and ask for what you like, and if he refuses just throw the stone I give you on the floor and the whole place will seem on fire. But don't be frightened; only wait your good luck.'

So Shawn went into the biggest shop there, and he spoke to the merchant quite stiff and proud.

'Show me the best suit of clothes you have,' said he. 'Never mind the price, that's of no consequence, only be very particular as to the fit.'

But the shopman laughed aloud.

THE MIDNIGHT RIDE

'We don't make clothes for beggars like you,' he said. 'Be off out of this.'

Then Shawn threw down the stone on the floor, and immediately the whole place seemed on fire, and the merchant ran out himself and all the shopmen after him to get pails of water, and Shawn laughed when he saw them all drenched.

'Now what will you give me,' said he, 'if I put out the fire for you?'

'You shall have the price of the best suit of clothes in the shop,' answered the merchant, 'all paid down in gold; only help me to put out the fire.'

So Shawn stooped down and picked up the stone, and put it quietly into his pocket, and instantly all the flames disappeared: and the merchant was so grateful that he paid him down all the gold for the clothes and more. And Shawn bid him good-night, and mounted the grey steed again quite happy in himself.

'Now,' said the black horseman, 'is there anything else you desire? for it is near ten o'clock, and we must be back by midnight; so just say what you would like to do.'

'Well,' said Shawn Ruadh, 'I would like of all things to see the Pope of Rome, for two of our priests are disputing as to who is to get the parish, and I want Father M'Grath to have it, for I have a great opinion of him, and if I ask his Holiness he'll settle it all in no time and for ever.'

'Come then,' said the black horseman; 'it is a long way to Rome, certainly, but I think we'll manage it in the two hours, and be back before twelve o'clock.'

So away they rode like the wind, and in no time Shawn found himself before the great palace of the Pope; and all the grand servants with gold sticks in their hands stared at him, and asked him what he wanted.

'Just go in,' said he, 'and tell his Holiness that Shawn Ruadh, all the way from Ireland, is here and wants to see him very particularly.'

But the servants laughed, and struck him with their gold sticks and hunted him away from the gate. Now the Pope hearing the rout looked out of the window, and seeing Shawn Ruadh he came down and asked him what he wanted.

'Just this, your Holiness,' answered Shawn, 'I want a letter on behalf of Father M'Grath bidding the Bishop give him the parish, and I'll wait till your Holiness writes it; and meanwhile let me have a little supper, for it's hungry I am after my long ride.'

Then the Pope laughed, and told the servants to drive the fellow away, for he was evidently out of his wits.

So Shawn grew angry, and flung down the stone on the floor, and instantly all the palace seemed on fire, and the Pope ordered the grand servants to go for water; and they had to run about like mad getting pails and jugs of water, whatever they could lay hands on; and all their fine clothes were spoiled, and the beautiful gold sticks were flung away in their fright, while they took the jugs and splashed and dashed the water over each other.

Now it was Shawn's turn to laugh till his sides ached, but his Holiness looked very grave.

'Well,' said Shawn, 'if I put out the fire what will you do for me? Will you write that letter?'

'Ay, I will,' said the Pope, 'and you shall have your supper also; only help us to put out the fire, my fine fellow.'

So Shawn quietly put the stone back in his pocket, and instantly all the flames disappeared.

'Now,' said the Pope, 'you shall have supper of the best in the palace; and I'll write a letter to the Bishop ordering him to give Father M'Grath the parish. And here, besides, is a purse of gold for yourself, and take it with my blessing.'

Then he ordered all the grand servants to get supper for the excellent young man from Ireland, and to make him comfortable. So Shawn was mightily pleased, and ate and drank like a prince. Then he mounted his grey steed again, and just as midnight struck he found himself at his own door, but all alone; for the grey steed and the black horseman had both vanished. But there stood his wife crying her eyes out and in great trouble.

'O Shawn, Agra! I thought you were dead or that evil had fallen on you.'

'Not a bit of it,' said Shawn, 'I've been supping with the Pope of Rome, and look here at all the gold I've brought home for you, my darling.'

And he put his hand in his pocket to get the purse; but lo! there was nothing there except a rough, grey stone. And from that hour to this his wife believes that he dreamed the whole story as he lay under the hayrick, on his way home from a carouse with the boys.

However, Father M'Grath got the parish, and Shawn took good care to tell him how he had spoken up boldly for him to the Pope of Rome, and made his Holiness write the letter to the Bishop about him. And Father M'Grath was a nice gentleman, and he smiled and told Shawn he thanked him kindly for his good word.

THE LEPREHAUN

The Leprehauns[7] are merry, industrious, tricksy little sprites, who do all the shoemaker's work and the tailor's and the cobbler's for the fairy gentry, and are often seen at sunset under the hedge singing and stitching. They know all the secrets of hidden treasure, and if they take a fancy to a person will guide him to the spot in the fairy rath where the pot of gold lies buried. It is believed that a family now living near Castlerea came by their riches in a strange way, all through the good offices of a friendly Leprehaun. And the legend has been handed down through many generations as an established fact.

There was a poor boy once, one of their forefathers, who used to drive his cart of turf daily back and forward, and make what money he could by the sale; but he was a strange boy, very silent and moody, and the people said he was a fairy changeling, for he joined in no sports and scarcely ever spoke to any one, but spent the nights reading

---

[7] Leprehaun, or Leith Brogan, means the 'Artisan of the Brogae.'

all the old bits of books he picked up in his rambles. The one thing he longed for above all others was to get rich, and to be able to give up the old weary turf cart, and live in peace and quietness all alone, with nothing but books round him, in a beautiful house and garden all by himself.

Now he had read in the old books how the Leprehauns knew all the secret places where gold lay hid, and day by day he watched for a sight of the little cobbler, and listened for the click, click of his hammer as he sat under the hedge mending the shoes.

At last, one evening just as the sun set, he saw a little fellow under a dock leaf, working away, dressed all in green, with a cocked hat on his head. So the boy jumped down from the cart and seized him by the neck.

'Now, you don't stir from this,' he cried, 'till you tell me where to find the hidden gold.'

'Easy now,' said the Leprehaun, 'don't hurt me, and I will tell you all about it. But mind you, I could hurt you if I chose, for I have the power; but I won't do it, for we are cousins once removed. So as we are near relations I'll just be good, and show you the place of the secret gold that none can have or keep except those of fairy blood and race. Come along with me, then, to the old fort of Lipenshaw, for there it lies. But make haste, for when the last red glow of the sun vanishes the gold will disappear also, and you will never find it again.'

'Come off, then,' said the boy, and he carried the Leprehaun into the turf cart, and drove off. And in a second they were at the old fort, and went in through a door made in the stone wall.

'Now, look round,' said the Leprehaun; and the boy saw the whole ground covered with gold pieces, and there were vessels of silver lying about in such plenty that all the riches of all the world seemed gathered there.

'Now take what you want,' said the Leprehaun, 'but hasten, for if that door shuts you will never leave this place as long as you live.'

So the boy gathered up his arms full of gold and silver, and flung them into the cart; and was on his way back for more when the door shut with a clap like thunder, and all the place became dark as night. And he saw no more of the Leprehaun, and had not time even to thank him.

So he thought it best to drive home at once with his treasure, and when he arrived and was all alone by himself he counted his riches, and all the bright yellow gold pieces, enough for a king's ransom.

And he was very wise and told no one; but went off next day to Dublin and put all his treasures into the bank, and found that he was now indeed as rich as a lord.

So he ordered a fine house to be built with spacious gardens, and he had servants and carriages and books to his heart's content. And he gathered all the wise men round him to give him the learning of a gentleman; and he became a great and powerful man in the country, where his memory is still held in high honour, and his descendants are living to this day rich and prosperous; for their wealth has never decreased though they have ever given largely to the poor, and are noted above all things for the friendly heart and the liberal hand.

But the Leprehauns can be bitterly malicious if they are offended, and one should be very cautious in dealing with them, and always treat them with great civility, or they will take revenge and never reveal the secret of the hidden gold.

One day a young lad was out in the fields at work when he saw a little fellow, not the height of his hand, mending shoes under a dock leaf. And he went over, never taking his eyes off him for fear he would vanish away; and when he got quite close he made a grab at the creature, and lifted him up and put him in his pocket.

Then he ran away home as fast as he could, and when he had the Leprehaun safe in the house, he tied him by an iron chain to the hob.

'Now, tell me,' he said, 'where am I to find a pot of gold? Let me know the place or I'll punish you.'

'I know of no pot of gold,' said the Leprehaun; 'but let me go that I may finish mending the shoes.'

'Then I'll make you tell me,' said the lad.

And with that he made down a great fire, and put the little fellow on it and scorched him.

'Oh, take me off, take me off!' cried the Leprehaun, 'and I'll tell you. Just there, under the dock leaf, where you found me, there is a pot of gold. Go; dig and find.'

So the lad was delighted, and ran to the door; but it so happened that his mother was just then coming in with the pail of fresh milk, and in his haste he knocked the pail out of her hand, and all the milk was spilled on the floor.

Then, when the mother saw the Leprehaun, she grew very angry and beat him. 'Go away, you little wretch!' she cried. 'You have overlooked the milk and brought ill-luck.' And she kicked him out of the house.

But the lad ran off to find the dock leaf, though he came back very sorrowful in the evening, for he had dug and dug nearly down to the middle of the earth; but no pot of gold was to be seen.

That same night the husband was coming home from his work, and as he passed the old fort he heard voices and laughter, and one said –

'They are looking for a pot of gold; but they little know that a crock of gold is lying down in the bottom of the old quarry, hid under the stones close by the garden wall. But whoever gets it must go of a dark night at twelve o'clock, and beware of bringing his wife with him.'

So the man hurried home and told his wife he would go that very night, for it was black dark, and she must stay at home and watch for him, and not stir from the house till he came back. Then he went out into the dark night alone.

'Now,' thought the wife, when he was gone, 'if I could only get to the quarry before him I would have the pot of gold all to myself; while if he gets it I shall have nothing.'

And with that she went out and ran like the wind until she reached the quarry, and than she began to creep down very quietly in the black dark. But a great stone was in her path, and she stumbled over it, and fell down and down till she reached the bottom, and there she lay groaning, for her leg was broken by the fall.

Just then her husband came to the edge of the quarry and began to descend. But when he heard the groans he was frightened.

'Cross of Christ about us!' he exclaimed; 'what is that down below? Is it evil, or is it good?'

'Oh, come down, come down and help me!' cried the woman. 'It's your wife is here, and my leg is broken, and I'll die if you don't help me.'

'And is this my pot of gold?' exclaimed the poor man. 'Only my wife with a broken leg lying at the bottom of the quarry.'

And he was at his wits' end to know what to do, for the night was so dark he could not see a hand before him. So he roused up a neighbour, and between them they dragged up the poor woman and carried her home, and laid her on the bed half dead from fright, and it was many a day before she was able to get about as usual; indeed she limped all her life long, so that the people said the curse of the Leprehaun was on her.

But as to the pot of gold, from that day to this not one of the family, father or son, or any belonging to them, ever set eyes on it. However, the little Leprehaun still sits under the dock leaf of the hedge and laughs at them as he mends the shoes with his little hammer – tick tack, tick tack – but they are afraid to touch him, for now they know he can take his revenge.

THE BRIDE'S DEATH-SONG

On a lone island by the West Coast there dwelt an old fisherman and his daughter, and the man had power over the water spirits, and he taught his daughter the charms that bind them to obey.

One day a boat was driven on the shore, and in it was a young handsome gentleman, half dead from the cold and the wet. The old fisherman brought him home and revived him, and Eileen the daughter nursed and watched him. Naturally the two young people soon fell in love, and the gentleman told the girl he had a beautiful house on the mainland ready for her, with plenty of everything she could desire

– silks to wear and gold to spend. So they were betrothed, and the wedding day was fixed. But Dermot, the lover, said he must first cross to the mainland and bring back his friends and relations to the wedding, as many as the boat would hold.

Eileen wept and prayed him not to leave, or at least to take her to steer the boat, for she knew there was danger coming, and she alone could have power over the evil spirits and over the waves and the winds. But she dared not tell the secret of the spell to Dermot or it would fail, and the charm be useless for ever after.

Dermot, however, only laughed at her fears, for the day was bright and clear, and he scorned all thought of danger. So he put off from the shore, and reached the mainland safely, and filled the boat with his friends to return to the island for the wedding. All went well till they were within sight of the island, when suddenly a fierce gust of wind drove the boat on a rock, and it was upset, and all who were in it perished.

Eileen heard the cry of the drowning men as she stood watching on the beach, but could give no help. And she was sore grieved for her lover, and sang a funeral wail for him in Irish, which is still preserved by the people. Then she lay down and died, and the old man, her father, disappeared. And from that day no one has ever ventured to live on the island, for it is haunted by the spirit of Eileen. And the mournful music of her wail is still heard in the nights when the winds are strong and the waves beat upon the rocks where the drowned men lay dead.

The words of the song are very plaintive and simple, and may be translated literally –

> 'I a virgin and a widow mourn for my lover.
> Never more will he kiss me on the lips;
> The cold wave is his bridal bed,
> The cold wave is his wedding shroud.
> O love, my love, had you brought me in the boat
> My spirit and my spells would have saved from harm.
> For my power was strong over waves and wind,

And the spirits of evil would have feared me.
O love, my love, I go to meet you in heaven.
I will ask God to let me see your face.
If the fair angels give me back my lover,
I will not envy the Almighty on His throne.'

THE FAIRY CHILD

An ancient woman living at Innis-Sark said that in her youth she knew a young woman who had been married for five years, but had no children. And her husband was a rough, rude fellow, and used to taunt her and beat her often, because she was childless. But in the course of time it came to pass that a man-child was born to her; and he was beautiful to look on as an angel from heaven. And the father was so proud of the child that he often stayed at home to rock the cradle, and help his wife at the work.

One day, however, as he rocked the cradle, the child looked up suddenly at him, and lo! there was a great beard on its face. Then the father cried out to his wife –

'This is not a child, but a demon! You have put an evil spell on him.'

And he struck her and beat her worse than ever he had done in his life before, so that she screamed aloud for help. On this the place grew quite dark, and thunder rolled over their heads, and the door flew wide open with a great crash, and in walked two strange women, with red caps on their heads and stout sticks in their hands. And they rushed at the man, and one held his arms while the other beat him till he was nearly dead.

'We are the avengers,' they said; 'look on us and tremble; for if you ever beat your wife again, we will come and kill you. Kneel down now, and ask her pardon.'

And when the poor wretch did so, all trembling with fright, they vanished away.

'Now,' said the man, when they were gone, 'this house is no fit place for me. I'll leave it for ever.'

So he went his way, and troubled his wife no more.

Then the child sat up in the cradle.

'Now, mother,' says he, 'since that man has gone, I'll tell you what you are to do. There is a holy well near this that you have never seen, but you will know it by the bunch of green rushes that grows over the mouth. Go there and stoop down and cry out aloud three times, and an old woman will come up, and whatever you want she will give it to you. Only tell no one of the well or of the woman, or evil will come of it.'

So the mother promised, and went to the well, and cried out three times; and an old woman came up, and said –

'Woman, why dost thou call me?'

And the poor mother was afraid, and answered all trembling –

'The child sent me, and I pray thee to do me good, and not evil.'

'Come down, then, with me into the well,' said the woman, 'and have no fear.'

So the mother held out her hand, and the other drew her down a flight of stone steps, and then they came to a massive closed door, and the old woman unlocked it and bade her enter. But the mother was afraid, and wept.

'Enter,' said the other, 'and fear nothing. For this is the gate of the king's palace, and you will see the queen of the fairies herself, for it is her son you are nursing; and the king, her husband, is with her on his golden throne. And have no fear, only ask no questions, and do as they order.'

Then they entered into a beautiful hall, and the floor was of marble, and the walls were of solid gold, and a great light shone over everything, so that the eyes could hardly see for the light. Then they passed on into another room, and at the end of it, on a golden throne, sat the king of the fairies. He was very handsome, and beside him sat his queen, fair and beautiful to look upon, all clad in silver.

'This, madam, is the nurse of your son, the young prince,' said the old woman.

THE FAIRY CHILD

The queen smiled, and bade the nurse to sit down, and asked her how she came to know of the place.

'My son it is who told her,' said the king, looking very angry. But the queen soothed him, and turning to one of her ladies, said –

'Bring here the other child.'

Then the lady brought in an infant, and placed him in the arms of the mother.

'Take him,' said the queen, 'he is your own child, that we carried away, for he was so beautiful; and the boy you have at home is mine, a little elfish imp. Still, I want him back, and I have sent a man to bring him here; and you may take your own lovely child home in safety, for the fairy blessings are on him for good. And the man that beat you was not your husband at all, but our messenger, that we sent to change the children. So now go back, and you will find your own true husband at home in your own place, watching and waiting for you by day and by night.'

With that the door opened, and the man who had beaten her came in; and the mother trembled and was afraid. But the man laughed, and told her not to fear, but to eat what was set before her, and then to go in peace.

So they brought her to another hall, where was a table covered with golden dishes and beautiful flowers, and red wine in crystal cups.

'Eat,' they said; 'this feast has been prepared for you. As to us, we cannot touch it, for the food has been sprinkled with salt.'

So she ate, and drank of the red wine, and never in all her life were so many things set before her that were lovely and good. And, as was right and proper, after dinner was over, she stood up, and folded her hands together to give God thanks. But they stopped her, and drew her down.

'Hush!' they said, 'that name is not to be named here.'

There was an angry murmur in the hall. But just then beautiful music was heard, and singing like the singing of priests, and the poor mother was so enchanted that she fell on her face as one dead. And when she came to herself it was noonday, and she was standing by the door of her own house. And her husband came out and took her by the hand, and brought her in. And there was her child, more beautiful than ever, as handsome as a young prince.

'Where have you been all this while?' asked the husband.

'It is only an hour since I went away, to look for my child, that the fairies stole from me,' she answered.

'An hour!' said the husband; 'you have been three years away with your child! And when you were gone, a poor sickly thing was laid in the cradle – not as big as a mushroom, and I knew well it was a fairy changeling. But it so happened that one day, a tailor came by, and stopped to rest; and when he looked hard at the child, the ugly misshapen thing sat up quite straight in the cradle, and called out –

'"Come now, what are you looking at? Give me four straws to play with."

'And the tailor gave him the straws. And when he got them, the child played and played such sweet music on them as if they were pipes, that all the chairs and tables began to dance; and when he grew tired, he fell back in the cradle and dropped asleep.

'"Now," said the tailor, "that child is not right; but I'll tell you what to do. Make down a great fire to begin with."

'So we made the fire. Then the tailor shut the door, and lifted the unlucky little wretch out of the cradle, and sat it on the fire. And no sooner had the flames caught it, than it shrieked aloud and flew up the chimney and disappeared. And when everything was burned that belonged to it, I knew you would come back to me with our own fine boy. And now let us name the name of God, and make the sign of the Cross over him, and ill luck will never again fall on our house – no more for ever.'

So the man and his wife lived happily from that day forth, and the child grew up and prospered, and was beautiful to look at and happy in his life; for the fairy blessings were on him of health, wealth, and prosperity, even as the queen of the fairies had promised to the mother.

THE DOOM

There was a young man of Innismore, named James Lynan, noted through all the island for his beauty and strength. Never a one could beat him at hunting or wrestling, and he was, besides, the best dancer in the whole townland. But he was bold and reckless, and ever foremost in all the wild wicked doings of the young fellows of the place.

One day he happened to be in chapel after one of these mad freaks, and the priest denounced him by name from the altar.

'James Lynan,' he said, 'remember my words; you will come to an ill end. The vengeance of God will fall on you for your wicked life; and by the power that is in me I denounce you as an evil liver and a limb of Satan, and accursed of all good men.'

The young man turned pale, and fell on his knees before all the people, crying out bitterly, 'Have mercy, have mercy; I repent, I repent,' and he wept like a woman.

'Go now in peace,' said the priest, 'and strive to lead a new life, and I'll pray to God to save your soul.'

From that day forth James Lynan changed his ways. He gave up drinking, and never a drop of spirits crossed his lips. And he began to attend to his farm and his business, in place of being at all the mad revels and dances and fairs and wakes in the island. Soon after he married a nice girl, a rich farmer's daughter, from the mainland, and they had four fine children, and all things prospered with him.

But the priest's words never left his mind, and he would suddenly turn pale and a shivering would come over him when the memory of the curse came upon him. Still he prospered, and his life was a model of sobriety and order.

One day he and his wife and their children were asked to the wedding of a friend about four miles off; and James Lynan rode to the place, the family going on their own car. At the wedding he was the life of the party as he always was; but never a drop of drink touched his lips. When evening came on, the family set out for the return home just as they had set out; the wife and children on the car, James Lynan riding his own horse. But when the wife arrived at home, she found her husband's horse standing at the gate riderless and quite still. They thought he might have fallen in a faint, and went back to search; when he was found down in a hollow not five perches from his own gate, lying quite insensible and his features distorted frightfully, as if seized while looking on some horrible vision.

They carried him in, but he never spoke. A doctor was sent for, who opened a vein, but no blood came. There he lay like a log, speechless as one dead. Amongst the crowd that gathered round was an old woman accounted very wise by the people.

'Send for the fairy doctor,' she said; 'he is struck.'

So they sent off a boy on the fastest horse for the fairy man. He could not come himself, but he filled a bottle with a potion. Then he said –

'Ride for your life; give him some of this to drink and sprinkle his face and hands also with it. But take care as you pass the lone bush on the round hill near the hollow, for the fairies are there and will hinder you if they can, and strive to break the bottle.'

Then the fairy man blew into the mouth and the eyes and the nostrils of the horse, and turned him round three times on the road and rubbed the dust off his hoofs.

'Now go,' he said to the boy; 'go and never look behind you, no matter what you hear.'

So the boy went like the wind, having placed the bottle safely in his pocket; and when he came to the lone bush the horse started and gave such a jump that the bottle nearly fell, but the boy caught it in time and held it safe and rode on. Then he heard a cluttering of feet behind him, as of men in pursuit; but he never turned or looked, for he knew it was the fairies who were after him. And shrill voices cried to him, 'Ride fast, ride fast, for the spell is cast!' Still he never turned round, but rode on, and never let go his hold of the fairy draught till he stopped at his master's door, and handed the potion to the poor sorrowing wife. And she gave of it to the sick man to drink, and sprinkled his face and hands, after which he fell into a deep sleep. But when he woke up, though he knew every one around him, the power of speech was gone from him; and from that time to his death, which happened soon after, he never uttered word more.

So the doom of the priest was fulfilled – evil was his youth and evil was his fate, and sorrow and death found him at last, for the doom of the priest is as the word of God.

THE CLEARING FROM GUILT

To prove innocence of a crime a certain ancient form is gone through, which the people look on with great awe, and call it emphatically – 'The Clearing.' It is a fearful ordeal, and instances are known of men who have died of fear and trembling from having passed through the terrors of the trial, even if innocent. And it is equally terrible for the accuser as well as the accused.

On a certain day fixed for the ordeal the accused goes to the churchyard and carries away a skull. Then, wrapped in a white sheet, and bearing the skull in his hand, he proceeds to the house of the accuser, where a great crowd has assembled; for the news of 'A Clearing' spreads like wildfire, and all the people gather together as witnesses of the ceremony. There, before the house of his accuser, he kneels down on his bare knees, makes the sign of the cross on his face, kisses the skull, and prays for some time in silence; the people also wait in silence, filled with awe and dread, not knowing what the result may be. Then the accuser, pale and trembling, comes forward and stands beside the kneeling man; and with uplifted hand adjures him to speak the truth. On which the accused, still kneeling and holding the skull in his hand, utters the most fearful imprecation known in the Irish language; almost as terrible as that curse of the Druids, which is so awful that it never yet was put into English words. The accused prays that if he fail to speak the truth all the sins of the man whose skull he holds may be laid upon his soul, and all the sins of his forefathers back to Adam, and all the punishment due to them for the evil of their lives, and all their weakness and sorrow both of body and soul be laid on him both in this life and in the life to come for evermore. But if the accuser has accused falsely and out of malice, then may all the evil rest on his head through this life for ever, and may his soul perish everlastingly.

It would be impossible to describe adequately the awe with which the assembled people listen to these terrible words, and the dreadful silence of the crowd as they wait to see the result. If nothing happens the man rises from his knees after an interval, and is pronounced innocent by the judgment of the people, and no word is ever again uttered against him, nor is he shunned or slighted by the neighbours. But the accuser is looked on with fear and dislike; he is considered unlucky, and seeing that his life is often made so miserable by the coldness and suspicion of the people, many would rather suffer wrong than force the accused person to undergo so terrible a trial as 'The Clearing.'

THE HOLY WELL AND THE MURDERER

The Well of St Brendan, in High Island, has great virtue, but the miraculous power of the water is lost should a thief or a murderer drink of it. Now a cruel murder had been committed on the mainland, and the priest noticed the people that if the murderer tried to conceal himself in the island no one should harbour him or give him food or drink. It happened at that time there was a woman of the island afflicted with pains in her limbs, and she went to the Holy Well to make the stations and say the prayers, and so get cured. But many a day passed and still she got no better, though she went round and round the well on her knees, and recited the paters and aves as she was told.

Then she went to the priest and told him the story, and he perceived at once that the well had been polluted by the touch of some one who had committed a crime. So he bade the woman bring him a bottle of the water, and she did as he desired. Then having received the water, he poured it out, and breathed on it three times in the name of the Trinity; when, lo! the water turned into blood.

'Here is the evil,' cried the priest. 'A murderer has washed his hands in the well.'

He then ordered her to make a fire in a circle, which she did, and he pronounced some words over it; and a mist rose up with the form of a spirit in the midst, holding a man by the arm.

'Behold the murderer,' said the spirit; and when the woman looked on him she shrieked –

'It is my son! my son!' and she fainted.

For the year before her son had gone to live on the mainland, and there, unknown to his mother, he had committed the dreadful murder for which the vengeance of God lay on him. And when she came to herself the spirit of the murderer was still there.

'Oh, my Lord! let him go, let him go! ' she cried.

'You wretched woman!' answered the priest. 'How dare you interpose between God and vengeance. This is but the shadowy form of your son; but before night he shall be in the hands of the law, and justice shall be done.'

Then the forms and the mist melted away, and the woman departed in tears, and not long after she died of a broken heart.

But the well from that time regained all its miraculous powers, and the fame of its cures spread far and wide through all the islands.

LEGENDS OF INNIS-SARK

A WOMAN'S CURSE

There was a woman of the Island of Innis-Sark who was determined to take revenge on a man because he called her by an evil name. So she went to the Saints' Well, and, kneeling down, she took some of the water and poured it on the ground in the name of the devil, saying, 'So may my enemy be poured out like water, and lie helpless on the earth!' Then she went round the well backwards on her knees, and at each station she cast a stone in the name of the devil, and said, 'So may the curse fall on him, and the power of the devil crush him!' After this she returned home.

Now the next morning there was a stiff breeze, and some of the men were afraid to go out fishing; but others said they would try their luck, and amongst them was the man on whom the curse rested. But they had not gone far from land when the boat was capsized by a heavy squall. The fishermen, however, saved themselves by swimming to shore; all except the man on whom the curse rested, and he sank like lead to the bottom, and the waves covered him, and he was drowned.

When the woman heard of the fate that had befallen her enemy, she ran to the beach and clapped her hands with joy and exulted. And as she stood there laughing with strange and horrid mirth, the corpse of the man she had cursed slowly rose up from the sea, and came drifting towards her till it lay almost at her very feet. On this she stooped down to feast her eyes on the sight of the dead man, when suddenly a storm of wind screamed past her, and hurled her from the point of rock where she stood. And when the people ran in all haste to help, no trace of her body could be seen. The woman and the corpse of the man she had cursed disappeared together under the waves, and were never seen again from that time forth.

Another woman in Shark Island was considered to have an evil influence over any one she disliked. One day a man called her a devil's hag in his anger. The woman answered nothing, but that night she went to a Holy Well near the place, and kneeling down, invoked a curse in the name of the devil. Then she went round the well three times backward on her knees, and each time threw a stone in the name of the devil, saying, 'So may the curse fall on his head!' Then she returned home, and told the people to wait for three days, and they would see her words had power. During this time the man was afraid to go out in his boat because of the curse. But on the third day as he was walking by the cliff he fell and broke his leg. And then every one knew that the woman had the witch-secret of evil; and she was held in much fear.

The most effective way of neutralizing the evil influence is to spit on the object and say, 'God bless it!' But another must do it at your request, and sometimes people refuse, fearing to anger the fairies by interfering with their work, whether for good or evil. But the islanders have such faith in the anointing with spittle that they will often solicit a passing stranger to spit on the afflicted person. Indeed, a stranger is considered to have more power than a neighbour.

A woman who kept a small day-school had reason to think that her son, a fine lad of twelve years old, was bewitched, for when he had eaten up the whole dish of stirabout at supper, he asked for more. And she said –

'My son, you had enough for three men. Go to your bed and sleep.'

But next morning he was worse and more ravenous, for he ate up all the bread that his mother had made for the scholars just as she took it from the oven, and not a single cake was left. Then she knew that witchcraft was on the boy, and she stood by the door to watch for a stranger. At last one came by, and she cried to him –

'Come in, come in, for the love of God, and spit on the face of my son!'

'Why should I spit on your son, O woman?' he answered; and he fled away, for he thought she was mad.

Then she sent for the priest, and his reverence poured holy water over him, and laid his hands upon his head while he prayed. So, after a time, the power of the witchcraft was broken, and the boy was restored to his right mind.

The islanders believe also that angels are constantly present amongst them, and all blessed things – the rain, and the dew, and the green crops – come from their power; but the fairies often bring sickness, and will do malicious tricks, and lame a horse, or steal the milk and butter, if they have been offended or deprived of their rights.

There are certain days on which it is not right to speak of the fairies. These days are Wednesdays and Fridays, for then they are present though invisible, and can hear everything, and lay their plans as to what they will carry off. On Friday especially their power for evil is very strong, and misfortunes are dreaded in the household. Therefore, on that day the children and cattle are strictly watched; a lighted wisp of straw is turned round the baby's head, and a quenched coal is set under the cradle and under the churn. And if the horses are restive in the stable, then the people know the fairies are riding on their backs. So they spit three times at the animal, when the fairies scamper off. This cure by the saliva is the most ancient of all superstitions, and the islanders still have the greatest faith in its mysterious power and efficacy.

At Innisboffin the fairies hold a splendid court, with revelry and dancing, when the moon is full; and it is very dangerous for young girls to be out at that time, for they will assuredly be carried off. And if they once hear the fairy music or drink of the fairy wine, they will never be the same again – a fate is on them, and before the year is out they will either disappear or die.

And the fairies are always on the watch for the handsome girls or children; for they look on mortals as of much higher race than themselves. And they are also glad to have the fine young men, the sons of mortal women, to assist them in their wars with each other; for there are two parties amongst the fairy spirits, one a gentle race that loves music and dancing, the other that has obtained power from the devil, and is always trying to work evil.

A young man lay down to sleep one Friday evening in summer under a hay-rick, and the fairies must have carried him off as he slept; for when he woke he found himself in a great hall, where a number of little men were at work – some spinning, some making shoes, some making spears and arrow-heads out of fish-bones and elf-stones; but all busy laughing and singing with much glee and merriment, while the little pipers played the merriest tunes.

Then an old man who sat in the corner came over, and looking very angry, told him he must not sit there idle; there were friends coming to dinner, and he must go down and help in the kitchen. So he drove the poor young fellow before him down into a great vaulted place, where a huge fire was burning, and a large pot was set over it.

'Now,' said the old man, 'prepare the dinner. There is the old hag we are going to eat.'

And true enough, to his horror, on looking round, there was an old woman hung up by the arms, and an old man skinning her.

'Now make haste and let the water boil,' said the old man; 'don't you see the pot on the fire, and I am nearly ready for you to begin. The company will soon be here, and there is no time to lose, for this old hag will take a good while to boil. Cut her up into little bits, and throw her into the pot.'

However, the young fellow was so frightened that he fell down on the floor speechless, and could neither move hand nor foot.

'Get up, you fool,' said another old man, who seemed to be the head over all; and he laughed at him. 'Do your work and never mind; this does not hurt her a bit. When she was there above in the world she was a wicked miser, hard to the world, and cruel and bitter in her words and works; so now we have her here, and her soul will never rest in peace, because we shall cut up the body in little bits, and the soul will not be able to find it, but wander about in the dark to all eternity without a body.'

Then the young man knew no more till he found himself in a beautiful hall, where a banquet was laid out; but, in place of the old hag, the table was covered with fruit, and chickens, and young turkeys, and butter, and cakes fresh from the oven, and crystal cups of bright red wine.

'Now sit down and eat,' said the prince, who sat at the top on a throne, with a red sash round his waist, and a gold band on his head. 'Sit down with this pleasant company and eat with us; you are welcome.'

And there were many beautiful ladies seated round, and grand noblemen, with red caps and sashes; and they all smiled at him and bade him eat.

'No,' said the young man; 'I cannot eat with you, for I see no priest here to bless the food. Let me go in peace.'

'Not at least till you taste our wine,' said the prince with a friendly smile.

And one of the beautiful ladies rose up and filled a crystal cup with the bright red wine, and gave it him. And when he saw it, the sight of it tempted him, and he could not help himself, but drank it all off without stopping; for it seemed to him the most delicious draught he ever had in his whole life.

But no sooner had he laid down the glass, than a noise like thunder shook the building, and all the lights went out; and he found himself alone in the dark night lying under the very same hay-rick where he had cast himself down to sleep, tired after his work. So he made his way home at last; but the taste of the fairy wine burned in his veins, and a fever was on him night and day for another draught; and he did no good, but pined away, seeking the fairy mansion, though he never found it any more. And so he died in his youth, a warning to all who eat of the fairy food, or drink of the fairy wine; for never more will they know peace or content, or be fit for their work, as in the days before the fairy spell was on them, which brings doom and death to all who fall under the fatal enchantment of its unholy power.

LEGENDS OF THE DEAD IN THE WESTERN ISLANDS

When young people die, either men or women, who were remarkable for beauty, it is supposed that they are carried off by the fairies to the fairy mansions under the earth, where they live in splendid palaces and are wedded to fairy queens or princes. But sometimes, if their kindred greatly desire to see them, they are allowed to visit the earth, though no enchantment has yet been discovered powerful enough to compel them to remain or resume again the mortal life.

Sometimes when the fishermen are out they meet a strange boat filled with people; and when they look on them they know that they are the dead who have been carried off by the fairies with their wiles and enchantments to dwell in the fairy palaces.

One day a man was out fishing, but caught nothing; and was just turning home in despair at his ill-luck when he suddenly saw a boat with three persons in it; and it seemed to him that they were his comrades, the very men who just a year before had been drowned in that spot, but whose bodies were never recovered, and he knew that he looked upon the dead. But the men were friendly, and called out to him –

'Cast your line as we direct, and you will have luck.'

So he cast his line as they bade him, and presently drew up a fine fish.

'Now, cast again,' they said, 'and keep beside us, and row to shore, but do not look on us.'

So he did as directed and hauled up fish after fish till his boat was full, and then he drew it up to the landing-place.

'Now,' they said, 'wait and see that no one is about before you land.'

So the man looked up and down the shore, but saw no one; then he turned to land his fish, when, behold, the men and the second boat had vanished, and he saw them no more. However, he landed his fish with much joy and brought them all safely home, though the wise people said that if he had not turned away his head that time, but kept his eyes steadily on the men till he landed, the enchantment would have been broken that held them in fairy-land, and the dead would have been restored to the earthly life, and to their kindred in the island who mourned for them.

THE DEATH SIGN

A woman was out one day looking after her sheep in the valley, and coming by a little stream she sat down to rest, when suddenly she seemed to hear the sound of low music, and turning round, beheld at some distance a crowd of people dancing and making merry. And she grew afraid and turned her head away not to see them. Then close by her stood a young man, pale and strange looking, and she beheld him with fear.

'Who are you?' she said at last; 'and why do you stand beside me?'

'You ought to know me,' he replied, 'for I belong to this place; but make haste now and come away, or evil will befall you.'

Then she stood up and was going away with him, when the crowd left off their dancing and ran towards them crying –

'Come back; come back; come back!'

'Don't stop; don't listen,' said the young man, 'but follow me.'

Then they both began to run, and ran on until they reached a hillock.

'Now we are safe,' said he; 'they can't harm us here.' And when they stopped he said to her again, 'Look me in the face and say if you know me now?'

'No,' she answered, 'you are a stranger to me.'

'Look again,' he said, 'look me straight in the face and you will know me.'

Then she looked, and knew instantly that he was a man who had been drowned the year before in the dark winter time, and the waves had never cast up his body on the shore. And she threw up her arms and cried aloud –

'Have you news of my child? Have you seen her, my fair-haired girl, that was stolen from me this day seven years. Will she come back to me never no more?'

'I have seen her,' said the man, 'but she will never come back, never more, for she has eaten of the fairy food and must now stay with the spirits under the sea, for she belongs to them body and soul. But go home now, for it is late, and evil is near you; and perhaps you will meet her sooner than you think.'

Then as the woman turned her face homeward, the man disappeared and she saw him no more.

When at last she reached the threshold of her house a fear and trembling came on her, and she called to her husband that some one stood in the doorway and she could not pass. And with that she fell down on the threshold on her face, but spake no word more. And when they lifted her up she was dead.

KATHLEEN

A young girl from Innis-Sark had a lover, a fine young fellow, who met his death by an accident, to her great grief and sorrow.

One evening at sunset, as she sat by the roadside crying her eyes out, a beautiful lady came by all in white, and tapped her on the cheek.

'Don't cry, Kathleen,' she said, 'your lover is safe. Just take this ring of herbs and look through it and you will see him. He is with a grand company, and wears a golden circlet on his head and a scarlet sash round his waist.'

So Kathleen took the ring of herbs and looked through it, and there indeed was her lover in the midst of a great company dancing on the hill; and he was very pale, but handsomer than ever, with the gold circlet round his head, as if they had made him a prince.

'Now,' said the lady, 'here is a larger ring of herbs. Take it, and whenever you want to see your lover, pluck a leaf from it and burn it; and a great smoke will arise, and you will fall into a trance; and in the trance your lover will carry you away to the fairy rath, and there you may dance all night with him on the greensward. But say no prayer, and make no sign of the cross while the smoke is rising, or your lover will disappear for ever.'

From that time a great change came over Kathleen. She said no prayer, and cared for no priest, and never made the sign of the cross, but every night shut herself up in her room, and burned a leaf of the ring of herbs as she had been told; and when the smoke arose she fell into a deep sleep and knew no more. But in the morning she told her people that, though she seemed to be lying in her bed, she was far away with the fairies on the hill dancing with her lover. And she was very happy in her new life, and wanted no priest nor prayer nor mass any more, and all the dead were there dancing with the rest, all the people she had known; and they welcomed her and gave her wine to drink in little crystal cups, and told her she must soon come and stay with them and with her lover for evermore.

Now Kathleen's mother was a good, honest, religious woman, and she fretted much over her daughter's strange state, for she knew the girl had been fairy-struck. So she determined to watch; and one night when Kathleen went to her bed as usual all alone by herself in the room, for she would allow no one to be with her, the mother crept up and looked through a chink in the door, and then she saw Kathleen take the round ring of herbs from a secret place in the press and pluck a leaf from it and burn it, on which a great smoke arose and the girl fell on her bed in a deep trance.

Now the mother could no longer keep silence, for she saw there was devil's work in it; and she fell on her knees and prayed aloud –

'O Maia, mother, send the evil spirit away from the child!'

And she rushed into the room and made the sign of the cross over the sleeping girl, when immediately Kathleen started up and screamed –

'Mother! Mother! the dead are coming for me. They are here! they are here!'

And her features looked like one in a fit. Then the poor mother sent for the priest, who came at once, and threw holy water on the girl, and said prayers over her; and he took the ring of herbs that lay beside her and cursed it for evermore, and instantly it fell to powder and lay like grey ashes on the floor. After this Kathleen grew calmer, and the evil spirit seemed to have left her, but she was too weak to move or to speak, or to utter a prayer, and before the clock struck twelve that night she lay dead.

NOVEMBER EVE

It is esteemed a very wrong thing amongst the islanders to be about on November Eve, minding any business, for the fairies have their flitting then, and do not like to be seen or watched; and all the spirits come to meet them and help them. But mortal people should keep at home, or they will suffer for it; for the souls of the dead have power over all things on that one night of the year; and they hold a festival with the fairies, and drink red wine from the fairy cups, and dance to fairy music till the moon goes down.

There was a man of the village who stayed out late one November Eve fishing, and never thought of the fairies until he saw a great number of dancing lights, and a crowd of people hurrying past with baskets and bags, and all laughing and singing and making merry as they went along.

'You are a merry set,' he said, 'where are ye all going to?'

'We are going to the fair,' said a little old man with a cocked hat and a gold band round it. Come with us, Hugh King, and you will have the finest food and the finest drink you ever set eyes upon.'

'And just carry this basket for me,' said a little red-haired woman.

So Hugh took it, and went with them till they came to the fair, which was filled with a crowd of people he had never seen on the island in all his days. And they danced and laughed and drank red wine from little cups. And there were pipers, and harpers, and little cobblers mending shoes, and all the most beautiful things in the world to eat and drink, just as if they were in a palace. But the basket was very heavy, and Hugh longed to drop it, that he might go and dance with a little beauty with long yellow hair, that was laughing up close to his face.

'Well, here put down the basket,' said the red-haired woman, 'for you are quite tired, I see;' and she took it and opened the cover, and out came a little old man, the ugliest, most misshapen little imp that could be imagined.

'Ah, thank you, Hugh,' said the imp, quite politely; 'you have carried me nicely; for I am weak on the limbs – indeed I have nothing to speak of in the way of legs: but I'll pay you well, my fine fellow; hold out your two hands,' and the little imp poured down gold and gold and gold into them, bright golden guineas. 'Now go,' said he, 'and drink my health, and make yourself quite pleasant, and don't be afraid of anything you see and hear.'

So they all left him, except the man with the cocked hat and the red sash round his waist

'Wait here now a bit,' says he, 'for Finvarra, the king, is coming, and his wife, to see the fair.'

As he spoke, the sound of a horn was heard, and up drove a coach and four white horses, and out of it stepped a grand, grave gentleman all in black and a beautiful lady with a silver veil over her face.

'Here is Finvarra himself and the queen,' said the little old man; but Hugh was ready to die of fright when Finvarra asked –

'What brought this man here?'

And the king frowned and looked so black that Hugh nearly fell to the ground with fear. Then they all laughed, and laughed so loud that everything seemed shaking and tumbling down from the laughter. And the dancers came up, and they all danced round Hugh, and tried to take his hands to make him dance with them.

'Do you know who these people are; and the men and women who are dancing round you?' asked the old man. 'Look well, have you ever seen them before?'

And when Hugh looked he saw a girl that had died the year before, then another and another of his friends that he knew had died long ago; and then he saw that all the dancers, men, women, and girls, were the dead in their long, white shrouds. And he tried to escape from them, but could not, for they coiled round him, and danced and laughed and seized his arms, and tried to draw him into the dance, and their laugh seemed to pierce through his brain and kill him. And he fell down before them there, like one faint from sleep, and knew no more till he found himself next morning lying within the old stone circle by the fairy rath on the hill. Still it was all true that he had been with the fairies; no one could deny it, for his arms were all black with the touch of the hands of the dead, the time they had tried to draw him into the dance; but not one bit of all the red gold, which the little imp had given him, could he find in his pocket. Not one single golden piece; it was all gone for evermore.

And Hugh went sadly to his home, for now he knew that the spirits had mocked him and punished him, because he troubled their revels on November Eve – that one night of all the year when the dead can leave their graves and dance in the moonlight on the hill, and mortals should stay at home and never dare to look on them.

THE DANCE OF THE DEAD

It is especially dangerous to be out late on the last night of November, for it is the closing scene of the revels – the last night when the dead have leave to dance on the hill with the fairies, and after that they must all go back to their graves and lie in the chill, cold earth, without music or wine till the next November comes round, when they all spring up again in their shrouds and rush out into the moonlight with mad laughter.

One November night, a woman of Shark Island, coming home late at the hour of the dead, grew tired and sat down to rest, when presently a young man came up and talked to her.

'Wait a bit,' he said, 'and you will see the most beautiful dancing you ever looked on there by the side of the hill.'

And she looked at him steadily. He was very pale, and seemed sad.

'Why are you so sad?' she asked, 'and as pale as if you were dead?'

'Look well at me,' he answered. 'Do you not know me?'

'Yes, I know you now,' she said. 'You are young Brien that was drowned last year when out fishing. What are you here for?'

'Look,' he said, 'at the side of the hill and you will see why I am here.'

And she looked, and saw a great company dancing to sweet music; and amongst them were all the dead who had died as long as she could remember – men, women, and children, all in white, and their faces were pale as the moonlight.

'Now,' said the young man, 'run for your life; for if once the fairies bring you into the dance you will never be able to leave them any more.'

But while they were talking, the fairies came up and danced round her in a circle, joining their hands. And she fell to the ground in a faint, and knew no more till she woke up in the morning in her own bed at home. And they all saw that her face was pale as the dead, and they knew that she had got the fairy-stroke. So the herb doctor was sent for, and every measure tried to save her, but without avail, for just as the moon rose that night, soft, low music was heard round the house, and when they looked at the woman she was dead.

It is a custom amongst the people, when throwing away water at night, to cry out in a loud voice, 'Take care of the water;' or, literally from the Irish, 'Away with yourself from the water' – for they say the spirits of the dead last buried are then wandering about, and it would be dangerous if the water fell on them.

One dark winter's night a woman suddenly threw out a pail of boiling water without thinking of the warning words. Instantly a cry was heard as of a person in pain, but no one was seen. However, the next night a black lamb entered the house, having the back all fresh scalded, and it lay down moaning by the hearth and died. Then they all knew this was the spirit that had been scalded by the woman. And they carried the dead lamb out reverently and buried it deep in the earth. Yet every night at the same hour it walked again into the house and lay down and moaned and died. And after this had happened many times, the priest was sent for, and finally, by the strength of his exorcism, the spirit of the dead was laid to rest, and the black lamb appeared no more. Neither was the body of the dead lamb found in the grave when they searched for it, though it had been laid by their own hands deep in the earth and covered with the clay.

Before an accident happens to a boat, or a death by drowning, low music is often heard, as if under the water, along with harmonious lamentations, and then every one in the boat knows that some young man or beautiful young girl is wanted by the fairies, and is doomed to die. The best safeguard is to have music and singing in the boat, for the fairies are so enamoured of the mortal voices and music that they forget to weave the spell till the fatal moment has passed, and then all in the boat are safe from harm.

SUPERSTITIONS CONCERNING THE DEAD

Many strange spells are effected by the means of a dead man's hand – chiefly to produce butter in the churn. The milk is stirred round nine times with the dead hand, the operator crying aloud all the time, 'Gather! gather! gather!' While a secret form of words is used which none but the initiated know.

Another use is to facilitate robberies. If a candle is placed in a dead hand, neither wind nor water can extinguish it. And if carried into a house the inmates will sleep the sleep of the dead as long as it remains under the roof, and no power on earth can wake them while the dead hand holds the candle.

For a mystic charm, one of the strongest known is the hand of an unbaptized infant fresh taken from the grave in the name of the Evil One.

A dead hand is esteemed also a certain cure for most diseases, and many a time sick people have been brought to a house where a corpse lay that the hand of the dead might be laid on them.

The souls of the dead who may happen to die abroad, greatly desire to rest in Ireland. And the relations deem it their duty to bring back the body to be laid in Irish earth. But even then the dead will not rest peaceably unless laid with their forefathers and their own people, and not amongst strangers.

A young girl happened to die of a fever while away on a visit to some friends, and her father thought it safer not to bring her home, but to have her buried in the nearest churchyard. However, a few nights after his return home, he was awakened by a mournful wail at the window, and a voice cried, 'I am alone; I am alone; I am alone!' Then the poor father knew well what it meant, and he prayed in the name of God that the spirit of his dead child might rest in peace until the morning. And when the day broke he arose and set off to the strange burial ground, and there he drew the coffin from the earth, and had it carried all the way back from Cork to Mayo; and after he had laid the dead in the old graveyard beside his people and his kindred, the spirit of his child had rest, and the mournful cry was no more heard in the night.

The corner of a sheet that has wrapped a corpse is a cure for headache if tied round the head.

The ends of candles used at wakes are of great efficacy in curing burns.

A piece of linen wrap taken from a corpse will cure the swelling of a limb if tied round the part affected.

It is believed that the spirit of the dead last buried has to watch in the churchyard until another corpse is laid there; or has to perform menial offices in the spirit world, such as carrying wood and water until the next spirit comes from earth. They are also sent on messages to earth, chiefly to announce the coming death of some relative, and at this they are glad, for then their time of peace and rest will come at last.

If any one stumbles at a grave it is a bad omen; but if he falls and touches the clay, he will assuredly die before the year is out.

Any one meeting a funeral must turn back and walk at least four steps with the mourners.

If the nearest relative touches the hand of a corpse it will utter a wild cry if not quite dead.

On Twelfth Night the dead walk, and on every tile of the house a soul is sitting, waiting for your prayers to take it out of purgatory.

There are many strange superstitions in the western islands of Connemara. At night the dead can be heard laughing with the fairies and spinning the flax. One girl declared that she distinctly heard her dead mother's voice singing a mournful Irish air away down in the heart of the hill. But after a year and a day the voices cease, and the dead are gone for ever.

It is a custom in the West, when a corpse is carried to the grave, for the bearers to stop half way, while the nearest relatives build up a small monument of loose stones, and no hand would ever dare to touch or disturb this monument while the world lasts.

When the grave is dug, a cross is made of two spades, and the coffin is carried round it three times before being placed in the clay. Then the prayers for the dead are said, all the people kneeling with uncovered head.

THE FATAL LOVE-CHARM

A potent love-charm used by women is a piece of skin taken from the arm of a corpse and tied on the person while sleeping whose love is sought. The skin is then removed after some time, and carefully put away before the sleeper awakes or has any consciousness of the transaction. And as long as it remains in the woman's possession the love of her lover will be unchanged. Or the strip of skin is placed under the head to dream on, in the name of the Evil One, when the future husband will appear in the dream.

A young girl who was servant in the large and handsome house of a rich family tried this charm for fun, thinking she would dream of one of her fellow-servants, and next morning her mistress asked the result.

'Throth, ma'am,' she answered, 'there never was such a foolish trick, for it was of the master himself I was dreaming all night, and of no one else.'

Soon after the lady died, and the girl, remembering her dream, watched her opportunity to tie a piece of skin taken from a corpse recently buried round the arm of her master while he slept. After this he became violently in love with the girl, though she was exceedingly ugly, and within the year he married her, his love all the while remaining fervent and unchanged.

But exactly one year and a day after her marriage her bedroom took fire by accident, and the strip of skin, which she had kept carefully hidden in her wardrobe, was burnt, along with all her grand wedding-clothes. Immediately the magic charm was broken, and the hatred of the gentleman for his low-born wife became as strong as the love he had once felt for her.

In her rage and grief at finding nothing but coldness and insult, she confessed the whole story; and, in consequence, the horror she inspired amongst the people was so great that no one would serve her with food or drink, or sit near her, or hold any intercourse with her; and she died miserably and half mad before the second year was out – a warning and a terror to all who work spells in the name of the Evil One.

THE FENIAN KNIGHTS

A LEGEND OF THE WEST

There is a fort near the Killeries in Connemara called *Lis-na-Keeran*. One day the powerful chief that lived there invited the great Fionn Ma-Coul, with his son Oscar and a band of Fenian knights, to a great banquet. But when the guests arrived they found no chairs prepared for them, only rough benches of wood placed round the table.

So Oscar and his father would take no place, but stood watching, for they suspected treachery. The knights, however, fearing nothing, sat down to the feast, but were instantly fixed to the benches so firmly by magic, that they could neither rise nor move.

Then Fionn began to chew his thumb, from which he always derived knowledge of the future, and by his magic power he saw clearly a great and terrible warrior riding fiercely towards the fort, and Fionn knew that unless he could be stopped before crossing a certain ford, they must all die, for they had been brought to *Lis-na-Keeran* only to be slain by their treacherous host; and unless the warrior was killed and his blood sprinkled on the Fenian knights, they must remain fixed on the wooden benches for ever.

So Oscar of the Lion heart rushed forth to the encounter. And he flung his spear at the mighty horseman, and they fought desperately till the setting of the sun. Then at last Oscar triumphed; victory was his; and he cut off the head of his adversary, and carried it on his spear all bleeding to the fort, where he let the blood drop down upon the Fenian knights that were transfixed by magic. On this they at once sprang up free and scatheless, all except one, for on him unhappily no blood had fallen, and so he remained fixed to the bench. His companions tried to drag him up by main force, but as they did so the skin of his thighs was left on the bench, and he was like to die.

Then they killed a sheep, and wrapped the fleece round him warm from the animal to heal him. So he was cured, but ever after, strange to relate, seven stone of wool were annually shorn from his body as long as he lived.

The manner in which Fionn learned the mystery of obtaining wisdom from his thumb was in this wise.

It happened one time when he was quite a youth that he was taken prisoner by a one-eyed giant, who at first was going to kill him, but then he changed his mind and sent him to the kitchen to mind the dinner. Now there was a great and splendid salmon broiling on the fire, and the giant said –

'Watch that salmon till it is done; but if a single blister rise on the skin you shall be killed.'

Then the giant threw himself down to sleep while waiting for the dinner.

So Fionn watched the salmon with all his eyes, but to his horror saw a blister rising on the beautiful silver skin of the fish, and in his fright and eagerness he pressed his thumb down on it to flatten it; then the pain of the burn being great, he clapped the thumb into his mouth and kept it there to suck out the fire. When he drew it back, however, he found, to his surprise that he had a knowledge of all that was going to happen to him, and a clear sense of what he ought to do. And it came into his mind that if he put out the giant's eye with an iron rod heated in the fire, he could escape from the monster. So he heated the rod, and while the giant slept he plunged it into his eye, and before the horrid being recovered from the shock, Fionn escaped, and was soon back safe amongst his own people, the Fenian knights; and ever after in moments of great peril and doubt, when he put his thumb into his mouth and sucked it, the vision of the future came on him, and he could foresee clearly whatever danger lay in his path, and how to avoid it. But it was only in such extreme moments of peril that the mystic power was granted to him. And thus he was enabled to save his own life and the lives of his chosen Fenian guard when all hope seemed well-nigh gone.

RATHLIN ISLAND

There is an old ruin called Bruce's Castle on this island, and the legend runs that Bruce and his chief warriors lie in an enchanted sleep in a cave of the rock on which stands the castle, and that one day they will rise up and unite the island to Scotland.

The entrance to this cave is visible only once in seven years. A man who happened to be travelling by at the time discovered it, and entering in he found himself all at once in the midst of the heavy-handed warriors. He looked down and saw a sabre half unsheathed in the earth at his feet, and on his attempting to draw it every man of the sleepers lifted up his head and put his hand on his sword. The man being much alarmed fled from the cave, but he heard voices calling fiercely after him; 'Ugh! ugh! Why could we not be left to sleep?' And they clanged their swords on the ground with a terrible noise, and then all was still, and the gate of the cave closed with a mighty sound like a clap of thunder.

THE STRANGE GUESTS

A company of strangers came one day to Rathlin island and the people distrusted them, but pretended to be friendly, and invited them to a feast, meaning to put an end to them all when they came unarmed to the festival, and the drink flowed freely. So the strangers came, but each man as he sat down drew his knife and stuck it in the table before him ere he began to eat. When the islanders saw their guests so well prepared, they were afraid; and the feast passed off quietly.

The next morning early, the strangers sailed away before any one was aware on the island; but on the table where each guest had sat, a piece of silver was found, covering the hole made by the knife. So the islanders rejoiced, and determined never again to plot evil against the wayfaring guests; but to be kind and hospitable to all wanderers for the sake of the Holy Mother who had sent them to the island to bring good luck to the people. But they never saw the strangers more.

The islanders have great faith in the power of the Virgin Mary, for our Lord Himself told St Bridget that His mother had a throne in heaven near His own; and whatever she asked of God it was granted, especially if it was any grace or favour for the Irish people, because He held them in great esteem on account of their piety and good works.

THE DEAD SOLDIER

There is an island in the Shannon, and if a mermaid is seen sitting on the rocks in the sunshine, the people know that a crime has been committed somewhere near; for she never appears but to announce ill-luck, and she has a spite against mortals, and rejoices at their misfortunes.

One day a young fisherman was drawn by the current towards the island, and he came on a long streak of red blood, and had to sail his boat through it till he reached the rocks where the mermaid was seated; and then the boat went round and round as in a whirlpool, and sank down at last under the waves.

Still he did not lose consciousness. He looked round and saw that he was in a beautiful country, with tall plants growing all over it; and the mermaid came and sang sweetly to him, and offered him wine to drink, but he would not taste it, for it was red like blood. Then he looked down, and to his horror he saw a soldier lying on the floor with his throat cut; and all round him was a pool of blood, and he remembered no more till he found himself again in his boat drifting against a hurricane, and suddenly he was dashed upon a rock, where his friends who were in search of him found him, and carried him home. There he heard a strange thing: a soldier, a deserter from the Athlone Barracks, being pursued had cut his throat and flung himself over the bridge into the river; and this was the very man the young fisher had seen lying a corpse in the mermaid's cave. After this he had no peace or comfort till he went to the priest, who exorcised him and gave him absolution; and then the wicked siren of the rocks troubled him no more, though she still haunts the islands of the Shannon and tries to lure victims to their death.

THE THREE GIFTS

A great, noble-looking man called one night at a cottage, and told the woman that she must come away with him then and there on the instant, for his wife wanted a nurse for her baby. And so saying, before she could answer, he swung her up on his great black horse on a pillion behind him. And she sat wondering at his tall, shadowy form, for she could see the moonlight through him.

'Do not fear,' he said, 'and no harm will happen to you. Only ask no questions whatever happens, and drink no wine that may be offered to you.'

On reaching the palace she saw the most beautiful ladies going about all covered with jewels, and she was led into a chamber hung with silk and gold, and lace as fine as cobwebs; and there on a bed supported by crystal pillars lay the mother, lovely as an angel, and her little baby beside her. And when the nurse had dressed the baby and handed it to the mother, the lady smiled and offered her wine; 'for then,' she said, 'you will never leave us, and I would love to have you always near me.'

But the woman refused, though she was sorely tempted by the beautiful bright red wine.

'Well, then,' said the lord and master, 'here are three gifts, and you may take them away in safety, for no harm will come to you by them. A purse, never to be opened, but while you have it, you will never want money; a girdle, and whoso wears it will never be slain in battle; and an herb that has power to cure all diseases for seven generations.'

So the woman was put again upon the horse with her three gifts, and reached her home safely. Then, from curiosity, the first thing she did was to open the purse, and behold, there was nothing in it but some wild flowers. On seeing this, she was so angry that she flung away the herb, 'for they were only making a fool of me,' she said, 'and I don't believe one word of their stories.' But the husband took the belt and kept it safe, and it went down in the family from father to son; and the last man who wore it was out in all the troubles of '98, and fought in every one of the battles, but he never got hurt or wound. However, after his death, no one knew what became of the belt; it was never seen more.

A woman was carried off one night to a fairy palace to attend one of the beautiful fairy ladies who lay sick on her golden bed.

And as she was going in at the gate a man whispered to her, 'Eat no food, and take no money from the fairies; but ask what you like and it will be granted.' So when the fairy lady was well, she bade the nurse ask what she pleased. The woman answered, 'I desire three things for my sons and their race – luck in fishing, luck in learning, and luck in gambling,' which things were granted – and to this day the family are the richest, the wisest, and the luckiest in the whole neighbourhood. They win at every game, and at every race, but always by fair play and without cheating; and not the priest himself can beat them at book learning. And every one knows that the power comes to them from the fairy gift, though good luck comes with it and not evil; and all the work of their hands has prospered through every generation since the day of the Three Wishes.

THE FAIRIES AS FALLEN ANGELS

The islanders, like all the Irish, believe that the fairies are the fallen angels who were cast down by the Lord God out of heaven for their sinful pride. And some fell into the sea, and some on the dry land, and some fell deep down into hell, and the devil gives to these knowledge and power, and sends them on earth where they work much evil. But the fairies of the earth and the sea are mostly gentle and beautiful creatures, who will do no harm if they are let alone, and allowed to dance on the fairy raths in the moonlight to their own sweet music, undisturbed by the presence of mortals. As a rule, the people look on fire as the great preservative against witchcraft, for the devil has no power except in the dark. So they put a live coal under the churn, and they wave a lighted wisp of straw above the cow's head if the beast seems sickly. But as to the pigs, they take no trouble, for they say the devil has no longer any power over them now. When they light a candle they cross themselves, because the evil spirits are then clearing out of the house in fear of the light. Fire and Holy Water they hold to be sacred, and are powerful; and the best safeguard against all things evil, and the surest test in case of suspected witchcraft.

THE FAIRY CHANGELING

One evening, a man was coming home late, and he passed a house where two women stood by a window, talking.

'I have left the dead child in the cradle as you bid me,' said one woman, 'and behold here is the other child, take it and let me go;' and she laid down an infant on a sheet by the window, who seemed in a secret sleep, and it was draped all in white.

'Wait,' said the other, 'till you have had some food, and then take it to the fairy queen, as I promised, in place of the dead child that we have laid in the cradle by the nurse. Wait also till the moon rises, and then you shall have the payment which I promised.'

They then both turned from the window. Now the man saw that there was some devil's magic in it all. And when the women turned away he crept up close to the open window and put his hand in and seized the sleeping child and drew it out quietly without ever a sound. Then he made off as fast as he could to his own home, before the women could know anything about it, and handed the child to his mother's care. Now the mother was angry at first, but when he told her the story, she believed him, and put the baby to sleep – a lovely, beautiful boy with a face like an angel.

Next morning there was a great commotion in the village, for the news spread that the first-born son of the great lord of the place, a lovely, healthy child, died suddenly in the night, without ever having had a sign of sickness. When they looked at him in the morning, there he laid dead in his cradle, and he was shrunk and wizened like a little old man, and no beauty was seen on him any more. So great lamentation was heard on all sides, and the whole country gathered to the wake. Amongst them came the young man who had carried off the child, and when he looked on the little wizened thing in the cradle he laughed. Now the parents were angry at his laughter, and wanted to turn him out.

But he said, 'Wait, put down a good fire,' and they did so.

Then he went over to the cradle and said to the hideous little creature, in a loud voice before all the people –

'If you don't rise up this minute and leave the place, I will burn you on the fire; for I know right well who you are, and where you came from.'

At once the child sat up and began to grin at him; and made a rush to the door to get away; but the man caught hold of it and threw it on the fire. And the moment it felt the heat it turned into a black kitten, and flew up the chimney and was seen no more.

Then the man sent word to his mother to bring the other child, who was found to be the true heir, the lord's own son. So there was great rejoicing, and the child grew up to be a great lord himself, and when his time came, he ruled well over the estate; and his descendants are living to this day, for all things prospered with him after he was saved from the fairies.

FAIRY WILES

When the fairies steal away a beautiful mortal child they leave an ugly, wizened little creature in its place. And these fairy changelings grow up malicious and wicked, and have voracious appetites. The unhappy parents often try the test of fire for the child, in this wise – placing it in the centre of the cabin, they light a fire round it, and fully expect to see it changed into a sod of turf. But if the child survives the ordeal it is accepted as one of the family, though very grudgingly; and it is generally hated by all the neighbours for its impish ways. But the children of the Sidhe and a mortal mother are always clever and beautiful, and specially excel in music and dancing. They are, however, passionate and wilful, and have strange, moody fits, when they desire solitude above all things, and seem to hold converse with unseen spiritual beings.

Fine young peasant women are often carried off by the fairies to nurse their little fairy progeny. But the woman is allowed to come back to her own infant after sunset. However, on entering the house, the husband must at once throw holy water over her in the name of God, when she will be restored to her own shape. For sometimes she comes with a hissing noise like a serpent; then she appears black, and shrouded like one from the dead; and, lastly, in her own shape, when she takes her old place by the fire and nurses her baby; and the husband must ask no questions, but give her food in silence. If she falls asleep the third night, all will be well, for the husband at once ties a red thread across the door to prevent the fairies coming in to carry her off, and if the third night passes over safely the fairies have lost their power over her for evermore.

SHAUN-MOR

A LEGEND OF INNIS-SARK

The islanders believe firmly in the existence of fairies who live in the caves by the sea – little men about the height of a sod of turf, who come out of the fissures of the rocks and are bright and merry, wearing green jackets and red caps, and ready enough to help any one they like, though often very malicious if offended or insulted.

There was an old man on the island called Shaun-Mor, who said that he had often travelled at night with the little men and carried their sacks for them; and in return they gave him strange fairy gifts and taught him the secret of power, so that he could always triumph over his enemies; and even as to the fairies, he was as wise as any of them, and could fight half a dozen of them together if he were so minded, and pitch them into the sea or strangle them with seaweed. So the fairies were angered at his pride and presumption, and determined to do him a malicious turn, just to amuse themselves when they were up for fun. So one night when he was returning home, he suddenly saw a great river between him and his house.

'How shall I get across now?' he cried aloud; and immediately an eagle came up to him.

'Don't cry, Shaun-Mor,' said the eagle, 'but get on my back and I'll carry you safely.'

So Shaun-Mor mounted, and they flew right up ever so high, till at last the eagle tumbled him off by the side of a great mountain in a place he had never seen before.

'This is a bad trick you have played me,' said Shaun; 'tell me where I am now?'

'You are in the moon,' said the eagle, 'and get down the best way you can, for now I must be off; so good-bye. Mind you don't fall off the edge. Good-bye,' and with that the eagle disappeared.

Just then a cleft in the rock opened, and out came a man as pale as the dead with a reaping-hook in his hand.

'What brings you here?' said he. 'Only the dead come here,' and he looked fixedly at Shaun-Mor so that he trembled like one already dying.

'O your worship,' he said, 'I live far from here. Tell me how I am to get down, and help me I beseech you.'

'Ay, that I will,' said the pale-faced man. 'Here is the help I give you,' and with that he gave him a blow with the reaping-hook which tumbled Shaun right over the edge of the moon; and he fell and fell ever so far till luckily he came in the midst of a flock of geese, and the old gander that was leading stopped and eyed him.

'What are you doing here, Shaun-Mor?' said he, 'for I know you well. I've often seen you down in Shark. What will your wife say when she hears of your being out so late at night, wandering about in this way. It is very disreputable, and no well brought up gander would do the like, much less a man; I am ashamed of you, Shaun-Mor.'

'O your honour,' said the poor man, 'it is an evil turn of the evil witches, for they have done all this; but let me just get up on your back, and if your honour brings me safe to my own house I shall be for ever grateful to every goose and gander in the world as long as I live.'

'Well then, get up on my back,' said the bird, fluttering its wings with a great clatter over Shaun; but he couldn't manage at all to get on its back, so he caught hold of one leg, and he and the gander went down and down till they came to the sea.

'Now let go,' said the gander, 'and find your way home the best way you can, for I have lost a great deal of time with you already, and must be away;' and he shook off Shaun-Mor, who dropped plump down into the sea, and when he was almost dead a great whale came sailing by, and flapped him all over with its fins. He knew no more till he opened his eyes lying on the grass in his own field by a great stone, and his wife was standing over him drenching him with a great pail of water, and flapping his face with her apron.

And then he told his wife the whole story, which he said was true as gospel, but I don't think she believed a word of it, though she was afraid to let on the like to Shaun-Mor, who affirms to this day that it was all the work of the fairies, though wicked people might laugh and jeer and say he was drunk.

THE CAVE FAIRIES

THE TUATHA-DE-DANANN

It is believed by many people that the cave fairies are the remnant of the ancient Tuatha-de-Dananns who once ruled Ireland, but were conquered by the Milesians.

These Tuatha were great necromancers, skilled in all magic, and excellent in all the arts as builders, poets, and musicians. At first the Milesians were going to destroy them utterly, but gradually were so fascinated and captivated by the gifts and power of the Tuatha that they allowed them to remain and to build forts, where they held high festival with music and singing and the chant of the bards. And the breed of horses they reared could not be surpassed in the world – fleet as the wind, with the arched neck and the broad chest and the quivering nostril, and the large eye that showed they were made of fire and flame, and not of dull, heavy earth. And the Tuatha made stables for them in the great caves of the hills, and they were shod with silver and had golden bridles, and never a slave was allowed to ride them. A splendid sight was the cavalcade of the Tuatha-de-Danann knights. Seven-score steeds, each with a jewel on his forehead like a star, and seven-score horsemen, all the sons of kings, in their green mantles fringed with gold, and golden helmets on their head, and golden greaves on their limbs, and each knight having in his hand a golden spear.

And so they lived for a hundred years and more, for by their enchantments they could resist the power of death.

EDAIN THE QUEEN

Now it happened that the king of Munster one day saw a beautiful girl bathing, and he loved her and made her his queen. And in all the land was no woman so lovely to look upon as the fair Edain, and the fame of her beauty came to the ears of the great and powerful chief and king of the Tuatha-de-Danann, Midar by name. So he disguised himself and went to the court of the king of Munster, as a wandering bard, that he might look on the beauty of Edain. And he challenged the king to a game of chess.

'Who is this man that I should play chess with him?' said the king.

'Try me,' said the stranger, 'you will find me a worthy foe.' Then the king said – 'But the chess-board is in the queen's apartment, and I cannot disturb her.'

However, when the queen heard that a stranger had challenged the king to chess, she sent her page in with the chess-board, and then came herself to greet the stranger. And Midar was so dazzled with her beauty, that he could not speak, he could only gaze on her. And the queen also seemed troubled, and after a time she left them alone.

'Now, what shall we play for?' asked the king.

'Let the conqueror name the reward,' answered the stranger, 'and whatever he desires let it be granted to him.'

'Agreed,' replied the monarch.

Then they played the game and the stranger won.

'What is your demand now?' cried the king. 'I have given my word that whatever you name shall be yours.'

'I demand the Lady Edain, the queen, as my reward,' replied the stranger. 'But I shall not ask you to give her up to me till this day year.' And the stranger departed.

Now the king was utterly perplexed and confounded, but he took good note of the time, and on that night just a twelvemonth after, he made a great feast at Tara for all the princes, and he placed three lines of his chosen warriors all round the palace, and forbade any stranger to enter on pain of death. So all being secure, as he thought, he took his

EDAIN THE QUEEN

place at the feast with the beautiful Edain beside him, all glittering with jewels and a golden crown on her head, and the revelry went on till midnight. Just then, to his horror, the king looked up, and there stood the stranger in the middle of the hall, but no one seemed to perceive him save only the king. He fixed his eyes on the queen, and coming towards her, he struck the golden harp he had in his hand and sang in a low sweet voice –

> 'O Edain, wilt thou come with me
> To a wonderful palace that is mine?
> White are the teeth there, and black the brows,
> And crimson as the mead are the lips of the lovers.
> O woman, if thou comest to my proud people,
> 'Tis a golden crown shall circle thy head.
> Thou shalt dwell by the sweet streams of my land,
> And drink of the mead and wine in the arms of thy lover.'

Then he gently put his arm round the queen's waist, and drew her up from her royal throne, and went forth with her through the midst of all the guests, none hindering, and the king himself was like one in a dream, and could neither speak nor move. But when he recovered himself, then he knew that the stranger was one of the fairy chiefs of the Tuatha-de-Danann who had carried off the beautiful Edain to his fairy mansion. So he sent round messengers to all the kings of Erin that they should destroy all the forts of the hated Tuatha race, and slay and kill and let none live till the queen, his young bride, was brought back to him. Still she came not. Then the king out of revenge ordered his men to block up all the stables where the royal horses of the Dananns were kept, that so they might die of hunger; but the horses were of noble blood, and no bars or bolts could hold them, and they broke through the bars and rushed out like the whirlwind, and spread all over the country. And the kings, when they saw the beauty of the horses, forgot all about the search for Queen Edain, and only strove how they could seize and hold as their own some of the fiery steeds with the silver hoofs and golden bridles. Then the king raged in his wrath, and sent for the chief of the Druids, and told him he should be put to death unless he discovered the place where the queen lay hid. So the Druid went over all Ireland, and searched, and made spells with oghams, and at last, having carved four oghams on four wands of a hazel-tree, it was revealed to him that deep down in a hill in the very centre of Ireland, Queen Edain was hidden away in the enchanted palace of Midar the fairy chief.

Then the king gathered a great army, and they circled the hill, and dug down and down till they came to the very centre; and just as they reached the gate of the fairy palace, Midar by his enchantments sent forth fifty beautiful women from the hillside, to distract the attention of the warriors, all so like the queen in form and features and dress, that the king himself could not make out truly, if his own wife were amongst them or not. But Edain, when she saw her husband so near her, was touched by love of him in her heart, and the power of the enchantment fell from her soul, and she came to him, and he lifted her up on his horse and kissed her tenderly, and brought her back safely to his royal palace of Tara, where they lived happily ever after.

But soon after the power of the Tuatha-de-Danann was broken for ever, and the remnant that was left took refuge in the caves where they exist to this day, and practise their magic, and work spells, and are safe from death until the judgment day.

THE ROYAL STEED

Of the great breed of splendid horses, some remained for several centuries, and were at once known by their noble shape and qualities. The last of them belonged to a great lord in Connaught, and when he died, all his effects being sold by auction, the royal steed came to the hammer, and was bought up by an emissary of the English Government, who wanted to get possession of a specimen of the magnificent ancient Irish breed, in order to have it transported to England.

THE ROYAL STEED

But when the groom attempted to mount the high-spirited animal, it reared, and threw the base-born churl violently to the ground, killing him on the spot.

Then, fleet as the wind, the horse galloped away, and finally plunged into the lake and was seen no more. So ended the great race of the mighty Tuatha-de-Danann horses in Ireland, the like of which has never been seen since in all the world for majesty and beauty.

Sometimes the cave fairies make a straight path in the sea from one island to another, all paved with coral, under the water; but no one can tread it except the fairy race. Fishermen coming home late at night, on looking down, have frequently seen them passing and re-passing – a black band of little men with black dogs, who are very fierce if any one tries to touch them.

There was an old man named Con, who lived on an island all alone, except for a black dog who kept him company. Now all the people knew right well that he was a fairy king, and could walk the water at night like the other fairies. So they feared him greatly, and brought him presents of cakes and fowls, for they were afraid of him and of his evil demon, the dog. For often, men coming home late have heard the steps of this dog and his breathing quite close to them, though they could not see him; and one man nearly died of fright, and was only saved by the priest who came and prayed over him.

But the cave fairies can assume many forms.

One summer's evening, a young girl, the daughter of the man who owned the farm, was milking the cows in the yard, when three beautiful ladies, all in white, suddenly appeared, and asked her for a drink of milk. Now the girl knew well that milk should not be given away without using some precaution against fairy wiles, so she hesitated, fearing to bring ill-luck on the cows.

'Is that the way you treat us?' said one of the ladies, and she slapped the girl on the face.

'But you'll remember us,' said the second lady, and she took hold of the girl's thumb and twisted it out of joint.

'And your lover will be false to you,' said the third, and with that she turned the girl's mantle crooked, the back to the front.

Then the first lady took a vessel and milked the cow, and they all drank of the milk as much as they wanted; after which they turned to the girl and bade her beware of again offending the spirits of the cave, for they were very powerful, and would not let her off so easily another time.

The poor girl fainted from fright, and was found quite senseless when they came to look for her; but the white ladies had disappeared. Though the story must have been true, just as she told it when she came to her senses, for not a drop of milk was left in the pail, nor could a drop more be got from the cows all that evening.

EVIL SPELLS

CATHAL THE KING

It is said by the wise women and fairy doctors that the roots of the elder tree, and the roots of an apple tree that bears red apples, if boiled together and drunk fasting, will expel any evil living thing or evil spirit that may have taken up its abode in the body of a man.

But an evil charm to produce a living thing in the body can also be made, by pronouncing a certain magic and wicked spell over the food or drink taken by any person that an enemy wishes to injure.

One should therefore be very cautious in accepting anything to eat from a person of known malicious tongue and spiteful heart, or who has an ill will against you, for poison lies in their glance and in the touch of their hands; and an evil spell is in their very presence, and on all they do, say, or touch.

Cathal, king of Munster, was the tallest and handsomest of all the kings of Erin, and he fell deeply in love with the beautiful sister of Fergus, king of Ulster; and the lovers were happy in their love and resolved on marriage. But Fergus, King of the North, had a mortal hatred to Cathal, King of the South, and wished, in secret, to prevent the marriage. So he set a watch over his sister, and by this means found out that she was sending a basket of the choicest apples to her lover, by the hands of a trusty messenger. On this Fergus managed to get hold of the basket of fruit from the messenger; and he changed them secretly for another lot of apples, over which he worked an evil spell. Furnished with these the messenger set out for Cashel, and presented them to

Cathal the king, who, delighted at this proof of love from his princess, began at once to eat the apples. But the more he ate, the more he longed for them, for a wicked spell was on every apple. When he had eaten them all up, he sent round the country for more, and ate, and ate, until there was not an apple left in Cashel, nor in all the country round.

Then he bade his chieftains go forth and bring in food to appease his appetite; and he ate up all the cattle and the grain and the fruit, and still cried for more; and had the houses searched for food to bring to him. So the people were in despair, for they had no more food, and starvation was over the land.

Now a great and wise man, the chief poet of his tribe, happened to be travelling through Munster at that time, and hearing of the king's state, he greatly desired to see him, for he knew there was devil's work in the evil spell. So they brought him to the king, and many strong invocations he uttered over him, and many powerful incantations, for poets have a knowledge of mysteries above all other men; until finally, after three days had passed, he announced to the lords and chiefs that on that night, when the moon rose, the spell would be broken, and the king restored to his wonted health. So all the chiefs gathered round in the courtyard to watch; but no one was allowed to enter the room where the king lay, save only the poet. And he was to give the signal when the hour had come and the spell was broken.

So as they watched, and just as the moon rose, a great cry was heard from the king's room, and the poet, flinging open the door, bade the chiefs enter; and there on the floor lay a huge dead wolf, who for a whole year had taken up his abode in the king's body; but was now happily cast forth by the strong incantations of the poet.

After this the king fell into a deep sleep, and when he arose he was quite well, and strong again as ever, in all the pride of his youth and beauty. At this the people rejoiced much, for he was greatly loved, and the poet who had restored him was honoured above all men in the land; for the king himself took off the golden torque from his own neck, and placed it on that of the poet, and he set him at his right hand at the feast.

Now a strange thing happened just at this time; for Fergus, King of the North, fell ill, and wasted away to a shadow, and of all the beautiful meats and wines they set before him he could taste nothing. So he died before a year had passed by; and then Cathal the king wedded his beloved princess, and they lived happily through many years.

THE POET'S MALEDICTION

The imprecations of the poets had often also a mysterious and fatal effect.

King Breas, the pagan monarch, was a fierce, cruel, and niggardly man, who was therefore very unpopular with the people, who hate the cold heart and the grudging hand.

Amongst others who suffered by the king's inhospitality, was the renowned Carbury the poet, son of Eodain, the great poetess of the Tuatha-de-Danann race; she who chanted the song of victory when her people conquered the Firbolgs, on the plains of Moytura; and the stone that she stood on, during the battle, in sight of all the warriors, is still existing, and is pointed out as the stone of Eodain, the poetess, with great reverence, even to this day.

It was her son, Carbury the poet, who was held in such high honour by the nation, that King Breas invited him to his court, in order that he might pronounce a powerful malediction over the enemy with whom he was then at war.

Carbury came on the royal summons, but in place of being treated with the distinction due to his high rank, he was lodged and fed so meanly that the soul of the poet raged with wrath; for the king gave him for lodgement only a small stone cell without fire or a bed; and for food he had only three cakes of meal without any flesh meat or sauce, and no wine was given him, such wine as is fit to light up the poet's soul before the divine mystic spirit of song can awake in its power within him. So very early the next morning, the poet rose up and departed, with much rage in his heart. But as he passed the king's house he stopped, and in place of a blessing, pronounced a terrible malediction over Breas and his race, which can still be found in the ancient books of Ireland, commencing thus –

> 'Without fire, without bed, on the surface of the floor!
> Without meat, without fowl, on the surface of the dish.
> Three little dishes and no flesh thereon,
> A cell without bed, a dish without meat, a cup without wine,
> Are these fit offerings from a king to a poet?
> May the king and his race be three times accursed for ever and for ever!'

Immediately three large blisters rose on the king's forehead, and remained there as a sign and mark of the poet's vengeance.

And from that day forth to his death, which happened not long after, the reign of Breas was a time of sore trouble and disaster, for he was three times defeated by his enemies, and from care and sorrow a grievous disease fell on him; for though hungry he could not swallow any food; and though all the meat and wine of the best was set before him, yet his throat seemed closed, and though raging with hunger yet not a morsel could pass his lips; and so he died miserably, starved in the midst of plenty, and accursed in all things by the power and malediction of the angry poet.

DRIMIAL AGUS THORIAL (A WICKED SPELL)

When a girl wishes to gain the love of a man, and to make him marry her, the dreadful spell is used called *Drimial Agus Thorial*. At dead of night, she and an accomplice go to a churchyard, exhume a newly-buried corpse, and take a strip of the skin from the head to the heel.

This is wound round the girl as a belt with a solemn invocation to the devil for his help.

After she has worn it for a day and a night she watches her opportunity and ties it round the sleeping man whose love she desires; during which process the name of God must not be mentioned.

When he awakes the man is bound by the spell; and is forced to marry the cruel and evil harpy. It is said the children of such marriages bear a black mark round the wrist, and are known and shunned by the people, who call them 'sons of the devil.'

AN IRISH ADEPT OF THE ISLANDS

Some persons, even at the present day amongst the peasants, have strange gifts and a knowledge of the hidden mysteries, but they can only impart this knowledge when they know that death is on them, and then it must be to a female, to an unmarried man, or to a childless woman, for these are the most susceptible to the mysterious power by which miracles can be worked.

A man now living at Innis-Sark has this strange and mystic gift. He can heal diseases by a word, even at a distance, and his glance sees into the very heart, and reads the secret thoughts of men. He never touched beer, spirits, or meat, in all his life, but has lived entirely on bread, fruit, and vegetables. A man who knew him thus describes him – 'Winter and summer his dress is the same, merely a flannel shirt and coat. He will pay his share at a feast, but neither eats nor drinks of the food and drink set before him. He speaks no English, and never could be made to learn the English tongue, though he says it might be used with great effect to curse one's enemy. He holds a burial-ground sacred, and would not carry away so much as a leaf of ivy from a grave. And he maintains that the people are right in keeping to their ancient usages, such as never to dig a grave on a Monday; and to carry the coffin three times round the grave, following the course of the sun, for then the dead rest in peace. Like the people, also, he holds suicides as accursed; for they believe that all the dead who have been recently buried turn over on their faces if a suicide is laid amongst them.

'Though well off he never, even in his youth, thought of taking a wife, nor was he ever known to love a woman. He stands quite apart from life, and by this means holds his power over the mysteries. No money will tempt him to impart this knowledge to another, for if he did he would be struck dead – so he believes. He would not touch a hazel stick, but carries an ash wand, which he holds in his hand when he prays, laid across his knees, and the whole of his life is devoted to works of grace and charity.'

Though now an old man he has never had a day's sickness. No one has ever seen him in a rage, nor heard an angry word from his lips but once; and then being under great irritation, he recited the Lord's Prayer backwards, as an imprecation on his enemy.

Before his death he will reveal the mystery of his power, but not till the hand of death is on him for certain.

THE MAY FESTIVAL

There were four great festivals held in Ireland from the most ancient pagan times, and these four sacred seasons were February, May, Midsummer, and November. May was the most memorable and auspicious of all; then the Druids lit the *Baal-Tinne*, the holy, goodly fire of Baal, the Sun-god, and they drove the cattle on a path made between two fires, and singed them with the flame of a lighted torch, and sometimes they cut them to spill blood, and then burnt the blood as a sacred offering to the Sun-god.

The great feast of Bel, or the Sun, took place on May Eve; and that of Samhain, or the Moon, on November Eve; when libations were poured out to appease the evil spirits, and also the spirits of the dead, who come out of their graves on that night to visit their ancient homes.

THE MAY FESTIVAL

The Phoenicians, it is known, adored the Supreme Being under the name of Bel-Samen, and it is remarkable that the peasants in Ireland, wishing you good luck, say in Irish, 'The blessing of Bel, and the blessing of Samhain, be with you," that is, of the sun and of the moon.

These were the great festivals of the Druids, when all domestic fires were extinguished, in order to be re-lit by the sacred fire taken from the temples, for it was deemed sacrilege to have any fires kindled except from the holy altar flame.

St Patrick, however, determined to break down the power of the Druids; and, therefore, in defiance of their laws, he had a great fire lit on May Eve, when he celebrated the paschal mysteries; and henceforth Easter, or the Feast of the Resurrection, took the place of the Baal festival.

The Baal fires were originally used for human sacrifices and burnt-offerings of the first-fruits of the cattle; but after Christianity was established the children and cattle were only passed between two fires for purification from sin, and as a safeguard against the power of the devil.

The Persians also extinguished the domestic fires on the Baal festival, the 21st of April, and were obliged to re-light them from the temple fires, for which the priests were paid a fee in silver money. A fire kindled by rubbing two pieces of wood together was also considered lucky by the Persians; then water was boiled over the flame, and afterwards sprinkled on the people and on the cattle. The ancient Irish ritual resembles the Persian in every particular, and the Druids, no doubt, held the traditional worship exactly as brought from the East, the land of the sun and of tree worship and well worship.

May Day, called in Irish *Là-Beltaine*, the day of the Baal fires, was the festival of greatest rejoicing held in Ireland. But the fairies have great power at that season, and children and cattle, and the milk and butter, must be well guarded from their influence. A spent coal must be put under the churn, and another under the cradle; and primroses must be scattered before the door, for the fairies cannot pass the flowers. Children that die in April are supposed to be carried off by the fairies, who are then always on the watch to abduct whatever is young and beautiful for their fairy homes.

Sometimes on the 1st of May, a sacred heifer, snow white, appeared amongst the cattle; and this was considered to bring the highest good luck to the farmer. An old Irish song that alludes to the heifer, may be translated thus –

> 'There is a cow on the mountain,
> A fair white cow;
> She goes East and she goes West,
> And my senses have gone for love of her;
> She goes with the sun and he forgets to burn,
> And the moon turns her face with love to her,
> My fair white cow of the mountain.'

The fairies are in the best of humours upon May Eve, and the music of the fairy pipes may be heard all through the night, while the fairy folk are dancing upon the rath. It is then they carry off the young people to join their revels; and if a girl has once danced to the fairy music, she will move ever after with such fascinating grace, that it has passed into a proverb to say of a good dancer, 'She has danced to fairy music on the hill.'

At the great long dance held in old times on May Day, all the people held hands and danced round a great May-bush erected on a mound. The circle sometimes extended for a mile, the girls wearing garlands, and the young men carrying wands of green boughs, while the elder people sat round on the grass as spectators, and applauded the ceremony. The tallest and strongest young men in the county stood in the centre and directed the movements, while the pipers and harpers, wearing green and gold sashes, played the most spirited dance tunes.

The oldest worship of the world was of the sun and moon, of trees, wells, and the serpent that gave wisdom. Trees were the symbol of knowledge, and the dance round the May-bush is part of the ancient ophite ritual. The Baila also, or waltz, is associated with Baal worship, where the two circling motions are combined; the revolution of the planet on its own axis, and also round the sun.

In Italy, this ancient festival, called *Calendi Maggio*, is celebrated in the rural districts much in the Irish way. Dante fell in love at the great May Day festival, held in the Portinari Palace. The Sclavonic nations likewise light sacred fires, and dance round a tree hung with garlands on May Day. This reverence for the tree is one of the oldest superstitions of humanity and the most universal, and the fires are a relic of the old pagan worship paid to the Grynian Apollo – fire above all things being held sacred by the Irish as a safeguard from evil spirits. It is a saying amongst them, 'Fire and salt are the two most sacred things given to man, and if you give them away on May Day, you give away your luck for the year.' Therefore no one will allow milk, or fire, or salt, to be carried away from the house on that day; and if people came in and asked for a lighted sod, they would be driven away with curses, for their purpose was evil.

The witches, however, make great efforts to steal the milk on May morning, and if they succeed, the luck passes from the family, and the milk and butter for the whole year will belong to the fairies. The best preventative is to scatter primroses on the threshold; and the old women tie bunches of primroses to the cows' tails, for the evil spirits cannot touch anything guarded by these flowers, if they are plucked before sunrise, not else. A piece of iron, also, made red hot, is placed upon the hearth; any old iron will do, the older the better, and branches of whitethorn and mountain ash are wreathed round the doorway for luck. The mountain ash has very great and mysterious qualities. If a branch of it be woven into the roof, that house is safe from fire for a year at least, and if a branch of it is mixed with the timber of a boat, no storm will upset it, and no man in it will be drowned for a twelvemonth certain. To save milk from witchcraft, the people on May morning cut and peel some branches of the mountain ash, and bind the twigs round the milk pails and the churn. No witch or fairy will then be able to steal the milk or butter. But all this must be done before sunrise. However, should butter be missed, follow the cow to the field, and gather the clay her hoof has touched; then, on returning home, place it under the churn with a live coal and a handful of salt, and your butter is safe from man or woman, fairy or fiend, for that year. There are other methods also to preserve a good supply of butter in the churn; a horse-shoe tied on it; a rusty nail from a coffin driven into the side: a cross made of the leaves of veronica placed at the bottom of the milk pail; but the mountain ash is the best of all safeguards against witchcraft and devil's magic. Without some of these precautions the fairies will certainly overlook the churn, and the milk and butter, in consequence, will fail all through the year, and the farmer suffer great loss. Herbs gathered on May Eve have a mystical and strong virtue for curing disease; and powerful potions are made then by the skilful herb women and fairy doctors, which no sickness can resist, chiefly of the yarrow, called in Irish 'the herb of seven needs' or cures, from its many and great virtues. Divination is also practised to a great extent by means of the yarrow. The girls dance round it singing –

> 'Yarrow, yarrow, yarrow,
> I bid thee good morrow,
> And tell me before to-morrow
> Who my true love shall be.'

The herb is then placed under the head at night, and in dreams the true lover will appear. Another mode of divination for the future fate in life is by snails. The young girls go out early before sunrise to trace the path of the snails in the clay, for always a letter is marked, and this is the initial of the true lover's name. A black snail is very unlucky to meet first in the morning, for his trail would read death; but a white snail brings good fortune. A white lamb on the right hand is also good; but the cuckoo is ominous of evil. Of old the year began with the 1st of May, and an ancient Irish rhyme says –

> 'A white lamb on my right side,
> So will good come to me;

THE MAY FESTIVAL

> But not the little false cuckoo
> On the first day of the year.'

Prophecies were also made from the way the wind blew on May mornings. In '98 an old man, who was drawing near to his end and like to die, inquired from those around him –

> 'Where did you leave the wind last night?' (May Eve.)
> They told him it came from the north.

'Then,' he said, 'the country is lost to the Clan Gael; our enemies will triumph. Had it been from the south, we should have had the victory; but now the Sassenach will trample us to dust.' And he fell back and died.

Ashes are often sprinkled on the threshold on May Eve; and if the print of a foot is found in the morning, turned inward, it betokens marriage; but if turned outward, death. On May Eve the fairy music is heard on all the hills, and many beautiful tunes have been caught up in this way by the people and the native musicians.

About a hundred years ago a celebrated tune, called *Moraleana*, was learnt by a piper as he traversed the hills one evening; and he played it perfectly, note by note, as he heard it from the fairy pipes; on which a voice spoke to him and said that he would be allowed to play the tune *three times* in his life before all the people, but never a fourth, or a doom would fall on him. However, one day he had a great contest for supremacy with another piper, and at last, to make sure of victory, he played the wonderful fairy melody; when all the people applauded and declared he had won the prize by reason of its beauty, and that no music could equal his. So they crowned him with the garland; but at that moment he turned deadly pale, the pipes dropped from his hand, and he fell lifeless to the ground. For nothing escapes the fairies; they know all things, and their vengeance is swift and sure.

It is very dangerous to sleep out in the open air in the month of May, for the fairies are very powerful then, and on the watch to carry off the handsome girls for fairy brides, and the young mothers as nurses for the fairy babies; while the young men are selected as husbands for the beautiful fairy princesses.

A young man died suddenly on May Eve while he was lying asleep under a hay-rick, and the parents and friends knew immediately that he had been carried off to the fairy palace in the great moat of Granard. So a renowned fairy man was sent for, who promised to have him back in nine days. Meanwhile he desired that food and drink of the best should be left daily for the young man at a certain place on the moat. This was done, and the food always disappeared, by which they knew the young man was living, and came out of the moat nightly for the provisions left for him by his people.

Now on the ninth day a great crowd assembled to see the young man brought back from Fairyland. And in the midst stood the fairy doctor performing his incantations by means of fire and a powder which he threw into the flames that caused a dense grey smoke to arise. Then, taking off his hat, and holding a key in his hand, he called out three times in a loud voice, 'Come forth, come forth, come forth!' On which a shrouded figure slowly rose up in the midst of the smoke, and a voice was heard answering, 'Leave me in peace; I am happy with my fairy bride, and my parents need not weep for me, for I shall bring them good luck, and guard them from evil evermore.'

Then the figure vanished and the smoke cleared, and the parents were content, for they believed the vision, and having loaded the fairy-man with presents, they sent him away home.

MAY-DAY SUPERSTITIONS

The marsh marigold is considered of great use in divination, and is called 'the shrub of Beltaine.' Garlands are made of it for the cattle and the door-posts to keep off the fairy power. Milk also is poured on the threshold, though none would be given away; nor fire, nor salt – these three things being sacred. There are many superstitions concerning May-time. It is not safe to go on the water the first Monday in May. Hares found on May morning are supposed to be witches, and should be stoned.

If the fire goes out on May morning it is considered very unlucky, and it cannot be re-kindled except by a lighted sod brought from the priest's house. And the ashes of this blessed turf are afterwards sprinkled on the floor and the threshold of the house.

Neither fire, nor water, nor milk, nor salt should be given away for love or money, and if a wayfarer is given a cup of milk, he must drink it in the house, and salt must be mixed with it. Salt and water as a drink is at all times considered a potent charm against evil, if properly prepared by a fairy doctor and the magic words said over it.

One day in May a young girl lay down to rest at noontide on a fairy rath and fell asleep – a thing of great danger, for the fairies are strong in power during the May month, and are particularly on the watch for a mortal bride to carry away to the fairy mansions, for they love the sight of human beauty. So they spirited away the young sleeping girl, and only left a shadowy resemblance of her lying on the rath. Evening came on, and as the young girl had not returned, her mother sent out messengers in all directions to look for her. At last she was found on the fairy rath, lying quite unconscious, like one dead.

They carried her home and laid her on her bed, but she neither spoke nor moved. So three days passed over. Then they thought it right to send for the fairy doctor. At once he said that she was fairy struck, and he gave them a salve made of herbs to anoint her hands and her brow every morning at sunrise, and every night when the moon rose; and salt was sprinkled on the threshold and round her bed where she lay sleeping. This was done for six days and six nights, and then the girl rose up suddenly and asked for food. They gave her to eat, but asked no questions, only watched her that she should not quit the house. And then she fixed her eyes on them steadily and said –

'Why did you bring me back? I was so happy. I was in a beautiful palace where lovely ladies and young princes were dancing to the sweetest music; and they made me dance with them, and threw a mantle over me of rich gold: and now it is all gone, and you have brought me back, and I shall never, never see the beautiful palace more.'

Then the mother wept and said –

'Oh, child, stay with me, for I have no other daughter, and if the fairies take you from me I shall die.'

When the girl heard this, she fell on her mother's neck and kissed her, and promised that she would never again go near the fairy rath while she lived, for the fairy doctor told her that if ever she lay down there again and slept, she would never return alive to her home any more.

FESTIVALS

CANDLEMAS

Candlemas day, the 2nd of February, used to be held in the old pagan times as a kind of saturnalia, with dances and torches and many unholy rites. But these gave occasion to so much ill conduct that in the ninth century the Pope abolished the festival, and substituted for it the Feast of the Purification of the Blessed Virgin, when candles were lit in her honour. Hence the name of Candlemas.

WHITSUNTIDE

Whitsuntide is a very fatal and unlucky time. Especially beware of water then, for there is an evil spirit in it, and no one should venture to bathe, nor to sail in a boat for fear of being drowned; nor to go a journey where water has to be crossed. And everything in the house must be sprinkled with holy water at Whitsuntide to keep away the fairies, who at that season are very active and malicious, and bewitch the cattle, and carry off the young children, and come up from the sea to hold strange midnight revels, when they kill with their fairy darts the unhappy mortal who crosses their path and pries at their mysteries.

WHITSUNTIDE LEGEND OF THE FAIRY HORSES

There was a widow woman with one son, who had a nice farm of her own close to a lake, and she took great pains in the cultivation of the land, and her corn was the best in the whole country. But when nearly ripe, and just fit for cutting, she found to her dismay that every night it was trampled down and cruelly damaged; yet no one could tell by what means it was done.

So she set her son to watch. And at midnight he heard a great noise and a rushing of waves on the beach, and up out of the lake came a great troop of horses, who began to graze the corn and trample it down madly with their hoofs.

When he told all this to his mother she bade him watch the next night also, but to take several of the men with him furnished with bridles, and when the horses rose from the lake they were to fling the bridles over as many as they could catch.

Now at midnight there was the same noise heard again, and the rush of the waves, and in an instant all the field was filled with the fairy horses, grazing the corn and trampling it down. The men pursued them, but only succeeded in capturing one, and he was the noblest of the lot. The rest all plunged back into the lake. However, the men brought home the captured horse to the widow, and he was put in the stable and grew big and strong, and never another horse came up out of the lake, nor was the corn touched after that night of his capture. But when a year had passed by the widow said it was a shame to keep so fine a horse idle, and she bade the young man, her son, take him out to the hunt that was held that day by all the great gentry of the country, for it was Whitsuntide.

And, in truth, the horse carried him splendidly at the hunt, and every one admired both the fine young rider and his steed. But as he was returning home, when they came within sight of the lake from which the fairy steed had risen, he began to plunge violently, and finally threw his rider. And the young man's foot being unfortunately caught in the stirrup, he was dragged along till he was torn limb from limb, while the horse still continued galloping on madly to the water, leaving some fragment of the unhappy lad after him on the road, till they reached the margin of the lake, when the horse shook off the last limb of the dead youth from him, and plunging into the waves disappeared from sight.

The people reverently gathered up the remains of the dead, and erected a monument of stones over the lad in a field by the edge of the lake; and every one that passes by still lays a stone and says a prayer that the spirit of the dead may rest in peace.

The phantom horses were never seen again, but the lake has an evil reputation even to this day amongst the people; and no one would venture a boat on it after sundown at Whitsuntide, or during the time of the ripening of the corn, or when the harvest is ready for the sickle, for strange sounds are heard at night, like the wild galloping of a horse across the meadow, along with the cries as of a man in his death agony.

NOVEMBER SPELLS

The ancient Irish divided the year into summer and winter – *Samrath* and *Gheimrath*; the former beginning in May, the latter in November, called also *Sam-fuim* (summer end). At this season, when the sun dies, the powers of darkness exercise great and evil influence over all things. The witch-women say they can then ride at night through the air with Diana of the Ephesians, and Herodias, and others leagued with the devil; and change men to beasts; and ride with the dead and cover leagues of ground on swift spirit-horses. Also on November Eve, by certain incantations, the dead can be made to appear and answer questions; but for this purpose blood must be sprinkled on the dead body when it rises; for it is said the spirits love blood. The colour excites them and gives them for the time the power and the semblance of life.

Divination by fire, by earth, and by water, is also largely practised; but, as an ancient writer has observed, 'All such divinations are accursed, for they are worked by the power of the fallen angels, who give knowledge only through malice, and to bring evil on the questioner. Neither should times and seasons be held lucky or unlucky, nor the course of the moon, nor the death of the sun, nor the so-called Egyptian days; for all things are blessed to a Christian. And this is the doctrine of the Holy Church, which all men should take to heart... But a prayer to God, written fine, may be worn tyed round the neck, for this is done in a holy spirit, and is not against the ordinances of the Church.'

The scapular here alluded to is a piece of cloth on which the name of Mary is written on one side and I.H.S. on the other. It preserves against evil spirits, and is a passport to heaven, and ensures against the pains of hell; for the Blessed Virgin takes the wearer under her especial care. It is placed in a little silk bag and worn tied round the neck, and is left upon the dead in their coffin for the angels to see at the resurrection. The scapular is never given to an evil liver, so it is a sign both of a pious life here and a blessed life hereafter.

NOVEMBER EVE

All the spells worked on November Eve are performed in the name of the devil, who is then forced to reveal the future fate of the questioner. The most usual spell is to wash a garment in a running brook, then hang it on a thorn bush, and wait to see the apparition of the lover, who will come to turn it. But the tricks played on this night by young persons on each other have often most disastrous consequences. One young girl fell dead with fright when an apparition really came and turned the garment she had hung on the bush. And a lady narrates that on the 1st of November her servant rushed into the room and fainted on the floor. On recovering, she said that she had played a trick that night in the name of the devil before the looking-glass; but what she had

NOVEMBER EVE

seen she dared not speak of, though the remembrance of it would never leave her brain, and she knew the shock would kill her. They tried to laugh her out of her fears, but the next night she was found quite dead, with her features horribly contorted, lying on the floor before the looking-glass, which was shivered to pieces.

Another spell is the building of the house. Twelve couples are taken, each being made of two holly twigs tied together with a hempen thread; these are all named and stuck round in a circle in the clay. A live coal is then placed in the centre, and whichever couple catches fire first will assuredly be married. Then the future husband is invoked in the name of the Evil One to appear and quench the flame.

On one occasion a dead man in his shroud answered the call, and silently drew away the girl from the rest of the party. The fright turned her brain, and she never recovered her reason afterwards. The horror of that apparition haunted her for ever, especially as on November Eve it is believed firmly that the dead really leave their graves and have power to appear amongst the living.

A young girl in a farmer's service was in the loft one night looking for eggs when two men came into the stable underneath, and through a chink in the boards she could see them quite well and hear all they said. To her horror she found that they were planning the murder of a man in the neighbourhood who was suspected of being an informer, and they settled how they would get rid of the body by throwing it into the Shannon. She crept home half dead with fright, but did not venture to tell any one what she had heard. Next day, however, the news spread that the man was missing, and it was feared he was murdered. Still the girl was afraid to reveal what she knew, though the ghost of the murdered man seemed for ever before her. Finally she could bear the place no longer, and, giving up her situation, she went to another village some miles off and took service. But on November Eve, as she was washing clothes in the Shannon, the dead body of the murdered man arose from the water and floated towards her, until it lay quite close to her feet. Then she knew the hand of God was in it, and that the spirit of the dead would not rest till he was avenged. So she went and gave information, and on her evidence the two murderers were convicted and executed.

If the cattle fall sick at this season, it is supposed that some old fairy man or woman is lying hid about the place to spy out the doings of the family and work some evil spells.

A farmer had a splendid cow, the pride of his farm, but suddenly it seemed ailing and gave no milk, though every morning it went and stood quite patiently under an old hawthorn-tree as if some one were milking her. So the man watched the time, and presently the cow came of herself and stood under the hawthorn, when a little old wizened woman came forth from the trunk of the tree, milked the cow, and then retreated into the tree again. On this the farmer sent at once for a fairy doctor, who exorcised the cow and gave it a strong potion, after which the spell was broken and the cow was restored to its usual good condition and gave the milk as heretofore.

The fairies also exercise a malign influence by making a path through a house, when all the children begin to pine and a blight falls on the family.

A farmer who had lost one son by heart disease (always a mysterious malady to the peasants) and another by gradual decay, consulted a wise fairy woman as to what should be done, for his wife also had become delicate and weak. The woman told him that on November Eve the fairies had made a road through the house, and were going back and forward ever since, and whatever they looked upon was doomed. The only remedy was to build up the old door and open another entrance. This the man did, and when the witch-women came as usual in the morning to beg for water or milk or meal they found no door, and were obliged to turn back. After this the spell was taken off the household, and they all prospered without fear of the fairies.

A TERRIBLE REVENGE

The fairies often take a terrible revenge if they are ever slighted or offended. A whole family once came under their ban because a fairy woman had been refused admittance into the house. The eldest boy lost his sight for some time, and though he recovered the use of his eyes yet they always had a strange expression, as if he saw some terrible object in the distance that scared him. And at last the neighbours grew afraid of the family, for they brought ill-luck wherever they went, and nothing prospered that they touched.

There were six children, all wizened little creatures with withered old faces and thin crooked fingers. Every one knew they were fairy changelings, and the smith wanted to put them on the anvil, and the wise women said they should be passed through the fire; but destiny settled the future for them, for one after another they all pined away and died, and the ban of the fairies was never lifted from the ill-fated house till the whole family lay in the grave.

MIDSUMMER

THE BAAL FIRES AND DANCES

This season is still made memorable in Ireland by lighting fires on every hill, according to the ancient pagan usage, when the Baal fires were kindled as part of the ritual of sun-worship, though now they are lit in honour of St John. The great bonfire of the year is still made on St John's Eve, when all the people dance round it, and every young man takes a lighted brand from the pile to bring home with him for good luck to the house.

In ancient times the sacred fire was lighted with great ceremony on Midsummer Eve; and on that night all the people of the adjacent country kept fixed watch on the western promontory of Howth, and the moment the first flash was seen from that spot the fact of ignition was announced with wild cries and cheers repeated from village to village, when all the local fires began to blaze, and Ireland was circled by a cordon of flame rising up from every hill. Then the dance and song began round every fire, and the wild hurrahs filled the air with the most frantic revelry.

Many of these ancient customs are still continued, and the fires are still lighted on St John's Eve on every hill in Ireland. When the fire has burned down to a red glow the young men strip to the waist and leap over or through the flames; this is done backwards and forwards several times, and he who braves the greatest blaze is considered the victor over the powers of evil, and is greeted with tremendous applause. When the fire burns still lower, the young girls leap the flame, and those who leap clean over three times back and forward will be certain of a speedy marriage and good luck in after life, with many children. The married women then walk through the lines of the burning embers; and when the fire is nearly burnt and trampled down, the yearling cattle are driven through the hot ashes, and their back is singed with a lighted hazel twig. These hazel rods are kept safely afterwards, being considered of immense power to drive the cattle to and from the watering places. As the fire diminishes the shouting grows fainter, and the song and the dance commence; while professional story-tellers narrate tales of fairy-land, or of the good old times long ago, when the kings and princes of Ireland dwelt amongst their own people, and there was food to eat and wine to drink for all comers to the feast at the king's house. When the crowd at length separate, every one carries home a brand from the fire, and great virtue is attached to the lighted brone which is safely carried to the house without breaking or falling to the ground. Many contests also arise amongst the young men; for whoever enters his house first with the sacred fire brings the good luck of the year with him.

On the first Sunday in Midsummer all the young people used to stand in lines after leaving chapel, to be hired for service – the girls holding white hands, the young men each with an emblem of his trade. The evening ended with a dance and the revelry was kept up until the dawn of the next day, called 'Sorrowful Monday,' because of the end of the pleasure and the frolic.

THE FAIRY DOCTRESS

But all this time the fairies were not idle; for it was at this very season of dances and festivals, when the mortals around them were happiest, that Finvarra the king and his chosen band were on the watch to carry off the prettiest girls to the fairy mansions.

There they kept them for seven years, and at the end of that time, when they grew old and ugly, they were sent back, for the fairies love nothing so much as youth and beauty. But as a compensation for the slight put on them, the women were taught all the fairy secrets and the magical mystery that lies in herbs, and the strange power they have over diseases. So by this means the women became all-powerful, and by their charms or spells or potions could kill or save as they chose.

There was a woman of the islands greatly feared, yet respected by the people for her knowledge of herbs, which gave her power over all diseases. But she never revealed the nature of the herb, and always gathered the leaves herself at night and hid them under the eaves of the house. And if the person who carried the herb home let it fall to the ground by the way, it lost its power; or if they talked of it or showed it to any one, all the virtue went out of it. It was to be used secretly and alone, and then the cure would be perfected without fail.

One time, a man who was told of this came over from the mainland in a boat with two other men to see the fairy woman; for he was lame from a fall and could do no work.

Now the woman knew they were coming, for she had a knowledge of all things through the power of divination she had learned from the fairies, and could see and hear though no man told her. So she went out and prepared the herb, and made a salve and brewed a potion, and had all ready for the man and his friends.

When they appeared she stood at the door and cried, 'Enter! This is the lucky day and hour; have no fear, for you will be cured by the power that is in me, and by the herb I give you.'

Then the man bowed down before her, and said, 'Oh, mother, this is my case.' And he told her, that being out one day on the mountains, he slipped and fell on his face. A mere slight fall, but when he rose up his leg was powerless though no bone seemed broken.

'I know how it happened,' she said. 'You trod upon a fairy herb under which the fairies were resting, and you disturbed them and broke in the top of their dwelling, so they were angry and struck you on the leg and lamed you out of spite. But my power is greater than theirs. Do as I tell you and you will soon be cured.'

So she gave him the salve and the bottle of potion, and bade him take it home carefully and use it in silence and alone, and in three days the power of the limb would come back to him.

Then the man offered her silver; but she refused.

'I do not sell my knowledge,' she said, 'I give it. And so the strength and the power remain with me.'

On this the men went their way. But after three days a message came from the man to say that he was cured. And he sent the wise woman a handsome present also; for a gift works no evil, though to sell the sacred power and mysteries of knowledge for money would be fatal; for then the spirit of healing that dwelt in the woman would have fled away and returned no more.

MARRIAGE RITES

In old times in Ireland it was thought right and proper to seem to use force in carrying off the bride to her husband. She was placed on a swift horse before the bridegroom, while all her kindred started in pursuit with shouts and cries. Twelve maidens attended the bride, and each was placed on horseback behind the young men who rode after the bridal pair. On arriving at her future home, the bride was met on the threshold by the bridegroom's mother, who broke an oaten cake over her head as a good augury of plenty in the future. In the mountains where horses cannot travel, the bridal party walk in procession; the young men carrying torches of dried bogwood to light the bride over the ravines, for in winter the mountain streams are rapid and dangerous to cross.

The Celtic ceremonial of marriage resembles the ancient Greek ritual in many points. A traveller in Ireland some fifty years ago, before politics had quite killed romance and ancient tradition in the hearts of the people, thus describes a rustic marriage festival which he came on by chance one evening in the wilds of Kerry:

A large hawthorn tree that stood in the middle of a field near a stream was hung all over with bits of coloured stuff, while lighted rush candles were placed here and there amongst the branches, to symbolize, no doubt, the new life of brightness preparing for the bridal pair. Then came a procession of boys marching slowly with flutes and pipes made of hollow reeds, and one struck a tin can with a stick at intervals, with a strong rhythmical cadence. This represented the plectrum. Others rattled slates and bones between their fingers, and beat time, after the manner of the Crotolistrai – a rude attempt at music, which appears amongst all nations of the earth, even the most savage. A boy followed, bearing a lighted torch of bogwood. Evidently he was Hymen, and the flame of love was his cognizance. After him came the betrothed pair hand-in-hand, a large square canopy of black stuff being held over their heads; the emblem, of course, of the mystery of love, shrouded and veiled from the prying light of day.

Behind the pair followed two attendants bearing high over the heads of the young couple a sieve filled with meal; a sign of the plenty that would be in their house, and an omen of good luck and the blessing of children.

A wild chorus of dancers and singers closed the procession; the chorus of the epithalamium, and grotesque figures, probably the traditional fauns and satyrs, nymphs and bacchanals, mingled together with mad laughter and shouts and waving of green branches.

The procession then moved on to a bonfire, evidently the ancient altar; and having gone round it three times, the black shroud was lifted from the bridal pair, and they kissed each other before all the people, who shouted and waved their branches in approval.

Then the preparations for the marriage supper began, on which, however, the traveller left them, having laid some money on the altar as an offering of good-will for the marriage future. At the wedding supper there was always plenty of eating and drinking, and dancing and the feast were prolonged till near morning, when the wedding song was sung by the whole party of friends standing, while the bride and bridegroom remained seated at the head of the table. The chorus of one of these ancient songs may be thus literally translated from the Irish –

> 'It is not day, nor yet day,
> It is not day, nor yet morning;
> It is not day, nor yet day,
> For the moon is shining brightly.'

Another marriage song was sung in Irish frequently, each verse ending with the lines –

> 'There is sweet enchanting music, and the golden harps
>   are ringing;
> And twelve comely maidens deck the bride-bed for the
>   bride.'

A beautiful new dress was presented to the bride by her husband at the marriage feast; at which also the father paid down her dowry before the assembled guests; and all the place round the house was lit by torches when night came on, and the song and the dance continued till daylight, with much speech-making and drinking of poteen. All fighting was steadily avoided at a wedding; for a quarrel would be considered a most unlucky omen. A wet day was also held to be very unlucky, as the bride would assuredly weep for sorrow throughout the year. But the bright warm sunshine was hailed joyfully, according to the old saying –

> 'Happy is the bride that the sun shines on;
> But blessed is the corpse that the rain rains on.'

THE DEAD

There are many strange superstitions concerning the dead. The people seem to believe in their actual presence, though unseen, and to have a great fear and dread of their fatal and mysterious power.

If a person of doubtful character dies, too bad for heaven, too good for hell, they imagine that his soul is sent back to earth, and obliged to obey the order of some person who bids him remain in a particular place until the Day of Judgment, or until another soul is found willing to meet him there, and then they may both pass into heaven together, absolved.

An incident is related that happened in the County Galway, concerning this superstition.

A gentleman of rank and fortune, but of a free and dissipated life, became the lover of a pretty girl, one of the tenant's daughters. And the girl was so devoted to him that perhaps he might have married her at last; but he was killed suddenly, when out hunting, by a fall from his horse.

Some time after, the girl, coming home late one evening, met the ghost of her lover, at a very lonesome part of the road. The form was the same as when living, but it had no eyes. The girl crossed herself, on which the ghost disappeared.

Again she met the same apparition at night, and a third time, when the ghost stood right before her in the path, so that she could not pass. Then she spoke, and asked in the name of God and the good angels, why he appeared to her; and he answered, that he could not rest in his grave till he had received some command from her, which he was bound to obey.

'Then,' she said, 'go stand by the gate of heaven till the Judgment Day, and look in at the blessed dead on their thrones, but you may not enter. This is my judgment on your soul.'

On this the ghost sighed deeply and vanished, and was seen no more. But the girl prayed earnestly that she soon might meet her lover at the gate of heaven, whither she had sent him, that so both might enter together into the blessed land. And thus it happened; for by that day year she was carried to her grave in the churchyard, but her soul went forth to meet her lover, where he waited for her by the gate of heaven; and through her love he was absolved, and permitted to enter within the gate before the Judgment Day.

It was considered disrespectful to the dead to take a short cut when carrying the coffin to the grave.

THE DEAD

In the Islands, when a person is dying, they place twelve lighted rushes round the bed. This, they say, is to prevent the devil coming for the soul; for nothing evil can pass a circle of fire. They also forbid crying for the dead until three hours have passed by, lest the wail of the mourners should waken the dogs who are waiting to devour the souls of men before they can reach the throne of God.

It is a very general custom during some nights after a death to leave food outside the house – a griddle cake, or a dish of potatoes. If it is gone in the morning, the spirits must have taken it; for no human being would touch the food left for the dead.

The great and old families of Ireland consider it right to be buried with their kindred, and are brought from any distance, however remote, to be laid in the ancient graveyard of the race.

A young man of family having died far away, from fever, it was thought advisable not to bring him home, but to bury him where he died. However, on the night of the funeral a phantom hearse with four black horses stopped at the churchyard. Some men then entered with spades and shovels and dug a grave, after which the hearse drove away. But next morning no sign of the grave was to be found, except a long line marked out, the length of a man's coffin.

It is unlucky and a bad omen to carry fire out of a house where any one is ill. A gentleman one day stopped at a cabin to get a light for his cigar, and having wished good morning in the usual friendly fashion, he took a stick from the fire, blew it into a blaze, and was walking away, when the woman of the house rose up fiercely and told him it was an evil thing to take fire away when her husband was dying. On looking round he saw a wretched skeleton lying on a bed of straw; so he flung back the stick at once, and fled from the place, leaving his blessing in the form of a silver offering, to neutralize the evil of the abducted fire.

After the priest has left a dying person, and confession has been made, all the family kneel round the bed reciting the Litany for the Dying, and holy water is sprinkled over the room until the soul departs.

Then they all rise and begin the mournful death-wail in a loud voice; and by this cry all the people in the village know the exact moment of the death, and each one that hears it utters a prayer for the departing soul.

At the wake the corpse is often dressed in the habit of a religious order. A cross is placed in the hands and the scapular on the breast. Candles are lighted all round in a circle, and the friends and relatives arrange themselves in due order, the nearest of kin being at the head. At intervals they all stand up and intone the death-wail, rocking back and forward over the dead, and reciting his virtues; while the widow and orphans frequently salute the corpse with endearing epithets, and recall the happy days they spent together.

When the coffin is borne to the grave each person present helps to carry it a little way; for this is considered a mode of showing honour to the dead. The nearest relatives take the front handles first; then after a little while they move to the back and others take their place, until every person in turn has borne the head of the coffin to the grave – for it would be dishonourable to the dead to omit this mark of respect.

As the coffin is lowered into the grave the death-cry rises up with a loud and bitter wail, and the excitement often becomes so great that women have fallen into hysterics; and at one funeral a young girl in her agony of grief jumped into her father's grave and was taken up insensible.

THE WAKE ORGIES

From ancient times the wakes, or funeral games, in Ireland were held with many strange observances carried down by tradition from the pagan era. Some of the rites, however, were so revolting and monstrous that the priesthood used all their influence to put them down. The old funeral customs, in consequence, have now been discontinued almost entirely amongst the people, and the ancient traditional usages are

THE WAKE ORGIES

unknown to the new generation, though the elders of the village can yet remember them. An old man still living thus described to an inquiring antiquary and lover of folk-lore, his experience of the ceremonial of a wake at which he had been present in the South of Ireland, when he was quite a youth, some fifty years before.

'One dark winter's night, about seven o'clock, a large party of us,' he said, 'young men and women, perhaps thirty or more, set out across the mountain to attend a wake at the house of a rich farmer, about three miles off. All the young men carried lighted torches, for the way was rugged and dangerous; and by their light we guided the women as best we could over the deep clefts and across the rapid streams, swollen by the winter's rain. The girls took off their shoes and stockings and walked barefoot, but where the water was heavy and deep the men carried them across in their arms or on their backs. In this way we all arrived at last at the farmhouse, and found a great assemblage in the large barn, which was hung throughout with branches of evergreen and festoons of laurel and holly.

'At one end of the barn, on a bed decorated with branches of green leaves, lay the corpse, an old woman of eighty, the mother of the man of the house. He stood by the head of the dead woman, while all the near relatives had seats round. Then the mourning women entered and sat down on the ground in a circle, one in the centre cloaked and hooded, who began the chant or funeral wail, all the rest joining in chorus. After an interval there would come a deep silence; then the chant began again, and when it was over the women rose up and went out, leaving the place free for the next comers, who acted a play full of ancient symbolic meaning. But, first, whisky was served round, and the pipers played; for every village had sent their best player and singer to honour the wake.

'When a great space was cleared in the centre of the barn, the first set of players entered. They wore masks and fantastic garments, and each carried a long spear and a bit of plaited straw on the arm for a shield. At once they began to build a fort, as it were, marking out the size with their spears, and using some rough play with the spectators.

While thus engaged a band of enemies appeared, also masked and armed. And now a great fight began and many prisoners were taken; but to save slaughter a horn was blown, and a fight demanded between the two best champions of the hostile forces. Two of the finest young men were then selected and placed at opposite ends of the barn, when they ran a tilt against one another with their spears, uttering fierce, loud cries, and making terrible demonstrations. At length one fell down as if mortally wounded; then all the hooded women came in again and keened over him, a male voice at intervals reciting his deeds, while the pipers played martial tunes. But on its being suggested that perhaps he was not dead at all, an herb doctor was sent for to look at him; and an aged man with a flowing white beard was led in, carrying a huge bundle of herbs. With these he performed sundry strange incantations, until finally the dead man sat up and was carried off the field by his comrades, with shouts of triumph. So ended the first play.

'Then supper was served and more whisky drunk, after which another play was acted of a different kind. A table was set in the middle of the barn, and two chairs, while all the people, about a hundred or more, gathered round in a circle. Then two men, dressed as judges, took their seats, with guards beside them, and called on another man to come forth and address the people. On this a young man sprang on the table and poured forth an oration in Irish, full of the most grotesque fun and sharp allusions, at which the crowd roared with laughter. Then he gave out a verse like a psalm, in gibberish Irish, and bade the people say it after him. It ran like this, being translated –

> "Yellow Macauly has come from Spain,
> He brought sweet music out of a bag,
> Sing *See-saw*, *Sulla Vick Dhau*,
> *Sulla, Sulla Vick Dhau righ.*"
> (That is, Solomon, son of David the King.)

'If any one failed to repeat this verse after him he was ordered to prison by the judges, and the guards seized him to cut off his head; or if any one laughed the judge sentenced him, saying in Irish, "Seize that man, he is a pagan: he is mocking the Christian faith. Let him die!"

'After this the professional story-teller was in great force, and held the listeners enchained by the wonders of his narration and the passionate force of his declamation. So the strange revelry went on, and the feasting and the drinking, till sunrise, when many of the guests returned to their homes, but others stayed with the family till the coffin was lifted for the grave.'

Full details of these strange wake orgies can seldom be obtained, for the people are afraid of the priesthood, who have vehemently denounced them. Yet the peasants cling to them with a mysterious reverence, and do not see the immorality of many of the wake practices. They accept them as mysteries, ancient usages of their forefathers, to be sacredly observed, or the vengeance of the dead would fall on them.

According to all accounts an immense amount of dramatic talent was displayed by the actors of these fantastic and symbolic plays.

An intelligent peasant, who was brought to see the acting at the Dublin theatre, declared on his return: 'I have now seen the great English actors, and heard plays in the English tongue, but poor and dull they seemed to me after the acting of our own people at the wakes and fairs; for it is a truth, the English cannot make us weep and laugh as I have seen the crowds with us when the players played and the poets recited their stories.'

The Celts certainly have a strong dramatic tendency, and there are many peasant families in Ireland who have been distinguished for generations as bards and actors, and have a natural and hereditary gift for music and song.

On the subject of wake orgies, a clever writer observes that they are evidently a remnant of paganism, and formed part of those Druidic rites meant to propitiate the evil spirits and the demons of darkness and doom; for the influence of Druidism lasted long after the establishment of Christianity. The Druid priests took shelter with the people, and exercised a powerful and mysterious sway over them by their magic spells. Druid practices were known to exist down to the time of the Norman invasion in the twelfth century, and even for centuries after; and to this Druidic influence may be traced the sarcasms on Christianity which are occasionally introduced into the mystery plays of the wake ceremonial. As in the one called 'Hold the Light,' where the passion of the Lord Christ is travestied with grotesque imitation. The same writer describes the play acted at wakes called 'The Building of the Ship,' a symbolic rite still older than Druidism, and probably a remnant of the primitive Arkite worship. This was followed by a scene called 'Drawing the Ship out of the Mud.' It was against these two plays that the anathemas of the Church were chiefly directed, in consequence of their gross immorality, and they have now entirely ceased to form any portion of the wake ceremonial of Ireland. Hindu priests would recognize some of the ceremonies as the same which are still practised in their own temples; and travellers have traced a similarity also in these ancient usages to the 'big canoe games' of the Mandan Indians.

In the next play, the Hierophant, or teacher of the games, orders all the men out of the room; a young girl is then dressed with a hide thrown over her, and horns on her head, to simulate a cow, while her maidens form a circle and slowly dance round her to music, on which a loud knocking is heard at the door. 'Who wants to enter?' asks the Hierophant. He is answered, 'The guards demand admittance for the bull who is without.' Admittance is refused, and the maidens and the cow affect great alarm. Still the knocking goes on, and finally the door is burst open and the bull enters. He also is robed with a hide and wears horns, and is surrounded by a band of young men as his guards. He endeavours to seize the cow, who is defended by her maidens, forming the dramatic incidents of the play. A general mock fight now takes place between the guards and the maidens, and the scene ends with uproarious hilarity and the capture of the cow.

There are other practices mentioned by writers on the subject, who trace in the Irish observances a tradition of the Cabyric rites, and also a striking similarity to the idolatrous practices of Hindustan as described in the 'Asiatic Researches,' and in Moore's 'Hindu Pantheon.'

It is remarkable also that in the Polynesian Islands the funeral rites were accompanied by somewhat similar ceremonies. These the early missionaries viewed with horror, and finally succeeded in extirpating them.

These ancient funeral rites have now disappeared in Ireland; still the subject remains one of intense interest to the ethnologist and antiquary, who will find in the details indications of the oldest idolatries of the world, especially of that primitive religion called Arkite, as in the dramatic performance called 'The Building of the Ship,' where one man prostrates himself on the ground as the ship, while two others sit head and foot to represent the prow and stern. This ship drama is, perhaps, a fragment of the earliest tradition of humanity represented by a visible symbol to illustrate the legend of the Deluge.

THE POWER OF THE WORD

The belief in the malific influence of the Evil Eye pervades all the Greek islands, and the same preventive measures are used as in Ireland. An old woman is employed to spit three times at the person affected, if she is a person learned in the mysteries and accounted wise. Salt and fire are also used as safeguards, precisely as the Irish peasant employs them to guard his cattle and children from the evil influence. But no superstition is more widely spread; it seems to pervade all the world, and to be instinctive to humanity. The educated are as susceptible to it as the illiterate, and no nerves are strong enough, apparently, to resist the impression made by an envious, malicious glance, for a poison that blights and withers seems to emanate from it. Reason appeals in vain; the feelings cannot be overcome that the presence and glance of some one person in a room can chill all the natural flow of spirits, while the presence of another seems to intensify all our mental powers, and transform us for the moment into a higher being.

But a malific power, stronger even than the glance of the Evil Eye, was exercised by the Bards of Erin: whom they would they blessed, but whom they would they also banned; and the poet's malison was more dreaded and was more fatal than any other form of imprecation – for the bard had the mystic prophet power: he could foresee, and he could denounce. And no man could escape from the judgment pronounced by a poet over one he desired to injure; for the poet had the knowledge of all mysteries and was Lord over the secrets of life by the power of The Word. Therefore poets were emphatically called the tribe of Duars, that is, The Men of the Word; for by a word the poets could produce deformities in those they disliked, and make them objects of scorn and hateful in the sight of other men.

THE POET AND THE KING

Nuadhé, the celebrated poet, is remembered in history by a memorable exercise of his malific power, and the punishment that fell on him in consequence; for Heaven is just, and even a bard cannot escape the penalty due for sin.

He was nephew to Caer, the king of Connaught, who reared him with all kindness and gentleness as his own son. But by an evil fate the wife of Caer the king loved the young man; and she gave him a silver apple in proof of her love, and further promised him the kingdom and herself if he could overthrow Caer and make the people depose him from the sovranty.

'How can I do this?' answered Nuadhé, 'for the king has ever been kind to me.'

'Ask him for some gift,' said the queen, 'that he will refuse, and then put a blemish on him for punishment, that so he can be no longer king;' for no one with a blemish was ever suffered to reign in Erin.

'But he refuses me nothing,' answered Nuadhé.

'Try him,' said the queen. 'Ask of him the dagger he brought from Alba, for he is under a vow never to part with it.'

So Nuadhé went to him, and asked for the dagger that came out of Alba as a gift.

'Woe is me!' said the king. 'This I cannot grant; for I am under a solemn vow never to part with it, or give it to another.' Then the poet by his power made a satire on him, and this was the form of the imprecation –

> 'Evil death, and a short life
>   Be on Caer the king!
> Let the spears of battle wound him,
> Under earth, under ramparts, under stones,
>   Let the malediction be on him!'

And when Caer rose up in the morning he put his hand to his face and found it was disfigured with three blisters, a white, a red, and a green. And when he saw the blemish he fled away filled with fear that any man should see him, and took refuge in a fort with one of his faithful servants, and no one knew where he lay hid.

So Nuadhé took the kingdom and held it for a year, and had the queen to wife. But then grievous to him was the fate of Caer, and he set forth to search for him.

And he was seated in the king's own royal chariot, with the king's wife beside him, and the king's greyhound at his feet, and all the people wondered at the beauty of the charioteer.

Now Caer was in the fort where he had found shelter, and when he saw them coming he said –

'Who is this that is seated in my chariot in the place of the champion, and driving my steeds?'

But when he saw that it was Nuadhé he fled away and hid himself for shame.

Then Nuadhé drove into the fort in the king's chariot, and loosed the dogs to pursue Caer. And they found him hid under the flagstone behind the rock even where the dogs tracked him. And Caer fell down dead from shame on beholding Nuadhé, and the rock where he fell flamed up and shivered into fragments, and a splinter leaped up high as a man, and struck Nuadhé on the eyes, and blinded him for life. Such was the punishment decreed, and just and right was the vengeance of God upon the sin of the poet.

THE SIDHE RACE

The Sidhe dwell in the Sifra, or fairy palace of gold and crystal, in the heart of the hill, and they have been given youth, beauty, joy, and the power over music, yet they are often sad; for they remember that they were once angels in heaven though now cast down to earth, and though they have power over all the mysteries of Nature, yet they must die without hope of regaining heaven, while mortals are certain of immortality. Therefore this one sorrow darkens their life, a mournful envy of humanity; because, while man is created immortal, the beautiful fairy race is doomed to annihilation.

One day a great fairy chief asked Columb-Kille if there were any hope left to the Sidhe that one day they would regain heaven and be restored to their ancient place amongst the angels. But the saint answered that hope there was none; their doom was fixed, and at the judgment-day they would pass through death into annihilation; for so had it been decreed by the justice of God.

On hearing this the fairy chief fell into a profound melancholy, and he and all his court sailed away from Ireland, and went back to their native country of Armenia, there to await the coming of the terrible judgment-day, which is fated to bring the fairy race certain death on earth, without any hope of regaining heaven.

The West of Ireland is peculiarly sacred to ancient superstitions of the Sidhe race. There is a poetry in the scenery that touches the heart of the people; they love the beautiful glens, the mountains rising like towers from the sea, the islands sanctified by the memory of a saint, and the green hills where Finvarra holds his court. Every lake and mountain has its legend of the spirit-land, some holy traditions of a saint, or some historic memory of a national hero who flourished in the old great days when Ireland had native chiefs and native swords to guard her; and amongst the Western Irish, especially, the old superstitions of their forefathers are reverenced with a solemn faith and fervour that is almost a religion. Finvarra the king is still believed to rule over all the fairies of the west, and Onagh is the fairy queen. Her golden hair sweeps the ground, and she is robed in silver gossamer all glittering as if with diamonds, but they are dew-drops that sparkle over it.

The queen is more beautiful than any woman of earth, yet Finvarra loves the mortal women best, and wiles them down to his fairy palace by the subtle charm of the fairy music, for no one who has heard it can resist its power, and they are fated to belong to the fairies ever after. Their friends mourn for them as dead with much lamentation, but in reality they are leading a joyous life down in the heart of the hill, in the fairy palace with the silver columns and the crystal walls.

Yet sometimes they are not drawn down beneath the earth, but remain as usual in the daily life, though the fairy spell is still on them; and the young men who have once heard the fairy harp become possessed by the spirit of music which haunts them to their death, and gives them strange power over the souls of men. This was the case with Carolan, the celebrated bard.

He acquired all the magic melody of his notes by sleeping out on a fairy rath at night, when the fairy music came to him in his dreams; and on awaking he played the airs from memory. Thus it was that he had power to madden men to mirth, or to set them weeping as if for the dead, and no one ever before or since played the enchanting fairy music like Carolan, the sweet musician of Ireland.

There was another man also who heard the fairy music when sleeping on a rath, and ever after he was haunted by the melody day and night, till he grew mad and had no pleasure in life, for he longed to be with the fairies again that he might hear them sing. So one day, driven to despair by the madness of longing, he threw himself from the cliff into the mountain lake near the fairy rath, and so died and was seen no more.

In the Western Islands they believe that the magic of fairy music is so strong that whoever hears it cannot choose but follow the sound, and the young girls are drawn away by the enchantment, and dance all night with Finvarra the king, though in the morning they are found fast asleep in bed, yet with a memory of all they had heard and seen; and some say that, while with the fairies, the young women learn strange secrets of love potions, by which they can work spells and dangerous charms over those whose love they desire; or upon any one who has offended and spoken ill of them.

It is a beautiful idea that the Irish airs, so plaintive, mournful, and tear-compelling, are but the remembered echoes of that spirit music which had power to draw souls away to the fairy mansions, and hold them captive by the sweet magic of the melody.

MUSIC

Music formed the chief part of education in ancient Ireland as in Greece, where the same word signified a song and a law. Laws, religion, sciences, and history were all taught in music to the Irish people by the *Ollamhs* or learned men. The Poets chanted the *Ros-Catha*, or song of battle, to incite the warriors to deeds of bravery. The Bards recited the deeds of the chiefs, or pleasant tales of love, at the festivals, and struck the harp to sustain the voice. The Brehons intoned the law in a recitative or monotone chant, seated on an eminence in the open air, while all the people were gathered round to listen. The Senachie chanted the history, genealogies, and traditions of the tribe, and the female mourners were instructed by the poets in the elegiac measure, or funeral wail over the dead.

The poet-power was also believed to confer the gift of prophecy; and no great expedition was undertaken by the tribe without the advice and sanction of the bard, and especially of the poet-priestess of the tribe. Thus Ethna the poetess stood on a high stone at the battle of Moytura, and gave inspiration by her chants to the warriors of the Tuatha-de-Dananns, and stimulated their courage by her prophecies of victory; and the stone she stood on is in existence to this day on the plain of the battle, and is still called by the people 'the Stone of the Prophetess.'

POET INSPIRATION

EODAIN THE POETESS

The *Leanan-Sidhe*, or the spirit of life, was supposed to be the inspirer of the poet and singer, as the *Ban-Sidhe* was the spirit of death, the foreteller of doom.

The Leanan-Sidhe sometimes took the form of a woman, who gave men valour and strength in the battle by her songs. Such was Eodain the poetess, by whom Eugene, king of Munster, gained complete victory over his foes. But afterwards he gave himself up to luxury and pleasure, and went away to Spain, where he remained nine years, and took to wife the daughter of the king of Spain. At the end of that time he returned to Ireland with a band of Spanish followers. But he found his kingdom plundered and ruined, and the revellers and drunkards were feasting in his banquet hall, and wasting his revenues for their pleasures while the people starved. And the whole nation despised the king, and would not hear his words when he sat down in his golden chair to give just judgment for iniquity. Then Eugene the king, in his deep sorrow and humiliation, sent for Eodain the poetess to come and give him counsel. So Eodain came to him, and upheld him with her strong spirit, for she had the power within her of the poet and the prophet, and she said –

'Arise now, O king, and govern like a true hero, and bring confusion on the evil workers. Be strong and fear not, for by strength and justice kings should rule.'

And Eugene the king was guided by her counsel and was successful. And he overthrew his enemies and brought back peace and order to the land. For the strength of the Leanan-Sidhe was in the words of Eodain, the power of the spirit of life which is given to the poet and the prophet, by which they inspire and guide the hearts of men.

THE BANSHEE

The Banshee means, especially, the woman of the fairy race, from *van*, 'The Woman – the Beautiful;' the same word from which comes *Venus*. Shiloh-Van was one of the names of Buddha – 'the son of the woman;' and some writers aver that in the Irish – *Sullivan* (Sulli-van), may be found this ancient name of Buddha.

As the Leanan-Sidhe was the acknowledged *spirit of life*, giving inspiration to the poet and the musician, so the Ban-Sidhe was the *spirit of death*, the most weird and awful of all the fairy powers.

But only certain families of historic lineage, or persons gifted with music and song, are attended by this spirit; for music and poetry are fairy gifts, and the possessors of them show kinship to the spirit race – therefore they are watched over by the spirit of life, which is prophecy and inspiration; and by the spirit of doom, which is the revealer of the secrets of death.

Sometimes the Banshee assumes the form of some sweet singing virgin of the family who died young, and has been given the mission by the invisible powers to become the harbinger of coming doom to her mortal kindred. Or she may be seen at night as a shrouded woman, crouched beneath the trees, lamenting with veiled face; or flying past in the moonlight, crying bitterly: and the cry of this spirit is mournful beyond all other sounds on earth, and betokens certain death to some member of the family whenever it is heard in the silence of the night.

THE BANSHEE

The Banshee even follows the old race across the ocean and to distant lands; for space and time offer no hindrance to the mystic power which is selected and appointed to bear the prophecy of death to a family. Of this a well-authenticated instance happened a few years ago, and many now living can attest the truth of the narrative.

A branch of the ancient race of the O'Gradys had settled in Canada, far removed, apparently, from all the associations, traditions, and mysterious influences of the old land of their forefathers.

But one night a strange and mournful lamentation was heard outside the house. No word was uttered, only a bitter cry, as of one in deepest agony and sorrow, floated through the air.

Inquiry was made, but no one had been seen near the house at the time, though several persons distinctly heard the weird, unearthly cry, and a terror fell upon the household, as if some supernatural influence had overshadowed them.

Next day it so happened that the gentleman and his eldest son went out boating. As they did not return, however, at the usual time for dinner, some alarm was excited, and messengers were sent down to the shore to look for them. But no tidings came until, precisely at the exact hour of the night when the spirit-cry had been heard the previous evening, a crowd of men were seen approaching the house, bearing with them the dead bodies of the father and the son, who had both been drowned by the accidental upsetting of the boat, within sight of land, but not near enough for any help to reach them in time.

Thus the Ban-Sidhe had fulfilled her mission of doom, after which she disappeared, and the cry of the spirit of death was heard no more.

At times the spirit-voice is heard in low and soft lamenting, as if close to the window.

Not long ago an ancient lady of noble lineage was lying near the death-hour in her stately castle. One evening, after twilight, she suddenly unclosed her eyes and pointed to the window, with a happy smile on her face. All present looked in the direction, but nothing was visible. They heard, however, the sweetest music, low, soft, and spiritual, floating round the house, and at times apparently close to the window of the sick room.

Many of the attendants thought it was a trick, and went out to search the grounds; but nothing human was seen. Still the wild plaintive singing went on, wandering through the trees like the night wind – a low, beautiful music that never ceased all through the night.

Next morning the noble lady lay dead; then the music ceased, and the lamentation from that hour was heard no more.

There was a gentleman also in the same country who had a beautiful daughter, strong and healthy, and a splendid horsewoman. She always followed the hounds, and her appearance at the hunt attracted unbounded admiration, as no one rode so well or looked so beautiful.

One evening there was a ball after the hunt, and the young girl moved through the dance with the grace of a fairy queen.

But that same night a voice came close to the father's window, as if the face were laid close to the glass, and he heard a mournful lamentation and a cry; and the words rang out on the air –

'In three weeks death; in three weeks the grave – dead – dead – dead!'

Three times the voice came, and three times he heard the words; but though it was bright moonlight, and he looked from the window over all the park, no form was to be seen.

Next day, his daughter showed symptoms of fever, and exactly in three weeks, as the Ban-Sidhe had prophesied, the beautiful girl lay dead.

The night before her death soft music was heard outside the house, though no word was spoken by the spirit-voice, and the family said the form of a woman crouched beneath a tree, with a mantle covering her head, was distinctly visible. But on approaching, the phantom disappeared, though the soft, low music of the lamentation continued till dawn.

Then the angel of death entered the house with soundless feet, and he breathed upon the beautiful face of the young girl, and she rested in the sleep of the dead, beneath the dark shadows of his wings.

Thus the prophecy of the Banshee came true, according to the time foretold by the spirit-voice.

QUEEN MAEVE

A remarkable account is given in the Bardic Legends of a form that appeared to Maeve, queen of Connaught, on the eve of battle.

Suddenly there stood before the queen's chariot, a tall and beautiful woman. She wore a green robe clasped with a golden bodkin, a golden fillet on her head, and seven braids for the Dead of bright gold were in her hand. Her skin was white as snow that falls in the night; her teeth were as pearls; her lips red as the berries of the mountain ash; her golden hair fell to the ground; and her voice was sweet as the golden harp-string when touched by a skilful hand.

'Who art thou, O woman?' asked the queen, in astonishment.

'I am Feithlinn, the fairy prophetess of the Rath of Cruachan,' she answered.

''Tis well, O Feithlinn the prophetess,' said Maeve; 'but what dost thou foresee concerning our hosts?'

'I foresee bloodshed; I foresee power; I foresee defeat!' answered the prophetess.

'My couriers have brought me good tidings!' said the queen; 'my army is strong, my warriors are well prepared. But speak the truth, O prophetess: for my soul knows no fear.'

'I foresee bloodshed; I foresee victory!' answered the prophetess the second time.

'But I have nothing to fear from the Ultonians,' said the queen, 'for my couriers have arrived, and my enemies are under dread. Yet, speak the truth, O prophetess, that our hosts may know it.'

'I foresee bloodshed; I foresee conquest; I foresee *death!*' answered the prophetess, for the third time.

'To me then it belongs not, thy prophecy of evil,' replied the queen, in anger.

'Be it thine, and on thy own head.'

And even as she spoke the prophet maiden disappeared, and the queen saw her no more.

But it so happened that, some time afterwards, Queen Maeve was cruelly slain by her own kinsman, at Lough Rea by the Shannon, to avenge the assistance she had given in war to the king of Ulster; there is an island in the lake where is shown the spot where the great queen was slain, and which is still known to the people as – *the stone of the dead queen*.

Maeve, the great queen of Connaught, holds a distinguished place in Bardic Legends. When she went to battle, it is said, she rode in an open car, accompanied by four chariots – one before, another behind, and one on each side – so that the golden *assion* on her head and her royal robes should not be defiled by the dust of the horses' feet, or the foam of the fiery steeds; for all the sovereigns of Ireland sat crowned with a diadem in battle, as they drove in their war-chariots, as well as in the festal and the public assemblies.

DEATH SIGNS

In one Irish family a cuckoo always appears before a death. A lady who arrived on a visit at a house observed one morning a cuckoo perched on the window-sill, but she felt no alarm, for there was no sickness in the family. Next day, however, one of the sons was carried home dead. He had been thrown from his horse when hunting, and killed on the spot.

In another family a mysterious sound is heard like the crashing of boards, and a rush of wind seems to pass through the house, yet nothing is broken or disturbed. The death of an officer in the Crimea was in this way announced to his family, for the news came immediately after the warning sound, and then they knew that the rush of the wind was the spirit of the dead which had passed by them, but without taking any visible form.

THE HARTPOLE DOOM

There is a tradition concerning the Hartpole family of Shrule Castle in the Queen's County (called the castle on the bloody stream, from the sanguinary deeds of the owner) that every male member of the family is doomed and fated to utter three screeches terrible to hear when dying. As to the origin of this doom the story goes that Sir Richard Hartpole about 300 years ago, in the time of the Elizabethan wars, committed many savage acts against the Irish, he being an upholder of the English faction.

One day a priest named O'More, having come to the castle on some friendly mission, the savage Hartpole ordered his retainers to seize him and hang him up in the courtyard.

'Good God!' exclaimed the priest. 'Give me at least a moment to pray!'

'Go then,' said Hartpole, 'you may pray.'

The priest kneeled down apart from the crowd. But Hartpole grew impatient, and ordered him to rise.

'You have prayed long enough,' he said, 'prepare for death.'

And when the priest heard the order for his death, and saw the man approach to seize him, he swayed from right to left and gave three fearful screams.

'Why do you screech?' asked the tyrant.

'So shall you scream, and all your descendants in your last agony,' exclaimed O'More, 'as a sign of the doom upon your race. You have murdered my people, you are now going to take my life; but I lay the curse of God on you and yours – your property shall pass away; your race shall perish off the earth; and by the three death screeches all men shall know that you and your posterity are accursed.'

The words of O'More only made the tyrant more furious, and the priest was hung at once in the courtyard before the eyes of Hartpole. But the prophecy of doom was fulfilled – the property perished, the castle became a ruin. The last Hartpole died miserably of want and hunger, and the whole race finally has become extinct.

SUPERSTITIONS

The two great festivals of the ancient Irish were *Lá Baal Tinné* or May Day (sacred to the Sun), and *Lá Samnah*, or November Eve (sacred to the Moon).

Food should be left out on November Eve for the dead, who are then wandering about. If the food disappears, it is a sign that the spirits have taken it, for no mortal would dare to touch or eat of the food so left.

Never turn your head to look if you fancy you hear footsteps behind you on that night; for the dead are walking then, and their glance would kill.

In November a distaff is placed under the head of a young man at night to make him dream of the girl he is destined to marry.

If a ball of worsted is thrown into a lime-kiln and wound up till the end is caught by invisible hands, the person who winds it calls out, 'Who holds the ball?' and the answer will be the name of the future husband or wife. But the experiment must be made only at midnight, and in silence and alone.

Whitsuntide is a most unlucky time; horses foaled then will grow up dangerous and kill some one.

A child born at Whitsuntide will have an evil temper, and may commit a murder.

Beware also of water at Whitsuntide, for an evil power is on the waves and the lakes and the rivers, and a boat may be swamped and men drowned unless a bride steers; then the danger ceases.

To turn away ill-luck from a child born at that time, a grave must be dug and the infant laid in it for a few minutes. After this process the evil spell is broken, and the child is safe.

If any one takes ill at Whitsuntide there is great danger of death, for the evil spirits are on the watch to carry off victims, and no sick person should be left alone at this time, nor in the dark. Light is a great safeguard, as well as fire, against malific influences.

In old times at Whitsuntide blood was poured out as a libation to the evil spirits; and the children and cattle were passed through two lines of fire.

SUPERSTITIONS

On May morning the Skellig rocks go out full sail to meet the opposite rocks, which advance half way to meet them, and then slowly retire like retreating ships.

At Midsummer the fairies try to pass round the Baal fires in a whirlwind in order to extinguish them, but the spirits may be kept off by throwing fire at them. Then the young men are free to leap over the burning embers and to drive the cattle through the flames, while coals of fire must also be passed three times over and three times under the body of each animal.

Foot-worship was a homage to Buddha, and it was always a Christian ceremony to wash the feet of the saints. The Irish had many superstitions about foot-water, and no woman was allowed to wash her feet in the sacred wells though the lavation was permitted to men.

If a child is fairy-struck, give it a cup of cold water in the name of Christ and make the sign of the cross over it.

On St Martin's Day when blood is spilt, whoever is signed with the blood is safe, for that year at least, from disease.

For the Evil Eye, a piece cut from the garment of the evil-eyed, burned to tinder and ground to powder, must be given to the person under the baneful spell, while his forehead is anointed with spittle thrice. So the Greeks spat three times in the face of the evil-eyed to break the spell.

Pass a red-hot turf three times over and under the body of an animal supposed to be fairy-struck, singeing the hair along the back. This drives off the fairies.

The Irish always went westward round a holy well, following the course of the sun, and creeping on their hands and knees. So did the ancient Persians when offering homage at the sacred fountains.

Red-haired people were held to be evil and malicious and unlucky, probably because Typhon, the evil principle, was red; and therefore a red heifer was sacrificed to him by the Egyptians.

In the mystic, or snake dance, performed at the Baal festival, the gyrations of the dancers were always westward, in the track of the sun, for the dance was part of the ancient ritual of sun worship.

THE FAIRY RATH

The ancient rath, or fort, or liss, generally enclosed about half an acre, and had two or more ramparts, formed by the heads of the tribe for defence. But when the race of the chieftains died out, then the Sidhe crowded into the forts, and there held their councils and revels and dances; and if a man put his ear close to the ground at night he could hear the sweet fairy music rising up from under the earth.

The rath ever after is sacred to the fairies, and no mortal is allowed to cut down a tree that grows on it, or to carry away a stone. But dangerous above all would it be to build on a fairy rath. If a man attempted such a rash act, the fairies would put a blast on his eyes, or give him a crooked mouth; for no human hand should dare to touch their ancient dancing grounds.

It is not right, the people say, to sing or whistle at night that old air, 'The pretty girl milking her cow;' for it is a fairy tune, and the fairies will not suffer a mortal to sing their music while they are dancing on the grass. But if a person sleeps on the rath the music will enter into his soul, and when he awakes he may sing the air he has heard in his dreams.

In this way the bards learned their songs, and they were skilled musicians, and touched the harp with a master hand, so that the fairies often gathered round to listen, though invisible to mortal eyes.

FAIRY NATURE

The *Siodh-Dune*, or the Mount of Peace, is also a favourite resort of the fairies. It is an ancient, sacred place, where the Druids in old time used to retire to pray, when they desired solitude; and the fairies meet there every seven years to perform the act of lamentation and mourning for having been cast out of heaven.

Earth, lake, and hill are peopled by these fantastic, beautiful gods of earth; the wilful, capricious child-spirits of the world. The Irish seem to have created this strange fairy race after their own image, for in all things they strangely resemble the Irish character.

The Sidhe passionately love beauty and luxury, and hold in contempt all the mean virtues of thrift and economy. Above all things they hate the close, niggard hand that gathers the last grain, and drains the last drop in the milk-pail, and plucks the trees bare of fruit, leaving nothing for the spirits who wander by in the moonlight. They like food and wine to be left for them at night, yet they are very temperate; no one ever saw an intoxicated fairy.

But people should not sit up too late; for the fairies like to gather round the smouldering embers after the family are in bed, and drain the wine-cup, and drink the milk which a good housewife always leaves for them, in case the fairies should come in and want their supper. A vessel of pure water should also be left for them to bathe in, if they like. And in all things the fairies are fond of being made much of, and flattered and attended to; and the fairy blessing will come back in return to the giver for whatever act of kindness he has done to the spirits of the hill and the cave. Some unexpected good fortune or stroke of luck will come upon his house or his children; for the fairy race is not ungrateful, and is powerful over man both for good and evil.

Therefore be kind to the wayfarer, for he may be a fairy prince in disguise, who has come to test the depth of your charity, and of the generous nature that can give liberally out of pure love and kindliness to those who are in need, and not in hope of a reward.

If treated well, the fairies will discover the hidden pot of gold, and reveal the mysteries of herbs, and give knowledge to the fairy women of the mystic spells that can cure disease, and save life, and make the lover loved.

All they ask in return is to be left in quiet possession of the rath and the hill and the ancient hawthorn trees that have been theirs from time immemorial, and where they lead a joyous life with music and dance, and charming little suppers of the nectar of flowers, down in the crystal caves, lit by the diamonds that stud the rocks.

But some small courtesies they require. Never drain your wine-glass at a feast, nor the poteen flask, nor the milk-pail; and never rake out all the fire at night, it looks mean, and the fairies like a little of everything going, and to have the hearth comfortable and warm when they come in to hold a council after all the mortal people have gone to bed. In fact, the fairies are born aristocrats, true ladies and gentlemen, and if treated with proper respect are never in the least malignant or ill-natured.

All the traditions of the fairies show that they love beauty and splendour, grace of movement, music and pleasure; everything, in fact, that is artistic, in contradistinction to violent, brutal enjoyment. Only an Aryan people, therefore, could have invented the Sidhe race.

IRISH NATURE

The Irish show their Aryan descent by the same characteristics as the Fairy race, for they also love everything that is artistic – the fascinations of life, beauty of form, music, poetry, song, splendour, and noble pleasures. Their kings in ancient times were elected for their personal beauty as much as for their chivalrous qualities. No man with a blemish or a deformity was allowed to reign. Then, their appreciation of intellect proved the value they set on the spiritual and ideal above the material and the brutal. The poet ranked next to the princes of the land. His person was sacred in battle; he was endowed with an estate, so that his soul might be free from sordid cares; and his robe of many colours, and the golden circlet on his brow at the festivals, showed his claim and right to rank next to royalty, and to sit at the right hand of the king. Poetry, learning, music, oratory, heroism, and splendour of achievement – these were the true objects of homage and admiration amongst the ancient Irish.

There was nothing brutal in their ideal of life; no hideous images or revolting cruelties; and the beautiful and graceful Sidhe race, with their plaintive music and soft melancholy, and aspirations for a lost heaven, is the expression in a graceful and beautiful symbol of the

IRISH NATURE

instinctive tendencies of the Irish nature to all that is most divine in human intellect, and soft and tender in human emotion.

Ireland is a land of mists and mystic shadows; of cloud-wraiths on the purple mountains; of weird silences in the lonely hills, and fitful skies of deepest gloom alternating with gorgeous sunset splendours. All this fantastic caprice of an ever-varying atmosphere stirs the imagination, and makes the Irish people strangely sensitive to spiritual influences. They see visions and dream dreams, and are haunted at all times by an ever-present sense of the supernatural. One can see by the form of the Irish head – a slender oval, prominent at the brows and high in the region of veneration, so different from the globular Teutonic head – that the people are enthusiasts, religious, fanatical; with the instincts of poetry, music, oratory, and superstition far stronger in them than the logical and reasoning faculties. They are made for worshippers, poets, artists, musicians, orators; to move the world by passion, not by logic. Scepticism will never take root in Ireland; infidelity is impossible to the people. To believe fanatically, trust implicitly, hope infinitely, and perhaps to revenge implacably – these are the unchanging and ineradicable characteristics of Irish nature, of Celtic nature, we may say; for it has been the same throughout all history and all ages. And it is these passionate qualities that make the Celt the great motive force of the world, ever striving against limitations towards some vision of ideal splendour; the restless centrifugal force of life, as opposed to the centipetal, which is ever seeking a calm quiescent rest within its appointed sphere.

The very tendency to superstition, so marked in Irish nature, arises from an instinctive dislike to the narrow limitations of common sense. It is characterized by a passionate yearning towards the vague, the mystic, the invisible, and the boundless infinite of the realms of imagination. Therefore the *Daine-Sidhe*, the people of the fairy mansions, have an irresistible attraction for the Irish heart. Like them, the Irish love youth, beauty, splendour, lavish generosity, music and song, the feast and the dance. The mirth and the reckless gaiety of the national temperament finds its true exponent in the mad pranks of the *Phouka* and the Leprehaun, the merry spirits that haunt the dells and glens, and look out at the wayfarer from under the dock-leaf with their glittering eyes. The inspiration that rises to poetry under the influence of excitement is expressed by the belief in the *Leanan-Sidhe*, who gives power to song; while the deep pathos of Irish nature finds its fullest representation in the tender, plaintive, spiritual music of the wail and lamentation of the *Ban-Sidhe*.

LEGENDS OF ANIMALS

There are no traces in Irish legend of animal worship, but many concerning the influence of animals upon human life, and of their interference with human affairs.

The peasants believe that the domestic animals know all about us, especially the dog and the cat. They listen to everything that is said; they watch the expression of the face, and can even read the thoughts. The Irish say it is not safe to ask a question of a dog, for he may answer, and should he do so the questioner will surely die.

The position of the animal race in the life scheme is certainly full of mystery. Gifted with extraordinary intelligence, yet with dumb souls vainly struggling for utterance, they seem like prisoned spirits in bondage, suffering the punishment, perhaps, for sin in some former human life, and now waiting the completion of the cycle of expiation that will advance them again to the human state.

The three most ancient words in the Irish language are, it is said, *Tor*, a tower; *Cu*, a hound, and *Bo*, a cow. The latter word is the same as is found in the Greek *Bosphorus*, and in the nomenclature of many places throughout Europe.

CONCERNING DOGS

Some very weird superstitions exist in Ireland concerning the howlings of dogs. If a dog is heard to howl near the house of a sick person, all hope of his recovery is given up, and the patient himself sinks into despair, knowing that his doom is sealed. But the Irish are not alone in holding this superstition. The Egyptians, Hebrews, Greeks, and Romans all looked on the howling of the dog as ominous. The very word howling may be traced in the Latin *ululu*, the Greek *holuluzo*, the Hebrew *hululue*, and the Irish *ulluloo*. In Ireland the cry raised at the funeral ceremony was called the Caoin, or keen, probably from χνων, a dog. And this doleful lamentation was also common to other nations of antiquity. The Hebrews, Greeks, and Romans had their hired mourners, who, with dishevelled hair and mournful cadenced hymns, led on the melancholy parade of death. Thus the Trojan women keened over Hector, the chorus being led by the beautiful Helen herself.

The howling of the dog was considered by these nations as the first note of the funeral dirge and the signal that the coming of death was near.

But the origin of the superstition may be traced back to Egypt, where dogs and dog-faced gods were objects of worship; probably because Sirius, the Dog-star, appeared precisely before the rising of the Nile, and thereby gave the people a mystic and supernatural warning to prepare for the overflow.

The Romans held that the howling of dogs was a fatal presage of evil, and it is noted amongst the direful omens that preceded the death of Caesar. Horace also says that Canidia by her spells and sorceries could bring ghosts of dogs from hell; and Virgil makes the dog to howl at the approach of Hecate.

It is remarkable that when dogs see spirits (and they are keenly sensitive to spirit influence) they never bark, but only howl. The Rabbins say that 'when the Angel of Death enters a city the dogs do howl. But when Elias appears then the dogs rejoice and are merry.' And Rabbi Jehuda the Just states, that once upon a time when the Angel of

Death entered a house the dog howled and fled; but being presently brought back he lay down in fear and trembling, and so died.

This strange superstition concerning the howling of dogs, when, as is supposed, they are conscious of the approach of the Spirit of Death, and see him though he is shrouded and invisible to human eyes, may be found pervading the legends of all nations from the earliest period down to the present time; for it still exists in full force amongst all classes, the educated, as well as the unlettered peasantry; and to this day the howling of a dog where a sick person is lying is regarded in Ireland in all grades of society with pale dismay as a certain sign of approaching death.

The Irish may have obtained the superstition through Egypt, Phoenicia, or Greece, for it is the opinion of some erudite writers that the Irish wolf-dog (*Canis gracius Hibernicus*) was descended from the dogs of Greece.

It is strange and noteworthy that although the dog is so faithful to man, yet it is never mentioned in the Bible without an expression of contempt; and Moses in his code of laws makes the dog an unclean animal, probably to deter the Israelites from the Egyptian worship of this animal. It was the lowest term of offence – 'Is thy servant a dog?' False teachers, persecutors, Gentiles, unholy men, and others sunk in sin and vileness were called dogs; while at the same time the strange prophetic power of these animals was universally acknowledged and recognized.

The Romans sacrificed a dog at the Lupercalia in February. And to meet a dog with her whelps was considered in the highest degree unlucky. Of all living creatures the name of 'dog' applied to any one expressed the lowest form of insult, contempt, and reproach. Yet, of all animals, the dog has the noblest qualities, the highest intelligence, and the most enduring affection for man.

The Irish wolf-dog had a lithe body, a slender head, and was fleet as the wind. The form of the animal is produced constantly in Irish ornamentation, but the body always terminates in endless twisted convolutions. The great Fionn Ma-Coul had a celebrated dog called 'Bran,' who is thus described in the bardic legends:

'A ferocious, small-headed, white-breasted, sleek-haunched hound; having the eyes of a dragon, the claws of a wolf, the vigour of a lion, and the venom of a serpent.'

In the same poem Fionn himself is described in highly ornate bardic language, as he leads the hound by a chain of silver attached to a collar of gold: A noble, handsome, fair-featured Fenian prince; young, courteous, manly, puissant; powerful in action; the tallest of the warriors; the strongest of the champions; the most beautiful of the human race.'

Bran, like his master, was gifted in a remarkable degree with the foreknowledge of evil, and thus he was enabled to give his young lord many warnings to keep him from danger.

Once, when victory was not for the Fenian host, Bran showed the deepest sorrow.

'He came to Fionn, wet and weary, and by this hand,' says the chronicler, 'his appearance was pitiful. He lay down before the chief, and cried bitterly and howled.

''Tis likely, my dog,' saith Fionn, 'that our heads are in great danger this day.'

Another time, the Fenian host having killed a huge boar, Ossian, the bard and prophet, ordered it to be burnt as of demon race. Bran, hearing this, went out readily and knowingly, and he brings in three trees in his paw; no one knew from whence; but the trees were put into the fire and the great pig was burnt, and the ashes of the beast were cast into the sea.

The Fenian princes generally went to the hunt accompanied altogether by about three thousand hounds; Bran leading, the wisest and fleetest of all. The chiefs formed a goodly army, a thousand knights or more – each wearing a silken shirt and a chotan of fine silk, a green mantle and fine purple cloak over to protect it; a golden diademed helmet on the head, and a javelin in each man's hand.

Once, a chief, being jealous of the splendour of the Fenian princes, became their bitter enemy, and set himself to curse Bran above all hounds in the land.

But Fionn answered, 'If thou shouldest curse Bran, my wise, intelligent dog, not a room east or west in thy great mansion but I will burn with fire.'

So Bran rested on the mountain with Fionn, his lord and master, and was safe from harm.

Yet, so fate decreed, Bran finally met his death by means of a woman. One day a snow-white hart, with hoofs that shone like gold, was scented on the hill, and all the hounds pursued, Bran leading. Hour after hour passed by, and still the hart fled on, the hounds following, till one by one they all dropped off from weariness, and not one was left save Bran. Then the hart headed for the lake, and reaching a high cliff, she plunged from it straight down into the water; the noble hound leaped in at once after her, and seized the hart as she rose to the surface; but at that instant she changed into the form of a beautiful lady, and laying her hand upon the head of Bran, she drew him down beneath the water, and the beautiful lady and Fionn's splendid hound disappeared together and were seen no more. But in memory of the event the cliff from which he leaped is called Coegg-y-Bran; while the lake and the castle beside it are called *Tiernach Bran* (the lordship of Bran) to this day. So the name and memory of Fionn's hound, and his wisdom and achievements are not forgotten by the people; and many dogs of the chase are still called after him, for the name is thought to bring luck to the hunter and sportsman. But the *Cailleach Biorar* (the Hag of the Water) is held in much dread, for it is believed that she still lives in a cave on the hill, and is ready to work her evil spells whenever opportunity offers, and her house is shown under the cairn, also the beaten path she traversed to the lake. Many efforts have been made to drain the lake, but the Druid priestess, the Hag of the Water, always interferes, and casts some spell to prevent the completion of the work. The water of the lake has, it is said, the singular property of turning the hair a silvery white; and the great Fionn having once bathed therein, he emerged a withered old man, and was only restored to youth by means of strong spells and incantations.

In Cormac's Glossary there is an interesting account of how the first lapdog came into Ireland, for the men of Britain were under strict orders that no lapdog should be given to the Gael, either of solicitation or of free will, for gratitude or friendship.

Now it happened that Cairbré Musc went to visit a friend of his in Britain, who made him right welcome and offered him everything he possessed, save only his lapdog, for that was forbidden by the law. Yet this beautiful lapdog was the one only possession that Cairbré coveted, and he laid his plans cunningly to obtain it.

There was a law at that time in Britain to this effect: 'Every criminal shall be given as a forfeit for his crime to the person he has injured.'

Now Cairbré had a wonderful dagger, around the haft of which was an adornment of silver and gold. It was a precious jewel, and he took fat meat and rubbed it all over the haft, with much grease. Then he set it before the lapdog, who began to gnaw at the haft, and continued gnawing all night till the morning, so that the haft was spoiled and was no longer beautiful.

Then on the morrow, Cairbré made complaint that his beautiful dagger was destroyed, and he demanded a just recompense.

'That is indeed fair,' said his friend, 'I shall pay a price for the trespass.'

'I ask no other price,' said Cairbré, 'than what the law of Britain allows me, namely, the criminal for his crime.'

So the lapdog was given to Cairbré, and it was called ever after *Mug-Eimé*, the slave of the haft, which name clung to it because it passed into servitude as a forfeit for the trespass.

Now when Cairbré brought it back to Erin with him, all the kings of Ireland began to wrangle and contend for possession of the lapdog, and the contention at last ended in this wise – it was agreed that the dog should abide for a certain time in the house of each king. Afterwards the dog littered, and each of them had a pup of the litter, and from this stock descends every lapdog in Ireland from that time till now.

After a long while the lapdog died, and the bare skull being brought to the blind poet Maer to try his power of divination, he at once exclaimed, through the prophetic power and vision in him, 'O Mug-

Eimé! this is indeed the head of Mug-Eimé, the slave of the haft, that was brought into Ireland and given over to the fate of a bondsman, and to the punishment of servitude as a forfeit.'

The word hound entered into many combinations as a name for various animals. Thus the rabbit was called, 'the hound of the brake;' the hare was 'the brown hound;' the moth was called 'the hound of fur,' owing to the voracity with which it devoured raiment. And the otter is still called by the Irish *Madradh-Uisgue* (the dog of the water).

The names of most creatures of the animal kingdom were primitive, the result evidently of observation. Thus the hedgehog was named 'the ugly little fellow.' The ant was the 'slender one.' The trout, Breac, or 'the spotted,' from the skin. And the wren was called 'the Druid bird,' because if any one understood the chirrup, they would have a knowledge of coming events as foretold by the bird.

CONCERNING CATS

Cats have been familiar to the human household from all antiquity, but they were probably first domesticated in Egypt, where, so far back as two thousand years ago, a temple was dedicated to the goddess of cats – Bubastis Pasht – represented with a cat's head. The Greeks had this feline pet of the house from Egypt, and from Greece the cat race, such as we have it now, was disseminated over Europe. It was a familiar element in Greek household life, and if anything was broken, according to Aristophanes, the phrase went then as now, 'The cat did it.' But cats were never venerated in Greece with religious adoration as in Egypt, the only country that gave them Divine honour, and where, if a cat died, the whole family shaved off their eyebrows in token of mourning.

The Irish have always looked on cats as evil and mysteriously connected with some demoniacal influence. On entering a house the usual salutation is, 'God save all here, except the cat.' Even the cake on the griddle may be blessed, but no one says, 'God bless the cat.'

It is believed that the devil often assumes the form of these animals. The familiar of a witch is always a black cat; and it is supposed that black cats have powers and faculties quite different from all other of the feline tribe. They are endowed with reason, can understand conversations, and are quite able to talk if they considered it advisable and judicious to join in the conversation. Their temperament is exceedingly unamiable, they are artful, malignant, and skilled in deception, and people should be very cautious in caressing them, for they have the venomous heart and the evil eye, and are ever ready to do an injury. Yet the liver of a black cat has the singular power to excite love when properly administered. If ground to powder and infused into potion, the recipient is fated to love passionately the person who offers it and has worked the charm.

An instance of this is narrated as having happened not very long ago. A farmer's daughter, a pretty coquette, attracted the attention of the young squire of the place. But though he was willing to carry on a flirtation, the young gentleman had no idea of debasing his proud lineage by an alliance. Yet a marriage was exactly what the girl desired, and which she was determined to accomplish. So she and a friend, an accomplice, searched the village till they found a black cat, black as night, with only three white hairs on the breast. Him they seized, and having tied up the animal in a bag, they proceeded to throw him from one to the other over a low wall, till the poor beast was quite dead. Then at midnight they began their unholy work. The liver and heart were extracted in the name of the Evil One, and then boiled down until they became so dry that they could easily be reduced to a powder, which was kept for use when opportunity offered. This soon came; the young squire arrived one evening as usual, to pay a visit to the pretty Nora, and began to make love to the girl with the ordinary amount of audacity and hypocrisy. But Nora had other views, so she made the tea by her little fire in a black teapot, for this was indispensable, and induced her lover to stay and partake of it with her, along with a fresh griddle cake. Then cunningly she infused the powder into his cup and watched him as he drank the tea with feverish anxiety. The result was even beyond her hopes. A violent and ardent passion seemed suddenly to have seized the young man, and he not only made earnest love to the pretty Nora, but offered her his hand in marriage, vowing that he would kill himself if she refused to become his lawful bride. To avoid such a catastrophe, Nora gently yielded to his request, and from that evening they were engaged. Daily visits followed from the young squire, and each time that he came Nora took care to repeat the charm of the love powder, so that the love was kept at fever heat, and finally the wedding day was fixed.

The family of the young squire were, however, not quite contented, especially as rumours of witchcraft and devil's dealings were bruited about the neighbourhood. And on the very eve of the marriage, just as the young man was pouring forth his vows of eternal love to the bride expectant, the door was burst open, and a body of men entered, headed by the nearest relations of the squire, who proceeded at once to belabour the young bridegroom with hazel sticks in the most vigorous manner. In vain the bride tried to interpose. She only drew the blows on herself, and finally the young man was carried away half stunned, lifted into the carriage and driven straight home, where he was locked up in his own room, and not allowed to hold any communication with the bride elect.

The daily doses of the powder having thus ceased, he began to recover from the love madness, and finally the fever passed away. And he looked back with wonder and horror on the fatal step he had so nearly taken. Now he saw there was really witchcraft in it, which the power of the hazel twigs had completely broken. And the accomplice having confessed the sorcery practised on him by Nora and herself, he hated the girl henceforth as much as he had once loved her.

And after a little he went away on foreign travel, and remained abroad for three years. When he returned, he found that Nora had degenerated into a withered little witch-faced creature, who was shunned by every one, and jeered at for the failure of her wicked spells, which had all come to nothing, though she had the Evil One himself to aid her; for such is the fate of all who deal in sorcery and devil's magic, especially with the help of Satan's chief instrument of witchcraft – the black cat.

But there is a certain herb of more power even than the cat's liver to produce love. Though what this herb is, only the adept knows and can reveal. The influence it exercises lasts, it is said, for twenty-one years, and then ceases and cannot be renewed.

A gentleman, now living, once ate of this herb, which was given to him by his wife's serving-maid, and in consequence he was fated to love the girl for the specified time. Not being then able to endure his wife's presence, he sent her away from the house, and devoted himself exclusively to the servant. Nineteen years have now passed by, and the poor lady is still waiting patiently to the end of the twenty-one years, believing that the witch-spell will then cease, and that her husband's love will be hers once more. For already he has been inquiring after her and his children, and has been heard lamenting the madness that forced him to drive them from the house for the sake of the menial, who usurped his wife's place by means of some wicked sorcery which he had no power to resist.

THE KING OF THE CATS

A most important personage in feline history is the King of the Cats. He may be in your house a common looking fellow enough, with no distinguishing mark of exalted rank about him, so that it is very difficult to verify his genuine claims to royalty. Therefore the best way is to cut off a tiny little bit of his ear. If he is really the royal personage, he will immediately speak out and declare who he is; and perhaps, at the same time, tell you some very disagreeable truths about yourself, not at all pleasant to have discussed by the house cat.

A man once, in a fit of passion, cut off the head of the domestic pussy, and threw it on the fire. On which the head exclaimed, in a fierce voice, 'Go tell your wife that you have cut off the head of the King of the Cats; but wait! I shall come back and be avenged for this insult,' and the eyes of the cat glared at him horribly from the fire.

THE KING OF THE CATS

And so it happened; for that day year, while the master of the house was playing with a pet kitten, it suddenly flew at his throat and bit him so severely that he died soon after.

*

A story is current also, that one night an old woman was sitting up very late spinning, when a knocking came to the door.

'Who is there?' she asked. No answer; but still the knocking went on. 'Who is there?' she asked a second time. No answer; and the knocking continued. 'Who is there?' she asked the third time, in a very angry passion.

Then there came a small voice – 'Ah, Judy, agrah, let me in, for I am cold and hungry; open the door, Judy, agrah, and let me sit by the fire, for the night is cold out here. Judy, agrah, let me in, let me in!'

The heart of Judy was touched, for she thought it was some small child that had lost its way, and she rose up from her spinning, and went and opened the door – when in walked a large black cat with a white breast, and two white kittens after her.

They all made over to the fire and began to warm and dry themselves, purring all the time very loudly; but Judy said never a word, only went on spinning.

Then the black cat spoke at last – 'Judy, agrah, don't stay up so late again, for the fairies wanted to hold a council here tonight, and to have some supper, but you have prevented them; so they were very angry and determined to kill you, and only for myself and my two daughters here you would be dead by this time. So take my advice, don't interfere with the fairy hours again, for the night is theirs, and they hate to look on the face of a mortal when they are out for pleasure or business. So I ran on to tell you, and now give me a drink of milk, for I must be off.'

And after the milk was finished the cat stood up, and called her daughters to come away.

'Good-night, Judy, agrah,' she said. 'You have been very civil to me, and I'll not forget it to you. Good-night, good-night.'

With that the black cat and the two kittens whisked up the chimney; but Judy looking down saw something glittering on the hearth, and taking it up she found it was a piece of silver, more than she ever could make in a month by her spinning, and she was glad in her heart, and never again sat up so late to interfere with the fairy hours, but the black cat and her daughters came no more again to the house.

THE DEMON CAT

The cat of the foregoing legend had evidently charming manners, and was well intentioned; but there are other cats of evil and wicked ways, that are, in fact, demons or witches, who assume the cat-form, in order to get easy entrance to a house, and spy over everything.

There was a woman in Connemara, the wife of a fisherman, and as he always had very good luck, she had plenty of fish at all times stored away in the house ready for market. But to her great annoyance she found that a great cat used to come in at night and devour all the best and finest fish. So she kept a big stick by her and determined to watch.

One day, as she and a woman were spinning together, the house suddenly became quite dark; and the door was burst open as if by the blast of the tempest, when in walked a huge black cat, who went straight up to the fire, then turned round and growled at them.

'Why, surely this is the devil!' said a young girl, who was by, sorting the fish.

'I'll teach you how to call me names,' said the cat; and, jumping at her, he scratched her arm till the blood came. 'There now,' he said, 'you will be more civil another time when a gentleman comes to see you.' And with that he walked over to the door and shut it close to prevent any of them going out, for the poor young girl, while crying loudly from fright and pain, had made a desperate rush to get away.

THE DEMON CAT

Just then a man was going by, and hearing the cries he pushed open the door and tried to get in, but the cat stood on the threshold and would let no one pass. On this, the man attacked him with his stick, and gave him a sound blow; the cat, however, was more than his match in the fight, for it flew at him and tore his face and hands so badly that the man at last took to his heels and ran away as fast as he could.

'Now it's time for my dinner,' said the cat, going up to examine the fish that was laid out on the tables. I hope the fish is good to-day. Now don't disturb me, nor make a fuss; I can help myself.' With that he jumped up and began to devour all the best fish, while he growled at the woman.

'Away, out of this, you wicked beast!' she cried, giving it a blow with the tongs that would have broken its back, only it was a devil; 'out of this! No fish shall you have to-day.'

But the cat only grinned at her, and went on tearing and spoiling and devouring the fish, evidently not a bit the worse for the blow. On this, both the women attacked it with sticks, and struck hard blows enough to kill it, on which the cat glared at them, and spit fire; then making a leap, it tore their hands and arms till the blood came, and the frightened women rushed shrieking from the house.

But presently the mistress returned, carrying with her a bottle of holy water; and looking in, she saw the cat still devouring the fish, and not minding. So she crept over quietly and threw the holy water on it without a word. No sooner was this done than a dense black smoke filled the place, through which nothing was seen but the two red eyes of the cat, burning like coals of fire. Then the smoke gradually cleared away, and she saw the body of the creature burning slowly till it became shrivelled and black like a cinder, and finally disappeared. And from that time the fish remained untouched and safe from harm, for the power of the Evil One was broken, and the demon cat was seen no more.

Cats are very revengeful, and one should be very careful not to offend them. A lady was in the habit of feeding the cat from her own table at dinner, and no doubt giving it choice morsels; but one day there was a dinner party, and pussy was quite forgotten. So she sulked and plotted revenge; and that night, after the lady was in bed, the cat, who had hid herself in the room, sprang at the throat of her friend and mistress, and bit her so severely that in a week the lady died of virulent blood poisoning.

Yet it is singular that the blood of the black cat is esteemed of wonderful power when mixed with herbs, for charms; and also of great efficacy in potions for the cure of disease; but three drops of the blood are sufficient, and it is generally obtained by nipping off a small piece of the tail.

CAT NATURE

The observation of cats is very remarkable, and also their intense curiosity. They examine everything in a house, and in a short time know all about it as well as the owner. They are never deceived by stuffed birds, or any such weak human delusions. They fathom it all at one glance, and then turn away with apathetic indifference, as if saying, in cat language – 'We know all about it.'

A favourite cat in a gentleman's house was rather fond of nocturnal rambles and late hours, perhaps copying his master, but no matter what his engagements were the cat always returned regularly next morning precisely at nine o'clock, which was the breakfast hour, and rang the house bell at the hall door. This fact was stated to me on undoubted authority; and, in truth, there is nothing too wonderful to believe about the intellect of cats; no matter what strange things may be narrated of them, nothing should be held improbable or impossible to their intelligence.

But cats are decidedly malific; they are selfish, revengeful, treacherous, cunning, and generally dangerous. The evil spirit in them is easily aroused. It is an Irish superstition that if you are going a journey, and meet a cat, you should turn back. But the cat must meet you on the road, not simply be in the house; and it must look you full

CAT NATURE

in the face. Then cross yourself and turn hack; for a witch or a devil is in your path.

It is believed also that if a black cat is killed and a bean placed in the heart, and the animal afterwards buried, the beans that grow from that seed will confer extraordinary power; for if a man places one in his mouth, he will become invisible, and can go anywhere he likes without being seen.

Cats have truly something awful in them. According to the popular belief they know everything that is said, and can take various shapes through their demoniac power. A cat once lived in a farmer's family for many years, and understood both Irish and English perfectly. Then the family grew afraid of it, for they said it would certainly talk some day. So the farmer put it into a bag, determined to get rid of it on the mountains. But on the way he met a pack of hounds, and the dogs smelt at the bag and dragged it open, on which the cat jumped out; but the hounds were on it in a moment, and tore the poor animal to pieces. However, before her death she had time to say to the farmer in very good Irish – 'It is well for you that I must die today, for had I lived I meant to have killed you this very night.' These were the last dying words of the cat uttered in her death agonies, before the face of many credible witnesses, so there can be no doubt on the matter.

Cats were special objects of mysterious dread to the ancient Irish. They believed that many of them were men and women metamorphosed into cats by demoniacal power. Cats also were the guardians of hidden treasure, and had often great battles among themselves on account of the hidden gold; when a demon, in the shape of the chief cat, led on the opposing forces on each side, and compelled all the cats in the district to take part in the conflict.

The Druidical or royal cat, the chief monarch of all the cats in Ireland, was endowed with human speech and faculties, and possessed great and singular privileges. 'A slender black cat, wearing a chain of silver,' so it is described.

There is a legend that a beautiful princess, a king's daughter, having gone down to bathe one day, was there enchanted by her wicked stepmother, who hated her; and by the spell of the enchantment she was doomed to be one year a cat, another a swan, and another an otter; but with the privilege of assuming her natural shape one day in each year, under certain conditions. It is to be regretted that we have no account as to the mode in which the Princess Faithlean exercised her brief enjoyment of human rights; for the narration would have had a mystic and deep psychological interest if the fair young victim had only retained during all her transformations the memory of each of her successive incarnations as the cat, the swan, and the otter.

This abnormal mode of existence, however, was not unusual amongst the Irish. Fionn himself had a wife who for seven years was alive by day and dead by night; and the Irish Princess Zeba, being enchanted by her wicked stepfather, the king of Munster, died and came to life again each alternate year.

All nations seem to have appreciated the mysterious and almost human qualities of cat nature; the profound cunning, the impertinent indifference, the intense selfishness, yet capable of the most hypocritical flatteries when some point has to be gained. Their traits are not merely the product of brute instinct with unvarying action and results, but the manifestation of a calculating intellect, akin to the human. Then their grace and flexile beauty make them very attractive; while the motherly virtues of the matron cat are singularly interesting as a study of order, education, and training for the wilful little kitten, quite on the human lines of salutary discipline. Humboldt declared that he could spend a whole day with immense profit and advantage to himself as a philosopher, by merely watching a cat with her kittens, the profound wisdom of the mother and the incomparable grace of the children. For cats are thoroughly well-bred, born aristocrats; never abrupt, fussy, or obtrusive like the dog, but gentle, grave, and dignified in manner. Cats never run, they glide softly, and always with perfect and beautiful curves of motion; and they express their affection, not violently, like the dog, but with the most graceful, caressing movements of the head.

Their intellect also is very remarkable, they easily acquire the meaning of certain words, and have a singular and exact knowledge of hours.

Mr St George Mivart, in his interesting and exhaustive work on cats, has devoted a whole chapter to the psychology of the cat; in which he shows that the race possesses evident mental qualities and peculiar intelligence, with also a decided and significant language of sounds and gestures to express the emotions of the cat mind. The highly reflective and observant nature of the cat is also admirably described in that very clever novel called 'The Poison Tree,' recently translated from the Bengalee. There the house-cat is drawn with the most lifelike touches, as she sits watching the noble and beautiful lady at work on her embroidery, while her little child is playing beside her with all the pretty toys scattered over the carpet: 'The cat's disposition was grave: her face indicated much wisdom, and a heart devoid of fickleness. She evidently was thinking – "the condition of human creatures is frightful; their minds are ever given to sewing of canvas, playing with dolls, or some such silly employment; their thoughts are not turned to good works, such as providing suitable food for cats. What will become of them hereafter!" Then, seeing no means by which the disposition of mankind could be improved, the cat, heaving a sigh, slowly departs.'

SEANCHAN THE BARD AND THE KING OF THE CATS

There is an amusing legend preserved in Ossianic tradition of the encounter between Seanchan, the celebrated chief poet of Ireland, and the King of all the Cats, who dwelt in a cave near Clonmacnoise.

In ancient Ireland the men of learning were esteemed beyond all other classes; all the great ollaves and professors and poets held the very highest social position, and took precedence of the nobles, and ranked next to royalty. The leading men amongst them lived luxuriously in the great Bardic House; and when they went abroad through the country they travelled with a train of minor bards, fifty or more, and were entertained free of cost by the kings and chiefs, who considered themselves highly honoured by the presence of so distinguished a company at their court. If the receptions were splendid and costly, the praise of the entertainer was chanted by all the poets at the feast; but if any slight were offered, then the Ard-Filé poured forth his stinging satire in such bitter odes, that many declared they would sooner die than incur the anger of the poets or be made the subject of their scathing satire.

All the learned men and professors, the ollaves of music, poetry, oratory, and of the arts and sciences generally, formed a great Bardic Association, who elected their own president, with the title of Chief Poet of all Ireland, and they also elected chief poets for each of the provinces. Learned women, likewise, and poetesses, were included in the Bardic Association, with distinct and recognized privileges, both as to revenue and costly apparel. Legal enactments even were made respecting the number of colours allowed to be worn in their mantles – the poet being allowed six colours, and the poetess five in her robe and mantle; the number of colours being a distinct recognition and visible sign of rank, and therefore very highly esteemed. But, in time, as a consequence of their many and great privileges, the pride and insolence of the learned class, the ollamhs, poets, and poetesses, became so insufferable, that even the kings trembled before them.

This is shown in the Ossianic tale, from which we may gather that Seanchan the Bard, when entertained at the court of King Guaire, grew jealous of the attention paid to the nobles while he was present. So he sulked at the festival, and made himself eminently disagreeable, as will be seen by the following legend: –

When Seanchan, the renowned Bard, was made *Ard-Filé*, or Chief Poet of Ireland, Guaire, the king of Connaught, to do him honour, made a great feast for him and the whole Bardic Association. And all the professors went to the king's house, the great ollaves of poetry and history and music, and of the arts and sciences; and the learned,

SEANCHAN THE BARD AND THE KING OF THE CATS

aged females, Grug and Grag and Grangait; and all the chief poets and poetesses of Ireland, an amazing number. But Guaire the king entertained them all splendidly, so that the ancient pathway to his palace is still called 'The Road of the Dishes.'

And each day he asked, 'How fares it with my noble guests?' But they were all discontented, and wanted things he could not get for them. So he was very sorrowful, and prayed to God to be delivered from 'the learned men and women, a vexatious class.'

Still the feast went on for three days and three nights. And they drank and made merry. And the whole Bardic Association entertained the nobles with the choicest music and professional accomplishments.

But Seanchan sulked and would neither eat nor drink, for he was jealous of the nobles of Connaught. And when he saw how much they consumed of the best meats and wine, he declared he would taste no food till they and their servants were all sent away out of the house.

And when Guaire asked him again, 'How fares my noble guest, and this great and excellent people?' Seanchan answered, 'I have never had worse days, nor worse nights, nor worse dinners in my life.' And he ate nothing for three whole days.

Then the king was sorely grieved that the whole Bardic Association should be feasting and drinking while Seanchan, the chief poet of Erin, was fasting and weak. So he sent his favourite serving-man, a person of mild manners and cleanliness, to offer special dishes to the bard.

'Take them away,' said Seanchan; 'I'll have none of them.'

'And why, oh, Royal Bard?' asked the servitor.

'Because thou art an uncomely youth,' answered Seanchan. 'Thy grandfather was chip-nailed – I have seen him; I shall eat no food from thy hands.'

Then the king called a beautiful maiden to him, his foster daughter, and said, 'Lady, bring thou this wheaten cake and this dish of salmon to the illustrious poet, and serve him thyself.' So the maiden went.

But when Seanchan saw her he asked: 'Who sent thee hither, and why hast thou brought me food?'

'My lord the king sent me, oh, Royal Bard,' she answered, 'because

I am comely to look upon, and he bade me serve thee with food myself.'

'Take it away,' said Seanchan, 'thou art an unseemly girl, I know of none more ugly. I have seen thy grandmother; she sat on a wall one day and pointed out the way with her hand to some travelling lepers. How could I touch thy food?' So the maiden went away in sorrow.

And then Guaire the king was indeed angry, and he exclaimed. 'My malediction on the mouth that uttered that! May the kiss of a leper be on Seanchan's lips before he dies!'

Now there was a young serving-girl there, and she said to Seanchan, 'There is a hen's egg in the place, my lord, may I bring it to thee, oh, Chief Bard?'

'It will suffice,' said Seanchan; 'bring it that I may eat.'

But when she went to look for it, behold the egg was gone.

'Thou hast eaten it,' said the bard, in wrath.

'Not so, my lord,' she answered; 'but the mice, the nimble race, have carried it away.'

'Then I will satirize them in a poem,' said Seanchan; and forthwith he chanted so bitter a satire against them that ten mice fell dead at once in his presence.

''Tis well,' said Seanchan; 'but the cat is the one most to blame, for it was her duty to suppress the mice. Therefore I shall satirize the tribe of the cats, and their chief lord, Irusan, son of Arusan. For I know where he lives with his wife Spit-fire, and his daughter Sharp-tooth, with her brothers, the Purrer and the Growler. But I shall begin with Irusan himself, for he is king, and answerable for all the cats.'

And he said – 'Irusan, monster of claws, who strikes at the mouse, but lets it go; weakest of cats. The otter did well who bit off the tips of thy progenitor's ears, so that every cat since is jagged-eared. Let thy tail hang down; it is right, for the mouse jeers at thee.'

Now Irusan heard these words in his cave, and he said to his daughter, Sharp-tooth: 'Seanchan has satirized me, but I will be avenged.'

'Nay, father,' she said, 'bring him here alive, that we may all take our revenge.'

SEANCHAN THE BARD AND THE KING OF THE CATS

'I shall go then and bring him,' said Irusan; 'so send thy brothers after me.'

Now when it was told to Seanchan that the King of the Cats was on his way to come and kill him, he was timorous, and besought Guaire and all the nobles to stand by and protect him.

And before long a vibrating, impressive, impetuous sound was heard, like a raging tempest of fire in full blaze. And when the cat appeared he seemed to them of the size of a bullock; and this was his appearance – rapacious, panting, jagged-eared, snub-nosed, sharp-toothed, nimble, angry, vindictive, glare-eyed, terrible, sharp-clawed. Such was his similitude. But he passed on amongst them, not minding till he came to Seanchan; and him he seized by the arm and jerked him up on his back, and made off the way he came before any one could touch him; for he had no other object in view but to get hold of the poet.

Now Seanchan, being in evil plight, had recourse to flattery. 'Oh, Irusan,' he exclaimed, 'how truly splendid thou art, such running, such leaps, such strength, and such agility! But what evil have I done, oh, Irusan, son of Arusan? spare me, I entreat. I invoke the saints between thee and me, oh, great King of the Cats.'

But not a bit did the cat let go his hold for all this fine talk, but went straight on to Clonmacnoise where there was a forge; and St Kieran happened to be there standing at the door.

'What!' exclaimed the saint; 'is that the Chief Bard of Erin on the back of a cat? Has Guaire's hospitality ended in this?' And he ran for a red-hot bar of iron that was in the furnace, and struck the cat on the side with it, so that the iron passed through him, and he fell down lifeless.

'Now my curse on the hand that gave that blow!' said the bard, when he got upon his feet.

'And wherefore?' asked St Kieran.

'Because,' answered Seanchan, 'I would rather Irusan had killed me, and eaten me every bit, that so I might bring disgrace on Guaire for the bad food he gave me; for it was all owing to his wretched dinners that I got into this plight.'

And when all the other kings heard of Seanchan's misfortunes, they sent to beg he would visit their courts. But he would have neither kiss nor welcome from them, and went on his way to the bardic mansion, where the best of good living was always to be had. And ever after the kings were afraid to offend Seanchan.

So as long as he lived he had the chief place at the feast, and all the nobles there were made to sit below him, and Seanchan was content. And in time he and Guaire were reconciled; and Seanchan and all the ollamhs, and the whole Bardic Association, were feasted by the king for thirty days in noble style, and had the choicest of viands and the best of French wines to drink, served in goblets of silver. And in return for his splendid hospitality the Bardic Association decreed, unanimously, a vote of thanks to the king. And they praised him in poems as 'Guaire the Generous,' by which name he was ever after known in history, for the words of the poet are immortal.

THE BARDS

The Irish kings in ancient times kept up splendid hospitality at their respective courts, and never sat down to an entertainment, it was said, without a hundred nobles at least being present. Next in rank and superb living to the royal race came the learned men, the ollamhs and poets; they were placed next the king, and above the nobles at the festivals, and very gorgeous was the appearance of the Ard-Filé on these occasions, in his white robes clasped with golden brooches, and a circlet of gold upon his head; while by his side lay the golden harp, which he seized when the poetic frenzy came upon him, and swept the chords to songs of love, or in praise of immortal heroes. The queen alone had the privilege to ask the poet to recite at the royal banquets, and while he declaimed, no man dared to interrupt him by a single word.

A train of fifty minor bards always attended the chief poet, and they

THE BARDS

were all entertained free of cost wherever they visited, throughout Ireland, while the Ard-Filé was borne on men's shoulders to the palace of the king, and there presented with a rich robe, a chain, and a girdle of gold. Of one bard, it is recorded that the king gave him, in addition, his horse and armour, fifty rings to his hand, one thousand ounces of pure gold, and his chess-board.

The game of chess is frequently referred to in the old bardic tales; and chess seems to have been a favourite pastime with the Irish from the most remote antiquity. The pieces must have been of great size, for it is narrated that the great Cuchullen killed a messenger who had told him a lie, by merely flinging a chessman at him, which pierced his brain. The royal chess-board was very costly and richly decorated. One is described in a manuscript of the twelfth century: 'It was a board of silver and pure gold, and every angle was illuminated with precious stones. And there was a man-bag of woven brass wire.' But the ancestors of the same king had in their hall a chess-board with the pieces formed of the *bones of their hereditary enemies*.

The dress of the bards added to their splendour, for the Brehon laws enacted that the value of the robes of the chief poet should be five milch cows, and that of the poetess three cows; the queen's robes being of the value of seven cows, including a diadem and golden veil, and a robe of scarlet silk, embroidered in divers colours. The scions of the royal house had also the right to seven colours in their mantle; while the poet was allowed six, and the poetess five – the number of colours being a sign of dignity and rank.

Learning was always highly esteemed in Ireland, and in ancient Erin the *literati* ranked next to the kings.

The great and wise *Ollamh-Fodla*, king of Ireland in Druidic times, built and endowed a college at Tara, near the royal palace, which was called *Mur-Ollamh*, 'the Wall of the Learned.' All the arts and sciences were represented there by eminent professors, the great ollaves of music, history, poetry, and oratory; and they lived and feasted together, and formed the great Bardic Association, ruled over by their own president, styled the Ard-Filé, or chief poet of Ireland, from *Filidecht* (philosophy or the highest wisdom); for the poets, above all men, were required to be pure and free from all sin that could be a reproach to learning. From them was demanded –

> 'Purity of hand,
> Purity of mouth,
> Purity of learning,
> Purity of marriage;'

and any ollamh that did not preserve these four purities lost half his income and his dignity, the poet being esteemed not only the highest of all men for his learning and intellect, but also as being the true revealer of the supreme wisdom.

Music was sedulously taught and cultivated at the college of the ollamhs; for all the ancient life of Ireland moved to music.

The Brehons seated on a hill intoned the laws to the listening people; the Senachies chanted the genealogies of the kings; and the Poets recited the deeds of the heroes, or sang to their gold harps those exquisite airs that still enchant the world, and which have been wafted down along the centuries, an echo, according to tradition, of the soft, pathetic, fairy music, that haunted the hills and glens of ancient Ireland.

The chief poet was required to know by heart four hundred poems, and the minor bards two hundred. And they were bound to recite any poem called for by the kings at the festivals. On one occasion a recitation was demanded of the legend of the *Taine-bo-Cuailne* or The Great Cattle Raid, of which Maeve, queen of Connaught, was the heroine, but none of the bards knew it. This was felt to be a great disgrace, and Seanchan and the bards set forth to traverse Ireland in search of the story of the Taine, under *Geasa*, or a solemn oath, not to sleep twice in the same place till it was found.

At length it was revealed to them that only the dead Fergus-Roy knew the poem, and forthwith they proceeded to his grave, and fasted and prayed for three days, while they invoked him to appear. And on their invocation Fergus-Roy uprose in awful majesty, and stood in his

THE BARDS

grave clothes before them, and recited the Taine from beginning to end to the circle of listening bards. Then, having finished, he descended again into the grave, and the earth closed over him.

During this expedition, Guaire the Generous took charge of all the wives and the poetesses of the Bardic Association, so as they should not trouble the bards while on their wanderings in search of the ballad of the Taine. Yet they do not seem to have been great feeders, these learned ladies; for it is related of one of them, Brigit the poetess, that although she only ate one hen's egg at a meal, yet she was called 'Brigit of the great appetite.'

It was on their return from the search for the Taine that the bards decreed a vote of thanks to Guaire the king.

In order to keep up the dignity of the great bardic clan, an income was paid by the State to each of the professors and poets according to his eminence; that of the chief poet being estimated by antiquarians at about five thousand a year of our money, for the lofty and learned Bardic Association disdained commerce and toil. The Fileas lived only on inspiration and the hospitality of their royal and noble patrons, which they amply repaid by laudatory odes and sonnets. But, if due homage were denied them, they denounced the ungenerous and niggard defaulter in the most scathing and bitter satires. Of one chief it is recorded that he absolutely went mad and died in consequence of the malignant poems that were made on him by a clever satirical bard.

At last the Brehons found it necessary to take cognizance of this cruel and terrible implement of social torture, and enactments were framed against it, with strict regulations regarding the quality and justice of the satires poured out by the poets on those who had the courage to resist their exactions and resent their insolence. Finally, however, the ollamhs, poets, and poetesses became so intolerable that the reigning king of Ireland about the seventh century made a great effort to extirpate the whole bardic race, but failed; they were too strong for him, though he succeeded in, at least, materially abridging their privileges, lessening their revenues, and reducing their numbers; and though they still continued to exist as the Bardic Association, yet they never afterwards regained the power and dignity which they once held in the land, before their pride and insolent contempt of all classes who were not numbered amongst the ollamhs and fileas, had aroused such violent animosity. The Brehon laws also decreed, as to the distraint of a poet, that his horsewhip be taken from him, 'as a warning that he is not to make use of it until he renders justice.' Perhaps by the horsewhip was meant the wand or staff which the poets carried, made of wood, on which it is conjectured they may have inscribed their verses in the Ogham character.

The Brehons seem to have made the most minute regulations as to the life of the people, even concerning the domestic cats. In the *Senchas Mor* (The Great Antiquity) it is enacted that the cat is exempt from liability for eating the food which he finds in the kitchen, 'owing to negligence in taking care of it.' But if it were taken from the security of a vessel, then the cat is in fault, and he may safely be killed. The cat, also, is exempt from liability for injuring an idler in catching mice while mousing; but *half-fines* are due from him for the profitable worker he may injure, and the excitement of his mousing takes the other half. For the distraint of a dog, a stick was placed over his trough in order that he be not fed. And there was a distress of two days for a black and white cat if descended from the great champion, which was taken from the ship of Breasal Breac, in which were white-breasted black cats; the same for the lapdog of a queen.

KING ARTHUR AND THE CAT

While on the subject of cats, the curious and interesting legend of 'King Arthur's Fight with the Great Cat' should not be passed over; for though not exactly Irish, yet it is at least Celtic, and belongs by affinity to our ancient race. It is taken from a prose romance of the fifteenth century, entitled, 'Merlin; or The Early Life of King Arthur,' recently edited, from the unique Cambridge Manuscript, by Mr Wheatly.

KING ARTHUR AND THE CAT

Merlin told the king that the people beyond the Lake of Lausanne greatly desired his help, 'for there repaireth a devil that destroyeth the country. It is a cat so great and ugly that it is horrible to look on.' For one time a fisher came to the lake with his nets, and he promised to give our Lord the first fish he took. It was a fish worth thirty shillings; and when he saw it so fair and great, he said to himself softly, 'God shall not have this; but I will surely give Him the next.' Now, the next was still better, and he said, 'Our Lord may wait yet awhile; but the third shall be His without doubt.' So he cast his net, but drew out only a little kitten, as black as any coal.

And when the fisher saw it he said he had need of it at home for rats and mice; and he nourished it and kept it in his house till it strangled him and his wife and children. Then the cat fled to a high mountain and destroyed and slew all that came in his way, and was great and terrible to behold.

When the king heard this he made ready and rode to the Lac de Lausanne and found the country desolate and void of people, for neither man nor woman would inhabit the place for fear of the cat.

And the king was lodged a mile from the mountain, with Sir Gawvain and Merlin and others. And they clomb the mountain, Merlin leading the way. And when they were come up, Merlin said to the king, 'Sir, in that rock liveth the cat;' and he showed him a great cave, large and deep, in the mountain.

'And how shall the cat come out?' said the king.

'That shall ye see hastily,' quoth Merlin; 'but look you, be ready to defend, for anon he will assail you.'

'Then draw ye all back,' said the king, 'for I will prove his power.'

And when they withdrew, Merlin whistled loud, and the cat leaped out of the cave, thinking it was some wild beast, for he was hungry and fasting; and he ran boldly to the king, who was ready with his spear, and thought to smite him through the body. But the fiend seized the spear in his mouth and broke it in twain.

Then the king drew his sword, holding his shield also before him. And as the cat leaped at his throat, he struck him so fiercely that the creature fell to the ground; but soon was up again, and ran at the king so hard that his claws gripped through the hauberk to the flesh, and the red blood followed the claws.

Now the king was nigh falling to earth; but when he saw the red blood he was wonder-wrath, and with his sword in his right hand and his shield at his breast, he ran at the cat vigorously, who sat licking his claws, all wet with blood. But when he saw the king coming towards him, he leapt up to seize him by the throat, as before, and stuck his fore-feet so firmly in the shield that they stayed there; and the king smote him on the legs, so that he cut them off to the knees, and the cat fell to the ground.

Then the king ran at him with his sword; but the cat stood on his hind-legs and grinned with his teeth, and coveted the throat of the king, and the king tried to smite him on the head; but the cat strained his hinder feet and leaped at the king's breast, and fixed his teeth in the flesh, so that the blood streamed down from breast and shoulder.

Then the king struck him fiercely on the body, and the cat fell head downwards, but the feet stayed fixed in the hauberk. And the king smote them asunder, on which the cat fell to the ground, where she howled and brayed so loudly that it was heard through all the host, and she began to creep towards the cave; but the king stood between her and the cave, and when she tried to catch him with her teeth he struck her dead.

Then Merlin and the others ran to him and asked how it was with him.

'Well, blessed be our Lord!' said the king, 'for I have slain this devil; but, verily, I never had such doubt of myself, not even when I slew the giant on the mountain; therefore I thank the Lord.'

(This was the great giant of St Michael's Mount, who supped all the season on seven knave children chopped in a charger of white silver, with powder of precious spices, and goblets full plenteous of Portugal wine.)

'Sir,' said the barons, 'ye have great cause for thankfulness.' Then they looked on the feet that were left in the shield and in the hauberk, and said, 'Such feet were never seen before!' And they took the shield and showed it to the host with great joy.

So the king let the shield be with the cat's feet; but the other feet he had laid in a coffin to be kept. And the mountain was called from that day, 'The Mountain of the Cat,' and the name will never be changed while the world endureth.

CONCERNING COWS

The most singular legends of Ireland relate to bulls and cows, and there are hundreds of places all commencing with the word *Bo* (one of the most ancient words in the Irish language), which recall some mystic or mythical story of a cow, especially of a white heifer, which animal seems to have been an object of the greatest veneration from all antiquity.

In old times there arose one day a maiden from the sea, a beautiful Berooch, or mermaid, and all the people on the Western Coast of Erin gathered round her and wondered at her beauty. And the great chief of the land carried her home to his house, where she was treated like a queen.

And she was very gentle and wise, and after some time she acquired the language, and could talk to the people quite well in their own Irish tongue, to their great delight and wonder. Then she informed them that she had been sent to their country by a great spirit, to announce the arrival in Ireland of the three sacred cows – *Bo-Finn, Bo-Ruadh* and *Bo-Dhu* – the white, the red, and the black cows, who were destined to fill the land with the most splendid cattle, so that the people should never know want while the world lasted.

This was such good news that the people in their delight carried the sea-maiden from house to house in procession, in order that she might tell it herself to every one; and they crowned her with flowers, while the musicians went before her, singing to their harps.

After dwelling with them a little longer she asked to be taken back to the sea, for she had grown sad at being away so long from her own kindred. So, on May Eve, a great crowd accompanied her down to the strand, where she took leave of them, telling them that on that day year they should all assemble at the same place to await the arrival of the three cows. Then she plunged into the sea and was seen no more.

However, on that day year all the people of Ireland assembled on the shore to watch, as they had been directed by the beautiful sea-maiden; and all the high cliffs and all the rocks were covered with anxious spectators from the early dawn. Nor did they wait in vain. Exactly at noon the waves were stirred with a mighty commotion, and three cows rose up from the sea – a white, a red, and a black – all beautiful to behold, with sleek skins, large soft eyes, and curved horns, white as ivory. They stood upon the shore for a while, looking around them. Then each one went in a different direction, by three roads; the black went south, the red went north, and the milk-white heifer – the *Bo-Finn* – crossed the plain of Ireland to the very centre, where stood the king's palace. And every place she passed was named after her, and every well she drank at was called *Lough-na-Bo*, or *Tober-Bo-Finn* (the well of the white cow), so her memory remains to this day.

In process of time the white heifer gave birth to twins, a male and female calf, and from them descended a great race, still existing in Ireland; after which the white cow disappeared into a great cave by the sea, the entrance to which no man knows. And there she remains, and will remain, in an enchanted sleep, until the true king of Eire, the lord of Ireland, shall come to waken her; but the lake near the cave is still known as *Lough-na-Bo-banna* (the lake of the snow-white cow). Yet some say that it was the king's daughter was carried off by enchantment to the cave, in the form of a cow, and she will never regain her form until she sleeps on the summit of each of the three highest mountains in Ireland; but only the true king of Eire can wake her from her sleep, and bring her to 'the rock of the high place,' when she will be restored at last to her own beautiful form.

Another legend says that a red-haired woman struck the beautiful

Bo-Finn with her staff, and smote her to death; and the roar which the white cow gave in dying was heard throughout the whole of Ireland, and all the people trembled. This is evidently an allegory. The beautiful *Bo-Finn* – the white cow – is Ireland herself; and the red-haired woman who smote her to death was Queen Elizabeth, 'in whose time, after her cruel wars, the cry of the slaughtered people was heard all over the land, and went up to heaven for vengeance against the enemies of Ireland; and the kingdom was shaken as by an earthquake, by the roar of the oppressed against the tyrant.'

The path of the white cow across Ireland is marked by small rude stone monuments, still existing. They show the exact spot where she rested each night and had her bed, and the adjoining lands have names connected with the tradition – as, 'The plain of the Fenian cows;' 'The hill of worship;' 'The pool of the spotted ox,' called after him because he always waited to drink till the white cow came, for they were much attached to each other.

There are also Druid stones at one resting-place, with Ogham marks on them. Some time ago an endeavour was made to remove and carry off the stones of one of the monuments; but the man who first put a spade in the ground was 'struck,' and remained bedridden for seven years.

The plain of the death of the *Bo-banna* (the white cow), where she gave the roar that shook all Ireland is called 'the plain of lamentation.' It never was tilled, and never will be tilled. The people hold it as a sacred spot, and until recently it was the custom to have dances there every Sunday. But these old usages are rapidly dying out; for though meant originally as mystic ceremonies, yet by degrees they degenerated to such licentious revelry that the wrath of the priesthood fell on them, and they were discontinued.

There is a holy well near 'the plain of lamentation,' called *Tobar-na-Bo* (the well of the white cow); and these ancient names, coming down the stream of time from the far-off Pagan era, attest the great antiquity of the legend of the coming to Ireland of the mystic and beautiful *Bo-Finn*.

There is another legend concerning the arrival of the three cows – the white, the red, and the black – which is said to be taken from the Book of Enoch.

Four cows sprang at once from the earth – two white, a red, and a black – and one of the four went over to the white cow and taught it a mystery. And it trembled and became a man, and this was the first man that appeared in Erin. And the man fashioned a ship and dwelt there with the cows while a deluge covered the earth. And when the waters ceased, the red and the black cows went their way, but the white remained.

The story is supposed by Bryant to be a literal rendering of some ancient hieroglyph, descriptive of the three races of mankind, and of the dispersion of the primal human family.

FAIRY WILES

The fairies are very desirous to abduct handsome cows and carry them off to the fairy palace under the earth; and if a farmer happens to find one of his stock ailing or diseased, the belief is that the fairies have carried off the real good animal, and sent an old wizened witch to take the form of the farmer's cow.

It is therefore to neutralize the fairy spells that the cattle are driven through the fire on St John's Eve; and other devices are employed – a bunch of primroses is very effective tied on the tail, or a hot coal run down the cow's back to singe the hair.

One evening a boy was driving home his father's cows when a fairy blast arose in the form of a whirlwind of dust, on which the cows took fright, and one of them ran upon a fairy rath. The boy followed to turn her back, when he was met and stopped by an old witch-woman.

'Let her alone, Alanna,' she cried, 'she is on our ground now, and you can't take her away. So just run home and tell your father that on this day twelvemonth the cow will be restored to him, and bring a fine young calf along with her. But the fairies want her badly now, for our beautiful queen down there is fretting her life out for want of some milk that has the scent of the green grass in it and of the fresh upper air. Now don't fret, Alanna, but trust my words. There, take yon hazel stick and strike the cow boldly three times on the head, that so the way may be clear we have to travel.'

With that the boy struck the animal as he was desired, for the old witch-woman was so nice and civil that he liked to oblige her, and immediately after she and the cow vanished away as if they had sunk into the earth.

However, the father minded the time, and when that day year came round he sent his son to the fairy rath to see if the witch had kept her promise, and there truly was the cow standing quite patiently, and a fine white calf by her side. So there were great rejoicings when he brought them home, for the fairies had kept their promise and behaved honourably, as indeed they always do when properly treated and trusted.

Not but that the fairies will do wicked things sometimes, and, above all, steal the milk when they get a chance, or skim the cream off the milk crocks.

A farmer had a fine cow that was the pride of his farm and gave splendid milk, but suddenly the animal seemed ailing and queer; for she gave no milk, but went every morning and stood under the old hawthorn-tree quite quietly as if some one were milking her.

So the man watched the place at milking time, and as usual down the field came the cow and took up her position close under the old hawthorn. Then the farmer beheld the trunk of the tree open, and out of the cleft came a little witch-woman all in red, who milked the cow in a vessel she had with her, and then she retreated into the tree again.

Here was devil's work in earnest, so thought the farmer, and he hastened off for the greatest fairy doctor in the country. And when he came the cow was singed all along its back with a live coal; and then an incantation was said over it, but no one heard the words the fairy doctor uttered; after this he gave the animal a strong potion to drink, but no one knew the herbs of which it was made. However, the next day the cow was quite restored, and gave her milk as heretofore, and the spell was broken for ever and ever, after they had drawn a circle round the old hawthorn-tree with a red-hot piece of iron taken from the hearth; for neither witch nor fairy can pass a circle of fire.

THE DEAD HAND

Witchcraft is sometimes practised by the people to produce butter in the churn, the most efficacious being to stir the milk round with the hand of a dead man, newly taken from the churchyard; but whoever is suspected of this practice is looked upon with great horror and dread by the neighbours.

A woman of the mainland got married to a fine young fellow of one of the islands. She was a tall, dark woman who seldom spoke, and kept herself very close and reserved from every one. But she minded her business; for she had always more butter to bring to market than any one else, and could therefore undersell the other farmers' wives. Then strange rumours got about concerning her, and the people began to whisper among themselves that something was wrong, and that there was witchcraft in it, especially as it was known that whenever she churned she went into an inner room off the kitchen, shut the door close, and would allow no one to enter. So they determined to watch and find out the secret, and one day a girl from the neighbourhood, when the woman was out, got in through a window and hid herself under the bed, waiting there patiently till the churning began.

At last in came the woman, and having carefully closed the door began her work with the milk, churning in the usual way without any strange doings that might seem to have magic in them. But presently she stopped, and going over to a box unlocked it, and from this receptacle, to the girl's horror, she drew forth the hand of a dead man, with which she stirred the milk round and round several times, going down on her knees and muttering an incantation all the while.

Seven times she stirred the milk with the dead hand, and seven times she went round the churn on her knees muttering some strange charm. After this she rose up and began to gather the butter from the churn with the dead hand, filling a pail with as much butter as the milk of ten cows. When the pail was quite full she dipped the dead hand three times in the milk, then dried it and put it back again in the box.

The girl, as soon as she could get away unperceived, fled in horror from the room, and spread the news amongst the people.

At once a crowd gathered round the house with angry cries and threats to break open the door to search for the dead hand.

At last the woman appeared calm and cold as usual, and told them they were taking a deal of trouble about nothing, for there was no dead hand in the house. However, the people rushed in and searched, but all they saw was a huge fire on the hearth, though the smell of burning flesh was distinctly perceptible, and by this they knew that she had burnt the dead hand. Yet this did not save her from the vengeance of the neighbours. She was shunned by every one; no one would eat with her, or drink with her, or talk to her, and after a while she and her husband quitted the island and were never more heard of.

However, after she left and the butter was brought to the market, all the people had their fair and equal rights again, of which the wicked witchcraft of the woman had defrauded them for so long, and there was great rejoicing in the island over the fall and punishment of the wicked witch of the dead hand.

THE WICKED WIDOW

The evil spells over milk and butter are generally practised by women, and arise from some feeling of malice or envy against a prosperous neighbour. But the spell will not work unless some portion of the milk is first given by consent. The people therefore are very reluctant to give away milk, unless to some friend that they could not suspect of evil. Tramps coming in to beg for a mug of milk should always be avoided, they may be witches in disguise; and even if milk is given, it must be drunk in the house, and not carried away out of it. In every case the person who enters must give a hand to the churn, and say, 'God bless all here.'

A young farmer, one of the fine handsome fellows of the West, named Hugh Connor, who was also well off and rich, took to wife a pretty young girl of the village called Mary, one of the Leydons, and there was no better girl in all the country round, and they were very comfortable and happy together. But Hugh Connor had been keeping company before his marriage with a young widow of the place, who had designs on him, and was filled with rage when Mary Leydon was selected for Connor's bride, in place of herself. Then a desire for vengeance rose up in her heart, and she laid her plans accordingly. First she got a fairy woman to teach her some witch secrets and spells, and then by great pretence of love and affection for Mary Connor, she got frequent admission to the house, soothing and flattering the young wife; and on churning days she would especially make it a point to come in and offer a helping hand, and if the cakes were on the griddle, she would sit down to watch and turn them. But it so happened that always on these days the cakes were sure to be burned and spoiled, and the butter would not rise in the churn, or if any did come, it was sour and bad, and of no use for the market. But still the widow kept on visiting, and soothing, and flattering, till Mary Connor thought she was the very best friend to her in the whole wide world, though it was true that whenever the widow came to the house something evil happened. The best dish fell down of itself off the dresser and broke; or the rain got in through the roof, and Mary's new cashmere gown, a present that had come to her all the way from Dublin, was quite ruined and spoiled. But worse came, for the cow sickened, and a fine young brood of turkeys walked straight into the lake and got drowned. And still worst of all, the picture of the Blessed Virgin Mother, that was pinned up to the wall, fell down one day, and was blown into the fire and burned.

After this, what luck could be on the house? and Mary's heart sank within her, and she fairly broke down, and cried her very life out in a torrent of tears.

Now it so happened that an old woman with a blue cloak, and the hood of it over her head, a stranger, was passing by at the time, and she stepped in and asked Mary kindly what ailed her. So Mary told her all her misfortunes, and how everything in the house seemed bewitched for evil.

'Now,' said the stranger, 'I see it all, for I am wise, and know the mysteries. Some one with the Evil Eye comes to your house. We must find out who it is.'

Then Mary told her that the nearest friend she had was the widow, but she was so sweet and kind, no one could suspect her of harm.

'We'll see,' said the stranger, 'only do as I bid you, and have everything ready when she comes.'

'She will be here soon,' said Mary, 'for it is churning day, and she always comes to help exactly at noon.'

'Then I'll begin at once; and now close the door fast,' said the stranger.

And with that she threw some herbs on the fire, so that a great smoke arose. Then she took all the plough irons that were about, and one of them she drove into the ground close beside the churn, and put a live coal beside it; and the other irons she heated red-hot in the fire, and still threw on more herbs to make a thick smoke, which Mary thought smelt like the incense in the church. Then with a hot iron rod from the fire, the strange woman made the sign of the cross on the threshold, and another over the hearth. After which a loud roaring was heard outside, and the widow rushed in crying out that a hot stick was running through her heart, and all her body was on fire. And then she dropped down on the floor in a fit, and her face became quite black, and her limbs worked in convulsions.

'Now,' said the stranger, 'you see who it is put the Evil Eye on all your house; but the spell has been broken at last. Send for the men to carry her back to her own house, and never let that witch-woman cross your threshold again.'

After this the stranger disappeared, and was seen no more in the village.

Now when all the neighbours heard the story, they would have no dealings with the widow. She was shunned and hated; and no respectable person would be seen talking to her, and she went by the name of the Evil Witch. So her life was very miserable, and not long after she died of sheer vexation and spite, all by herself alone, for no one would go near her; and the night of the wake no one went to offer a prayer, for they said the devil would be there in person to look after his own. And no one would walk with her coffin to the grave, for they said the devil was waiting at the churchyard gate for her; and they firmly believe to this day that her body was carried away on that night from the graveyard by the powers of darkness. But no one ventured to test the truth of the story by opening the coffin, so the weird legend remains still unsolved.

But as for Hugh Connor and the pretty Mary, they prospered after that in all things, and good luck and the blessing of God seemed to be evermore on them and their house, and their cattle, and their children. At the same time, Mary never omitted on churning days to put a red-hot horse-shoe under the churn according as the stranger had told her, who she firmly believed was a good fairy in disguise, who came to help her in the time of her sore trouble and anxiety.

THE BUTTER MYSTERY

There were two brothers who had a small farm and dairy between them, and they were honest and industrious, and worked hard to get along, though they had barely enough, after all their labour, just to keep body and soul together.

THE BUTTER MYSTERY

One day while churning, the handle of the dash broke, and nothing being near to mend it, one of the brothers cut off a branch from an elder-tree that grew close to the house, and tied it to the dash for a handle. Then the churning went on, but to their surprise, the butter gathered so thick that all the crocks in the house were soon full, and still there was more left. The same thing went on every churning day, so the brothers became rich, for they could fill the market with their butter, and still had more than enough for every buyer.

At last, being honest and true men, they began to fear that there was witchcraft in it, and that they were wronging their neighbours by abstracting their butter, and bringing it to their own churn in some strange way. So they both went off together to a great fairy doctor, and told him the whole story, and asked his advice.

'Foolish men,' he said to them, 'why did you come to me? For now you have broken the spell, and you will never have your crocks filled with butter any more. Your good fortune has passed away, for know the truth now. You were not wronging your neighbours; all was fair and just that you did, but this is how it happened. Long ago, the fairies passing through your land had a dispute and fought a battle, and having no arms, they flung lumps of butter at each other, which got lodged in the branches of the elder-tree in great quantities, for it was just after May Eve, when butter is plenty. This is the butter you have had, for the elder-tree has a sacred power which preserved it until now, and it came down to you through the branch you cut for a handle to the dash. But the spell is broken now that you have uttered the mystery, and you will have no more butter from the elder-tree.'

Then the brothers went away sorrowful, and never after did the butter come beyond the usual quantity. However, they had already made so much money that they were content. And they stocked their farm, and all things prospered with them, for they had dealt uprightly in the matter, and the blessing of the Lord was on them.

CONCERNING BIRDS

In all countries superstitions of good or evil are attached to certain birds. The raven, for instance, has a wide-world reputation as the harbinger of evil and ill-luck. The wild geese portend a severe winter; the robin is held sacred, for no one would think of harming a bird who bears on his breast the blessed mark of the blood of Christ; while the wren is hunted to death with intense and cruel hate on St Stephen's Day.

THE MAGPIE

There is no Irish name for the Magpie. It is generally called *Francagh*, a Frenchman, though no one knows why. Many queer tales are narrated of this bird, arising from its quaint ways, its adroit cunning and habits of petty larceny. Its influence is not considered evil, though to meet one alone in the morning when going a journey is an ill omen, but to meet more than one magpie betokens good fortune, according to the old rhyme which runs thus–

> 'One for Sorrow,
> Two for Mirth,
> Three for Marriage,
> Four for a Birth.'

THE WREN

The wren is mortally hated by the Irish; for on one occasion, when the Irish troops were approaching to attack a portion of Cromwell's army, the wrens came and perched on the Irish drums, and by their tapping and noise aroused the English soldiers, who fell on the Irish troops and killed them all. So ever since the Irish hunt the wren on St Stephen's Day, and teach their children to run it through with thorns and kill it whenever it can be caught. A dead wren was also tied to a pole and carried from house to house by boys, who demanded money; if nothing was given the wren was buried on the door-step, which was considered a great insult to the family and a degradation.

THE RAVEN AND WATER WAGTAIL

If ravens come cawing about a house it is a sure sign of death, for the raven is Satan's own bird; so also is the water wagtail, yet beware of killing it, for it has three drops of the devil's blood in its little body, and ill-luck ever goes with it, and follows it.

THE CUCKOO AND ROBIN REDBREAST

It is very unlucky to kill the cuckoo or break its eggs, for it brings fine weather; but most unlucky of all things is to kill the robin redbreast. The robin is God's own bird, sacred and holy, and held in the greatest veneration because of the beautiful tradition current amongst the people, that it was the robin plucked out the sharpest thorn that was piercing Christ's brow on the cross; and in so doing the breast of the bird was dyed red with the Saviour's blood, and so has remained ever since a sacred and blessed sign to preserve the robin from harm and make it beloved of all men.

CONCERNING LIVING CREATURES

THE CRICKET

The crickets are believed to be enchanted. People do not like to express an exact opinion about them, so they are spoken of with great mystery and awe, and no one would venture to kill them for the whole world. But they are by no means evil; on the contrary, the presence of the cricket is considered lucky, and their singing keeps away the fairies at night, who are always anxious, in their selfish way, to have the whole hearth left clear for themselves, that they may sit round the last embers of the fire, and drink the cup of milk left for them by the farmer's wife, in peace and quietness. The crickets are supposed to be hundreds of years old, and their talk, could we understand it, would no doubt be most interesting and instructive.

THE BEETLE

The beetle is not killed by the people for the following reason: they have a tradition that one day the chief priests sent messengers in every direction to look for the Lord Jesus, and they came to a field where a man was reaping, and asked him –

'Did Jesus of Nazareth pass this way?'

'No,' said the man, 'I have not seen him.'

'But I know better,' said a little clock running up, 'for He was here to-day and rested, and has not long gone away.'

'That is false,' said a great big black beetle, coming forward; 'He has not passed since yesterday, and you will never find Him on this road; try another.'

So the people kill the clock because he tried to betray Christ; but they spare the beetle and will not touch him, because he saved the Lord on that day.

THE HARE

Hares are considered unlucky, as the witches constantly assume their form in order to gain entrance to a field where they can bewitch the cattle. A man once fired at a hare he met in the early morning, and having wounded it, followed the track of the blood till it disappeared within a cabin. On entering he found Nancy Molony, the greatest witch in all the county, sitting by the fire, groaning and holding her side. And then the man knew that she had been out in the form of a hare, and he rejoiced over her discomfiture.

Still it is not lucky to kill a hare before sunrise, even when it crosses your path; but should it cross three times, then turn back, for danger is on the road before you.

A tailor one time returning home very late at night from a wake, or better, very early in the morning, saw a hare sitting on the path before him, and not inclined to run away. As he approached, with his stick raised to strike her, he distinctly heard a voice saying, 'Don't kill it.' However, he struck the hare three times, and each time heard the voice say, 'Don't kill it.' But the last blow knocked the poor hare quite dead; and immediately a great big weasel sat up, and began to spit at him. This greatly frightened the tailor who, however, grabbed the hare, and ran off as fast as he could. Seeing him look so pale and frightened, his wife asked the cause, on which he told her the whole story; and they both knew he had done wrong, and offended some powerful witch, who would be avenged. However, they dug a grave for the hare and buried it; for they were afraid to eat it, and thought that now perhaps the danger was over. But next day the man became suddenly speechless, and died off before the seventh day was over, without a word evermore passing his lips; and then all the neighbours knew that the witch-woman had taken her revenge.

THE WEASEL

Weasels are spiteful and malignant, and old withered witches sometimes take this form. It is extremely unlucky to meet a weasel the first thing in the morning; still it would be hazardous to kill it, for it might be a witch and take revenge. Indeed one should be very cautious about killing a weasel at any time, for all the other weasels will resent your audacity, and kill your chickens when an opportunity offers. The only remedy is to kill one chicken yourself, make the sign of the cross solemnly three times over it, then tie it to a stick hung up in the yard, and the weasels will have no more power for evil, nor the witches who take their form, at least during the year, if the stick is left standing; but the chicken may be eaten when the sun goes down.

A goose is killed on St Michael's Day because the son of a king, being then at a feast, was choked by the bone of a goose; but was restored by St Patrick. Hence the king ordered a goose to be sacrificed every year on the anniversary of the day to commemorate the event, and in honour of St Michael.

A fowl is killed on St Martin's Day, and the blood sprinkled on the house. In Germany a black cock is substituted.

A crowing hen, a whistling girl, and a black cat, are considered most unlucky. Beware of them in a house.

If a cock comes on the threshold and crows, you may expect visitors.

To see three magpies on the left hand when on a journey is unlucky; but two on the right hand is a good omen.

If you hear the cuckoo on your right hand you will have luck all the year after.

Whoever kills a robin redbreast will never have good luck were they to live a thousand years.

A water wagtail near the house betokens bad news on its way to you.

If the first lamb of the season is born black, it foretells mourning garments for the family within the year.

It is very lucky for a hen and her chickens to stray into your house. Also it is good to meet a white lamb in the early morning with the sunlight on its face.

It is unlucky to meet a magpie, a cat, or a lame woman when going a journey. Or for a cock to meet a person in the doorway and crow before him – then the journey should be put off.

If one magpie comes chattering to your door it is a sign of death; but if two prosperity will follow. For a magpie to come to the door and look at you is a sure death-sign, and nothing can avert the doom.

A flight of rooks over an army betokens defeat; if over a house, or over people when driving or walking, death will follow.

It is very unlucky to ask a man on his way to fish where he is going. And many would turn back, knowing that it was an evil spell.

When a swarm of bees suddenly quits the hive it is a sign that death is hovering near the house. But the evil may be averted by the powerful prayers and exorcism of the priest

The shoe of a horse or of an ass nailed to the door-post will bring good luck; because these animals were in the stall when Christ was born, and are blessed for evermore. But the shoe must be found, not given, in order to bring luck.

In whatever quarter you are looking when you first hear the cuckoo in the season, you will be travelling in that direction before the year is over.

THE WEASEL

It was the privilege of the chief bards to wear mantles made of birds' plumage. A short cape flung on the shoulders made of mallards' necks and crests must have been very gorgeous in effect, glittering like jewels, when the torch-light played on the colours at the festivals.

OMENS AND SUPERSTITIONS

Auguries and prophecies of coming fate may also he obtained from the flight of birds, the motion of the winds, from sneezing, dreams, lots, and the signs from a verse of the Psalter or Gospels. The peasantry attach great importance to the first verses of St John's Gospel, and maintain that when the cock crows in the morning he is repeating these verses (from the 1st to the 14th), and if we understood the language of animals and birds, we could often hear them quoting these same verses.

A charm against sickness is an amulet worn round the neck, enclosing a piece of paper, on which is written the first three verses of St John's Gospel.

OMENS THAT FORBODE EVIL

To stick a penknife in the mast of a boat when sailing is most unlucky.

To meet a man with red hair, or a woman with a red petticoat, the first thing in the morning.

To kill the robin redbreast.

To pass a churn and not give a helping hand.

To meet a funeral and not go back three steps with it.

To have a hare cross your path before sunrise.

To take away a lighted sod on May days or churning days; for fire is the most sacred of all things, and you take away the blessing from the house along with it.

OMENS THAT FORBODE EVIL

The Irish are very susceptible to omens. They say, 'Beware of a childless woman who looks fixedly at your child.'

Fire is the holiest of all things. Walk three times round a fire on St John's Eve, and you will be safe from disease for all that year.

It is particularly unlucky to meet a red-haired man the first thing in the morning. There is a tradition that Judas Iscariot had red hair, and it is from this the superstitious dread of the evil interference of a red-haired man may have originated.

Never begin work on a Friday.

Never remove from a house or leave a situation on Saturday.

Never begin to make a dress on Saturday, or the wearer will die within the year.

Never mend a rent in a dress while on, or evil and malicious reports will be spread about you.

Some days are unlucky to certain families – as Tuesday to the Tudors. Henry VIII., Edward, Mary, and Elizabeth all died upon a Tuesday.

To throw a slipper after a party going a journey is lucky. Also to breakfast by candle-light on Christmas morning.

It is fatal at a marriage to tie a knot in a red handkerchief, and only an enemy would do it. To break the spell the handkerchief should be burned.

The first days of the year and of the week are the luckiest. Never begin a journey on a Friday or Saturday, nor move from your residence, nor change a situation. Never cut out a dress or begin to make it on a Friday, nor fix a marriage, for of all days the fairies have the most malific power on a Friday. They are present then, and hear all that is said, therefore beware of speaking ill of them, for they will work some evil if offended.

Never pay away money on the first Monday of the year, or you will lose your luck in gaining money all the year after.

Presents may be given on New Year's Day, but no money should be paid away.

Those who marry in autumn will die in spring.

The yew-tree, the ash, and the elder-tree were sacred. The willow has a mystery in it of sound. The harp of King Brian-Boru was made of willow-wood.

When a servant leaves her place, if her mistress gives her a piece of bread let her put by some of it carefully, for as long as she has it good luck will follow her.

TO ATTRACT BEES

Gather foxglove, raspberry leaves, wild marjoram, mint, camomile, and valerian; mix them with butter made on May Day, and let the herbs also be gathered on May Day. Boil them all together with honey; then rub the vessel into which the bees should gather, both inside and out, with the mixture; place it in the middle of a tree, and the bees will soon come. Foxglove or 'fairy fingers' is called 'the great herb' from its wondrous properties.

SUPERSTITIONS OF THE ISLANDS

CONCERNING THE DEAD

It is ill luck when going with a funeral to meet a man on a white horse. No matter how high the rank of the rider may be, the people must seize the reins and force him to turn back and join the procession at least for a few yards.

The three most powerful divinations are by fire, by water, and by clay. These are the three great powers – the power that ascends, which is fire; the power that falls, which is water; and the power that lies level on the earth, and has the mystery of the dead, which is clay.

If a short cut should be taken while carrying a corpse to the grave the dead will be disturbed in the coffin, for it is a slight and an insult to the corpse.

When a death was expected it was usual to have a good deal of bread ready baked in the house in order that the evil spirits might be employed eating it, and so let the soul of the dying depart in peace. Twelve candles stuck in clay should also be placed round the dying.

If two funerals meet at the same churchyard, the last corpse that enters will have to supply the dead with water till the next corpse arrives.

Never take a child in your arms after being at a wake where a corpse was laid out unless you first dip your hands in holy water.

The moment the soul leaves the body the evil spirits try to seize it, but the guardian angel fights against them, and those around must pray earnestly that the angel may conquer. After death the body must not be disturbed, nor should the funeral chant be raised for one hour.

There are many superstitions prevalent in the Western Islands which are implicitly believed and acted on. Fishermen when going to sea must always enter the boat by the right side, no matter how inconvenient.

A coal of fire thrown after the fisherman brings him good fortune.

A sick person must not be visited on a Friday, nor by any person who has just quitted a wake and looked upon the dead. The hair and nails of a sick person must not be cut till after recovery.

If a corpse falls to the ground the most fatal events will happen to the family.

The lid must not be nailed on the coffin of a new-born child, or the mother that bore it will never have another.

THE COASTGUARD'S FATE

One day a coastguard man was out in his boat with some of the islanders when a terrible storm arose with thunder and lightning. The poor people fell on their knees and prayed devoutly, but the man laughed at them, called them fools and cowards, and said he also could make lightning and thunder as well as the God they were praying to. So he immediately prepared a small cannon he had on board, and set a match to the powder and fired it off. But before the echo died away a stream of lightning passed over him, and he fell dead in the boat a blackened corpse – a dreadful sign of the vengeance of heaven on his blasphemous daring.

RELICS

If a false oath is taken upon a relic the vengeance of God falls upon the swearer, and the doom that few can bear and live rests upon him and upon all his descendants even to the seventh generation. They are shunned by the people, and looked upon as unlucky and accursed. There are some living even now from whom the curse of the past is not lifted, because the seventh generation has not yet passed by.

MYSTERIES OF FAIRY POWER

THE EVIL STROKE

Some persons are possessed naturally with the power of the Evil Stroke, but it is not considered at all so unlucky as the Evil Eye; for the person who has it does not act from intentional malice but from necessity, from a force within him which acts without his will, and often to his deep regret: as in hurling matches, where a chance stroke of his may do serious injury, and even the dust of the earth raised by his foot has blinded his opponent for a week.

One day a young man, while wrestling with another in play at a fair, where they met by chance, struck him on the arm, which immediately became fixed and powerless as stone. His friends brought him home, but nothing would restore the power of the arm or bring back the life; so after he had lain in this state for three days his family sent for the young man who had struck him, to ask for his help. When he came and saw the arm stiff as stone, he anointed it all over with spittle, making also the sign of the cross; and after some time the arm began to move again with life, and finally was quite restored. But the young man of the Evil Stroke was so dismayed at this proof of the strange power in him, that

THE EVIL STROKE

he would never again join in sports for fear of some unlucky accident.

The power, however, is sometimes very useful, as in the case of attack from a bull or a ferocious dog; for a touch from the hand of a person possessing the Evil Stroke at once quells the madness in the animal, who will crouch down trembling with fear, and become as incapable of doing injury as if suddenly and powerfully mesmerized.

But the power does not come by volition, only at intervals; and the person possessing it does not himself know the moment when it can be effectively exercised.

Women, also, have the mysterious gift of this strange occult force, and one young girl was much dreaded in the country in consequence; for anything struck by her, beast or man, became instantly paralyzed, as if turned to stone. One day, at a hurling match, she threw a lump of clay at the winner in anger, because her own lover had failed to win the prize. Immediately the young victor fell down stunned and lifeless, and was so carried home to his mother. Then they sent in all haste for the young girl to restore him to consciousness; but she was so frightened at her own evil work that she went and hid herself. Finding it then impossible to bring her, his friends sent for the fairy doctor, who, by dint of many charms and much stroking, at last restored the young man to life. The girl, however, was in such dread of the curses of the mother, that she fled, and took service in a distant part of the country. And all the people rejoiced much over her departure from amongst them.

Yet it was considered lucky in some ways to have a fairy-stricken child in the house, for the fairies generally did a good turn by the family to compensate for the evil. And so there was always plenty of butter in the churn, and the cattle did not sicken wherever there was a stricken child.

It is also lucky to employ a half-simpleton about the farm, and to be kind to the deaf and dumb, and other afflicted creatures. No one in Ireland would harm them or turn them out of their way, and they always get food and drink for the asking, without any payment being thought of or accepted.

THE CHANGELING

A woman was one night lying awake while her husband slept, when the door suddenly opened and a tall dark man entered, of fierce aspect, followed by an old hag with a child in her arms – a little, misshapen, sickly-looking little thing. They both sat down by the fire to warm themselves, and after some time the man looked over at the cradle that stood beside the mother's bed with her boy in it, and kept his eyes on it for several minutes. Then he rose, and when the mother saw him walking over direct to the cradle, she fainted and knew no more.

When she came to herself she called to her husband, and bade him light a candle; this he did, on which the old hag in the corner rose up at once and blew it out. Then he lit it a second time, and it was blown out; and still a third time he lit the candle, when again it was blown out, and a great peal of laughter was heard in the darkness.

On this the man grew terribly angry, and taking up the tongs he made a blow at the hag; but she slipped away, and struck him on the arm with a stick she held in her hand. Then he grew more furious, and beat her on the head till she roared, when he pushed her outside and locked the door.

After this he lit the candle in peace; but when they looked at the cradle, lo! in place of their own beautiful boy, a hideous little creature, all covered with hair, lay grinning at them. Great was their grief and lamentation, and both the man and his wife wept and wailed aloud for the loss of their child, and the cry of their sorrow was bitter to hear.

Just then the door suddenly opened, and a young woman came in, with a scarlet handkerchief wound round her head.

'What are you crying for,' she asked, 'at this time of night, when every one should be asleep?'

'Look at this child in the cradle,' answered the man, 'and you will cease to wonder why we mourn and are sad at heart.' And he told her all the story.

When the young woman went over to the cradle and looked at the child, she laughed, but said nothing.

THE CHANGELING

'Your laughter is stranger than our tears,' said the man. 'Why do you laugh in the face of our sorrows?'

'Because,' she said, 'this is my child that was stolen from me to-night; for I am one of the fairy race, and my people, who live under the fort on the hill, thought your boy was a fine child, and so they changed the babies in the cradle; but, after all, I would rather have my own, ugly as he is, than any mortal child in the world. So now I'll tell you how to get back your own son, and I'll take away mine at once. Go to the old fort on the hill when the moon is full, and take with you three sheaves of corn and some fire, and burn them one after the other. And when the last sheaf is burning, an old man will come up through the smoke, and he will ask you what it is you desire. Then tell him you must have your child back, or you will burn down the fort, and leave no dwelling-place for his people on the hill. Now, the fairies cannot stand against the power of fire, and they will give you back your child at the mere threat of burning the fort. But mind, take good care of him after, and tie a nail from a horse-shoe round his neck, and then he will be safe.'

With that the young woman took up the ugly little imp from the cradle in her arms, and was away before they could see how she got out of the house.

Next night, when the moon was full, the man went to the old fort with the three sheaves of corn and the fire, and burned them one after the other; and as the second was lighted there came up an old man and asked him what was his desire.

'I must have my child again that was stolen,' he answered, 'or I'll burn down every tree on the hill, and not leave you a stone of the fort where you can shelter any more with your fairy kindred.'

Then the old man vanished, and there was a great silence, but no one appeared.

On that the father grew angry, and he called out in a loud voice, 'I am lifting the third sheaf now, and I'll burn and destroy and make desolate your dwelling-place, if my child is not returned.'

Then a great tumult and clamour was heard in the fort, and a voice said, 'Let it be. The power of the fire is too strong for us. Bring forth the child.'

And presently the old man appeared, carrying the child in his arms.

'Take him,' he said. 'By the spell of the fire, and the corn you have conquered. But take my advice, draw a circle of fire, with a hot coal this night, round the cradle when you go home, and the fairy power cannot touch him any more, by reason of the fire.'

So the man did as he was desired, and by the spell of fire and of corn the child was saved from evil, and he grew and prospered. And the old fort stands to this day safe from harm, for the man would allow no hand to move a stone or harm a tree; and the fairies still dance there on the rath, when the moon is full, to the music of the fairy pipes, and no one hinders them.

THE FAIRY DOCTOR

If a healthy child suddenly droops and withers, that child is fairy-struck, and a fairy doctor must be at once called in. Young girls also, who fall into rapid decline, are said to be fairy-struck; for they are wanted in Fairy-land as brides for some chief or prince, and so they pine away without visible cause till they die.

The other malign influences that act fatally on life are the Wind and the Evil Eye. The evil power of the Wind is called a fairy-blast; while, of one suffering from the Evil Eye, they say he has been 'overlooked.'

The fairy doctor must pronounce from which of these three causes the patient is suffering. The fairy-stroke, or the fairy-blast, or the Evil Eye; but he must take no money for the opinion given. He is paid in some other way; by free gracious offerings in gratitude for help given.

A person who visited a great fairy doctor for advice, thus describes the process of cure at the interview: –

'The doctor always seems as if expecting you, and had full knowledge of your coming. He bids you be seated, and after looking fixedly on your face for some moments, his proceedings begin. He takes three rods of witch hazel, each three inches long, and marks them separately, 'For the Stroke,' 'For the Wind,' 'For the Evil Eye.' This is to ascertain from which of these three evils you suffer. He then takes off his coat, shoes, and stockings; rolls up his shirt sleeves, and stands with his face to the sun in earnest prayer. After prayer he takes a dish of pure water and sets it by the fire, then kneeling down, he puts the three hazel rods he had marked into the fire, and leaves them there till they are burned black as charcoal. All the time his prayers are unceasing; and when the sticks are burned, he rises, and again faces the sun in silent prayer, standing with his eyes uplifted and hands crossed. After this he draws a circle on the floor with the end of one of the burned sticks, within which circle he stands, the dish of pure water beside him. Into this he flings the three hazel rods, and watches the result earnestly. The moment one sinks he addresses a prayer to the sun, and taking the rod out of the water he declares by what agency the patient is afflicted. Then he grinds the rod to powder, puts it in a bottle which he fills up with water from the dish, and utters an incantation or prayer over it, in a low voice, with clasped hands held over the bottle. But what the words of the prayer are no one knows, they are kept as solemn mysteries, and have been handed down from father to son through many generations, from the most ancient times. The potion is then given to be carried home, and drunk that night at midnight in silence and alone. Great care must be taken that the bottle never touches the ground; and the person carrying it must speak no word, and never look round till home is reached. The other two sticks he buries in the earth in some place unseen and unknown. If none of the three sticks sink in the water, then he uses herbs as a cure. Vervain, eyebright, and yarrow are favourite remedies, and all have powerful properties known to the adept; but the words and prayers he utters over them are kept secret, and whether they are good or bad, or addressed to Deity or to a demon, none but himself can tell.'

These are the visible mysteries of the fairy doctor while working out his charms and incantations. But other fairy doctors only perform the mysteries in private, and allow no one to see their mode of operation or witness the act of prayer.

If a potion is made up of herbs it must be paid for in silver but charms and incantations are never paid for, or they would lose their power. A present, however, may be accepted as an offering of gratitude.

THE POET'S SPELL

A very ancient story, as old as the tenth century, is narrated, and firmly believed by the people, that once on a time when the reapers were at work, a fine handsome young married woman, who was in the field with them, suddenly fell down dead. This caused a great fear and consternation, especially as it was asserted that just before the fatal event, a fairy blast had passed over the field, carrying a cloud of dust and stones with it; and there could be no doubt but that the fairies had rushed by in the cloud, and struck the woman dead as they passed.

Then her people sent for the great wise poet of the tribe, who was reputed to have the power by his song to break the strongest fairy spells: and he chanted low music over her, and uttered mystic incantations, the words of which no man heard; but after a while the woman unclosed her eyes and rose up, restored to life.

When they questioned her, she told them all she knew.

'In sickness I was,' she said, 'and I appeared to be dead, for I could neither speak nor move, till the song of the poet gave me power. Then the life rose up in me again, and the strength, and I was healed.'

CHARM FOR THE FAIRY STROKE

There is a very ancient and potent charm which may be tried with great effect in case of a suspected fairy-stroke.

CHARM FOR THE FAIRY STROKE

Place three rows of salt on a table in three lines, three equal measures to each row. The person performing the spell then encloses the rows of salt with his arm, leaning his head down over them, while he repeats the Lord's Prayer three times over each row – that is, nine times in all. Then he takes the hand of the one who has been fairy-struck, and says over it, 'By the power of the Father, and of the Son, and of the Holy Spirit, let this disease depart, and the spell of the evil spirits be broken! I adjure, I command you to leave this man [naming him]. In the name of God I pray; in the name of Christ I adjure; in the name of the Spirit of God I command and compel you to go back and leave this man free! Amen! Amen! Amen!'

THE FARMER'S FATE

The peasants have the greatest dread of the fairy-stroke, and consider it the most dangerous indication of fairy hostility. When a person is struck, he becomes wholly insensible to external things, as if his soul had been taken out of him and carried away.

A farmer once began to build a barn on a fairy circle, to the great horror of the neighbours, who warned him of the danger; but he only laughed at their nonsense, and built and finished his barn on the fairy rath.

However, riding home one evening after sunset, he was suddenly struck, and fell insensible to the ground. They carried him home and laid him on his bed, where he lay for several days, his eyes fixed and staring without any motion of the eyelids, and no indication of life remaining, except his colour which never changed.

All the doctors came and looked at him, but could do nothing. There was no fracture nor injury of any kind to his frame; so the doctors shook their heads and went their way, saying they would call again in a day or two. But the family objected to delay, and sent at once for the great fairy doctor of the district. The moment he came he threw herbs on the fire, when a fragrant smell filled the room like church incense. Then he pounded some herbs and mixed a liquid with them, but what the herbs were, no one knew. And with this mixture he touched the brow and the lips and the hands of the man, and sprinkled the rest over his insensible form. After this he told them to keep silence round him for two hours, when he would return and finish the cure. And so it happened, for in two hours the life came back to the man, though he could not speak. But strength came gradually; and by the next day he rose up, and said he had dreamed a dream, and heard a voice saying to him, 'Pull down the barn, for ill-luck is on it.' Accordingly he gave orders to his men, and every stick and stone was carried away, and the fairy rath left free again for the fairies to dance on, as in the olden time, when they were the gods of the earth, long before men came to dispute their rights, and take possession of their ancient pleasure grounds – an indignity no high-spirited fairy could calmly endure. For in their councils they had decreed that the fairy rath, at least, should be sacred for all time, and woe to the man who builds his house thereon. An evil fate is on him and on the house for evermore. Down it must come, or the evil spell will never be lifted. There is no hope for it, for the most dangerous and subtle of all enemies is an angry fairy.

Nor should the paths even be crossed by work of human hand, which the fairies traverse from one palace to another. Their line of march must not be impeded. Finvarra and his men would resent such a gross insult to the royal fairy rights, and severely punish the audacious and offending mortal. Not even the Grand Jury would be allowed to interfere, for if they did, every man of them would be demolished in some way or other by fairy power.

THE FAIRY RATH

The fairies, beside being revengeful, are also very arrogant, and allow no interference with their old-established rights.

THE FAIRY RATH

There is a rath in the Queen's County, only four yards in diameter, but held so sacred as the fairies' dancing ground that no one dared to remove a handful of earth from the mound; and at night the sweetest low music may be heard floating round the hill, as if played by silver bagpipes.

One evening a boy lay down on the rath to listen to the music, and, without thinking, began to gather up balls of the clay and fling them hither and thither in sport, when suddenly he was struck down by a violent blow and became senseless.

There he was found by his people, who went to search for him; and when he came to himself he bleated like a calf, and it was a long time before he recovered his reason, for the power of the fairies is great, and none can resist it.